INNOVATIVE
FLIES AND
TECHNIQUES

**Al & Gretchen
Beatty**

INNOVATIVE
FLIES AND
TECHNIQUES

Al & Gretchen
Beatty

Frank Amato
PORTLAND

DEDICATION

We would like to dedicate this book to the many great fly tiers from the Federation of Fly Fishers who continue to share so willingly. We have learned much over the years and many of the skills we have today are a direct result of our exposure to them. Gretchen wants to especially recognize her father "Dub" Evans for teaching a young daughter the magic of hooks, thread, and materials. Al thanks Bruce Staples for giving an unknown fly tier from north Idaho his start in the world of demonstration fly dressing.

Published in 2005 by
Frank Amato Publications, Inc.
PO Box 82112
Portland, Oregon 97282
(503) 653-8108
www.amatobooks.com

Softbound ISBN: 1-57188-347-9 • Softbound UPC: 0-81127-00181-1
Spiral Hardbound ISBN: 1-57188-348-7 • Spiral Hardbound UPC: 0-81127-00182-8
Limited Hardbound ISBN: 1-57188-349-5 • Limited Hardbound UPC: 0-81127-00183-5

All photographs taken by the author unless otherwise noted.
Book Design: Tony Amato

Printed in Singapore

1 3 5 7 9 10 8 6 4 2

Contents

ACKNOWLEDGEMENTS

This book is the result of our efforts, to be sure, but more importantly it exists because of the group of people you see on these pages. They are people who were willing to take time from their busy lives to share with others, and we are pleased to call them friends. What we found so amazing while preparing each person's profile was how little we really knew about their lives; what they do for a living, other hobbies, family members, etc. Yes, they are friends, but in a fly-tying sense. When we talk with them we speak the language of hooks, fur, feathers, and other materials, never realizing they are also lawyers, doctors, construction workers, college professors, etc. We suggest you take a few minutes to review each person's profile before studying their flies to see a bit of the soul coming through those patterns; we certainly look at those flies differently than we did a couple of years ago at the start of this project.

Many of the people featured here are fellow members of the Federation of Fly Fishers and others are not, but no matter we all have the same screw loose (a love of fly tying).

We also must recognize the good people at Frank Amato Publications for working with us throughout this project. It would not have happened with out their knowledge and help. A special thank you has to go to Jim Schollmeyer who put us through a crash photography course so we could shoot the pictures herein.

We must certainly acknowledge ourselves as well. Not every married couple would take the time away from their personal lives needed to complete a project such as this book. Thank God, we enjoy each other's company whether it's at the computer keyboard, at the vise, or on the water. For the past couple of years we've spent a lot more time at the keyboard than we did on the water. We certainly hope you find our efforts worthwhile.

—*Al & Gretchen Beatty*
Boise, Idaho

ABOUT THIS BOOK

While Gretchen and I were working on the Federation of Fly Fishers' *Fly Pattern Encyclopedia* it soon became evident there were flies featured that needed more exposure than a single recipe and photograph could accomplish. Long before that book was completed we had decided to write another book to further explain some of the patterns in a step-by-step format.

When the *Fly Pattern Encyclopedia* was complete we took a much-needed rest and enjoyed each other's company on every body of water we could find near our home in Delta, Colorado. Near the end of 2001 we decided it was time write the next book. I started contacting fly tiers whose patterns needed more explanation than they received in the first book.

Fly tiers responded with the patterns requested, but also with requests to include flies that had evolved since the last publication date. You might think we'd have stayed with the original plan with this one slight modification, but that did not happen. By May 2002 we were in the middle of moving our home and business from Colorado to Boise, Idaho (Gretchen's home town). I contacted Frank Amato Publications advising them there would be a delay with this manuscript, and they agreed to allow us to put the project on hold.

During the time these pages were laying in a storage building they decided to change their direction while Gretchen and I were otherwise occupied. Like a lot of projects, this one took on a life of its own. We had friends of fly tiers from the first book coming out of the woodwork wanting to share some of their ideas. The patterns we saw were awesome for a wide range of reasons—an innovative design, a simple but effective idea, or improvements on an existing fly. These flies convinced us to change the book's content to what you are now reading.

—Al Beatty

AL & GRETCHEN BEATTY

Al and Gretchen Beatty

The authors are best friends, on and off the water, at the keyboard, or working side by side. They make their home in Boise, Idaho; Gretchen's hometown. Al often remarks that his home will be anywhere Gretchen is so you all know where his heart is. There they operate the family business (BT's Fly Fishing Products), write, and operate a video production company (fly fishing and tying videos, of course). They got married on April Fool's Day in 1993 and are as much in love today as when they walked down the aisle together. You might ask, "Why April Fool's Day?" That's so Al won't forget his wedding anniversary, anyone should know that!

Their lives came together with starts at opposite ends of the country; Oregon for Gretchen and Arkansas for Al. Born a war baby in 1943 in Fort Smith, Arkansas Al's journey to recognition within the fly-fishing community had very meager beginnings on a dairy farm in north-western Iowa, his mother's home state. Milking cows at four-o-clock, morning and evening seven days a week, did not leave much time for fishing. But he was bit by the fishing bug at an early age and did manage several times a week to hitch a ride to a near by lake to fish for crappie with worms and a bobber. There Al observed his first fly fisher catch a crappie right next to his location on the bank and he was hooked! Fly-fishing was the sport for him. He just needed to figure out how to get started.

At the start of all of his fly tying or casting clinics, Al describes himself as "a fly-tier who fly-fishes." That proclamation is a reflection on his early years in Iowa. He received a Herter's fly tying kit for his fourteenth birthday and a month later was selling flies to a local hardware store. Since that start as a commercial fly tier, Al has sold flies every year for the past forty-plus years. That includes 1968 spent with the US Army in Vietnam, his least profitable commercial tying year when he only tied three dozen flies for an officer who wanted to fly fish the Mekong River. Other years your authors have produced near 3000 dozen flies but today tend keep the amount to around 500 dozen per year.

It was more than a year after Al started selling flies that he finally put the money together to buy a fly rod, reel, and line. Al often pokes fun at him self by saying, "It took me a year to get that first fly rod and another twenty to learn how to cast it." There weren't any casting instructors or fly-fishing clubs in the Iowa farm country in the mid 1950's.

After twenty-plus years struggling to learn fly-casting Al encountered a life-altering experience when he discovered the Federation of Fly Fishers at their Conclave in Spokane, Washington. Al learned more at that one show about fly casting and tying than he had acquired teaching himself during the previous years. From that day forward Al has dedicated himself to the Federation of Fly Fisher's goals, *Conserving—Restoring—Educating Through Fly Fishing.* At first he learned from the best of the best; Dave Whitlock, Lefty Kreh, and Mel Krieger just to name a few. In time he graduated from the roll of student to that of an instructor.

Al and Gretchen generously share their skills with people the world over. Today they are sought after instructors/demonstrators for organizations on a local, regional, national, and inter-national basis. Both of your authors have been recognized for their contribution. Al has received the Buz Buszek Memorial Award & the Man of the Year Award and Gretchen was recognized with the Woman of the Year Award in 2001.

Though both of your authors are recognized today in the small world of fly-fishing, Gretchen's start along this path was much different from Al's. She was born in 1944 in Klamath Falls, Oregon to the fly-fishing Evans family. Her father Dub worked in various locations during the war years on "critical construction" as a plumbing and heating contractor for the US Government.

At the end of the war the Evans family returned home to Boise to resume life. Besides keeping busy with his plumbing & heating business Dub made certain to find time to fly fish and tie flies on a commercial basis. Gretchen fondly remembers sitting next to him at the tender age of six sorting hackle/materials for him as he constructed flies in the "rotary fashion" on a converted treadle sewing machine. Years later when Gretchen started tying with Al she asked, "What's all this?" when he introduced to her tying tools like hackle pliers, a bodkin, and a bobbin. The only tools she had needed up to that time was a pair of scissors and the rotating-treadle vise she got from her father.

Gretchen also well remembers Dub carrying her across the steam on his shoulders so she could fish her Royal Coachman on the other side. In the early years her rod of choice (what dad gave her) was a trimmed willow stick and a section of leader. With that rig she terrorized the fish in the central Idaho streams near her home.

The years passed and Gretchen became a young lady who still loved to fly-fish with the family and downhill ski with her brother Bill. Eventually college, marriage, a career, and a family placed demands on her time so fly-fishing and tying went on a back burner for several years. They remained on that back burner until…!

In the late 1970's both Al and Gretchen went to work as managers for GTE (later to become Verizon). Their careers bounced around each other for the next fifteen years. Often while at a meeting or working on a project, Gretchen would speak of her early years as a fly-fisher and fly tier. At those times the soft, far-away look in her eyes reached out to him. Al learned the tough manager really had a heart of gold. In time, their passion for a sport developed into a love for each other.

In 1993 they married, retired from GTE, and entered the full-time fly-fishing world. This book is the forth and hopefully not the last they will write together. Read, enjoy, and learn from it; they certainly did in writing it.

ELK DRAGON

Gretchen brought this pattern to life based on a panic attack. Not hers, it was Al's! He was guiding on a farm pond near their home and was experiencing a real tough day while another guide on the same water was having a great day. After an hour of frustration, Al asked the other group what fly they were using. The response was, "A hair-wing dragonfly" but they never did show it to him. Al called Gretchen on the cell phone and asked her to tie him a couple of hair-wing dragonflies and bring to him as soon as possible.

She went to the tying table where she was working on an order of Elk Hair Humpies. Using what was close at hand, in short order she assembled the pattern you see here; a combination of foam, elk hair, and plastic bead chain. Two hours later Gretchen delivered several to Al and saved the day.

She was the hero, but it cost him dearly later. She seems to remember a steak dinner; he remembers several steak dinners. No matter what the pay-off, the real point is Gretchen tied a fly that fit the need using materials lying right in front of her. You can too!

Elk Dragon

Hook:	Dry fly, size 8
Thread:	Blue
Tail:	Elk, tied extended-body style
Body:	Blue closed-cell foam
Wings:	Elk, tied spent style
Eyes:	Black plastic bead chain
Head:	Trimmed foam

Step 1: Tie a thread base that covers the front half of the hook shank. Leave the thread hanging in the center of the hook.

Step 2: Select, clean, and stack a small clump of elk hair. Tie it on with the tips pointing to the rear of the hook. The fibers should be twice as long as the complete hook. Trim any excess hair ends.

Step 3: Wrap the thread out on the elk hair (forming the extended body) until you are close to the tips. Then wrap back to the hook. Use open spirals when completing this part of the operation. It is easiest to hold the hair fibers with the left hand keeping them under tension while wrapping the thread with the right hand.

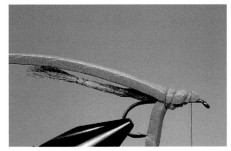

Step 4: Cut two strips of foam that are as wide as the distance of the hook gape and trim a point on each. Bind them to the front part of the hook with one on top and the other on the bottom.

Step 5: Select, clean, and stack a clump of hair about twice as big as the unit you used for the tail in Step Two. Bind this clump to the top of the shank and trim the excess ends.

Step 6: Cut two connected beads from a section of plastic bead chain. Tie them on the hooks lightly back of the hook eye. Pull the bottom foam forward and bind it to the bottom of the hook just behind the hook eye. Trim away the excess bottom section of foam.

Step 7: Divide the clump of elk hair located on top of the hook into two segments. Pull the top foam up, over, and through the hair segments.

Step 8: Bind the top foam to the hook at the eye and trim the excess to form the head. Whip finish, trim the thread, and apply head cement.

EZY Crayfish

We first stumbled on this fly after moving to Montana in 1993. Local fly-fishers told us the Madison River below Ennis Lake was a good brown-trout fishery early or late in the season. The section below Warm Springs fishing access had a large population of crayfish and a brown Woolly Bugger was the go-to-fly for the locals. We found it to really produce when dead-drifted between the weed beds. It really was a heart stopper to observe a big brown trout attack your Bugger as the fly drifted over the tan sandy area between the deep-green weed beds.

Like many innovative fly tiers, we just couldn't leave the brown Bugger alone, there really had to be an improvement that would fish better or at least make us think so. While Al spent his days guiding on the Madison and Yellowstone rivers, Gretchen spent her days tying flies for his next-day needs.

Each morning she would give him his lunch for the day which contained food, but more importantly several dozen flies he figured he would need for the day's fishing. The flies were standard Montana guide flies, the ones that always produce like the Prince Nymph (BH), the brown Woolly Bugger, GRHE, etc. Gretchen always included two or three "idea flies" she though might improve on the brown Bugger as a crayfish pattern. After several false starts, the pattern you see here crawled out of her vise and into Al's box of guide flies.

He well remembers a great day on the lower Madison when the clients in his boat were catching many more fish than anyone else on the river. Up to this time the fly did not have a name, but the client that day ended up providing a name without realizing it when he said something to the effect of, "This fly sure makes catching those brown trout easy." The EZY Crayfish was born. Today it remains a favorite crayfish pattern. We feel it it's a must-have fly in either warm- or cold-water fishing applications. Try it, you won't be disappointed.

EZY Crayfish

Hook:	Streamer, 4-8
Thread:	Brown
Weight:	Lead wire
Eyes:	Bead chain, brown or black
Claws/Tail:	Four Chickabou feathers, brown
Rib:	Copper wire
Body:	Brown Crystal Chenille
Shell Back:	Poly yarn, brown
Hackle:	Palmered saddle, brown
Tail:	Trimmed shell back

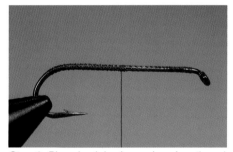

Step 1: Place hook in vise and apply a thread base that covers the complete hook shank and extends down slightly into the bend. Wrap forward to the middle of the shank and leave the bobbin hanging there.

Step 2: Bind a section of brown poly yarn to the back part of the hook and trim any excess material. Attach the bead chain eyes at the end of the shank. Note: They are tied to the under side of the hook shank. Leave the thread hanging in the center of the hook.

Step 3: Tie on four chickabou feathers (two per side) with the natural curve sweeping away from each other, to form the claws. Trim any excess material. Wrap several turns of lead wire behind the eye and trim any waste ends. Attach a section of Crystal Chenille to wrap later as the body and trim any excess. Bind a section of copper wire to use later as the rib.

Step 4: Wrap the chenille around the eyes and tie it off directly in front of them. Leave the excess there and tie on a brown saddle hackle feather. Continue wrapping the chenille forward to the eye, tie it off, and trim the excess. Palmer the hackle forward, tie it off, and trim any waste ends. Note: The materials and lead wire help form a natural crayfish profile.

Step 5: Pull the brown poly yarn up and over to form the shell back and bind it in place directly behind the hook eye. Be sure the poly goes between the chickabou feathers that are forming the claws. Trim the excess poly yarn long to form the crayfish's tail.

Step 6: Wrap the copper wire forward as a rib and tie it off at the hook eye. It also provides segmentation to the shell back. Trim the waste end, whip finish, and apply a coating of head cement.

Ghost Wing Wulff

This pattern did not appear in the, *Fly Pattern Encyclopedia* because it was developed after the book was published. The authors, however, have been so impressed with the fly and the concept it represents they decided to include it. The Ghost Wing Wulff came from a situation often encountered when fly-fishing into the evening hours, the time just before the sun goes down over the horizon and the glare is on the water. If the fly-fisher can get the setting sun to his/her back, then dealing with the low-light glare is no longer a problem. But Murphy's Law invariably intervenes and puts them in a situation where the best fishing includes looking directly into the surface glare.

Over the years we've tested many different material colors in an attempt to beat the problem. Logic suggests white, orange, and lime as good candidates, but the color that works best is a surprise—black! Not only do black-colored flies work very well in low-light surface glare, they are even easier to see after dark if you like to fish long into the evening like your authors often do. Let's put this bit of information in our mental filing cabinet for a moment.

Shortly after this revelation Al answered a phone call. The voice on the other end was good friend Dave Corcoran from The River's Edge fly shop in Bozeman, Montana. He had a "work in" order of flies for a customer from Argentina who was coming to Montana to fish. One of the flies this customer requested was a black-bodied Wulff with calf-tail hair incorporated into the wings.

As we tied the ordered flies it quickly became evident that the white hair silhouetted against the black stood out like a flashing light on a dark night. Could this fly be an all-around pattern that was easily seen in both high and low light situations? We just had to find out. With a dozen extra white/black-winged Wulffs in our fly boxes we headed to the river near our home. Those patches of white in the wings were easy to see during the afternoon hours and as evening approached the black provided the much-needed profile against the low-light glare.

We were excited! A fly readily visible in almost all light situations had just fallen into our laps. We couldn't keep calling it the white/black-winged Wulff, so Gretchen named it the Ghost Wing Wulff. The next evening they returned to the river armed several different standard Wulffs and the new Ghost Wing. The GW provided the best visibility in the low light conditions, but the white on black wings worked in all light conditions equally as well as the standard patterns we used as the benchmark.

We continue to use the mixed-wing design today. Now the only time you'll find a standard Wulff in our fly boxes is if it's there by mistake. The Ghost Wing is our favorite hair wing.

Ghost Wing Wulff

Hook:	Dry fly, size 2-20
Thread:	Black size A thread
Tail:	Moose body hair
Body:	Black size A thread
Wings:	Moose body hair
Ghost Wing:	White calf-tail hair
Hackle:	Black
Head:	Black size 6/0

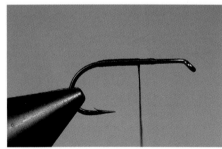

Step 1: Mentally divide the hook shank into four parts. Apply a thread base to the back three-fourths, ending up slightly short of your starting point. This stop point is important, so take notice.

Step 2: Stack and attach a moose-hair tail that is equal in length to the hook shank. Notice when the waste ends are trimmed they tend to creep forward. The purpose for stopping at the point illustrated in Step 1 is to leave room for the wings in the next step.

Step 3: Select, clean, and stack a clump of moose hair for the wings. Bind them to the hook with several tight thread wrap. Divide them with one figure-eight wrap to keep them apart for the next step.

Step 4: Trim a piece of calf-tail hair, clean out the under fur, and even the tips in a hair stacker. Tie them on the hook so they extend between the divided moose-hair clumps. The calf fibers should be a bit shorter than the moose. Trim the excess calf-tail fibers and cover-wrap this area. Half-hitch the size "A" thread and switch to the black size 6/0.

Step 5: Divide the calf-tail fibers into two equal clumps. Bind each to the divided moose fibers and post the two-part wings with several thread wraps. Note: Often you will need to reverse the direction of the "posting wraps" to position the ghost wings on the "inside" of the wing assembly—the white to the inside and black to the outside.

Step 6: Tie on a black hackle, or color of choice. Wrap several turns both behind and in front of the wings. Tie it off at the eye, trim the excess, whip finish, and cut off the thread. Apply a coating of head cement or Aqua Head.

Little Sunrise

Like many flies this is an adaptation of several different patterns, with probably eighty percent of the influence coming from a series of Harvester flies developed by Bill Marts from the Blue Dun Fly Shop in Spokane, Washington. We first learned of them when he asked Gretchen to tie an order of Harvesters for his shop. After completing the order, Gretchen tied several extras and put them in her fly box.

The next weekend on the river she kicked Al's rear end using them; Gretchen three, Al zip! She finally did share the pattern with him the next day and his success rate improved as well. Over the years the Harvester has remained an important steelhead pattern for us and still is today.

When Al accepted a marketing director's position with Whiting Farms in Delta, Colorado access to feathers became a fly-tier's dream. Tom Whiting had just about every kind of hackle-producing bird in either a production or experimental status, and we made good use of the ready feather availability. They experimented with many different feathers and fell in love with Tom's product, Soft Hackle with Chickabou, which is basically a smaller version of marabou.

Bringing Soft Hackle with Chickabou into the Harvester fly series seemed only natural to Gretchen as she spent hours at the vise while Al was working at Whiting Farms. Its smaller size lent well to low water style flies and the "Little" series was born all incorporating Chickabou in the hackle collar.

The Skykomish Sunrise has always been a favorite fly so it was only a matter of time before its influence slipped into the Little fly series. The Little Sunrise quickly proved itself in a riffle near Heller's Bar on the Snake River up stream from Asotin, Washington. On its maiden voyage there the pattern devastated the steelhead and a couple of nice trout. Since that trip, its decedents have enticed many cold-, warm-, and saltwater species, including trout, steelhead, bonefish, bass, panfish, and carp (one of our favorite species).

Little Sunrise

Hook:	Salmon, size 2/0-6
Thread:	Red
Tag:	Copper wire
Body:	Pink & orange yarn, braided
Wing:	Orange fur, orange Krystal Flash
Hackle:	Red guinea over red & orange Chickabou
Head:	Thread

Step 1: Place a hook in the vise; use a style appropriate for the expected fishing environment. Here we are using a salmon hook. Apply a thread base that covers the looped-eye platform. Trim the excess thread and tie a section of copper wire to the bottom of the shank. Wrap toward the back of the hook binding the copper wire to the underside of the shank. Stop just slightly in front of the hook point then wrap forward several thread turns. Wrap the wire forward to form a tag; we used eight turns even though five is the more traditional number. Tie the tag off to the bottom of the shank then advance the thread forward binding the wire to the underside of the hook. Trim the wire near the start of the looped-eye platform.

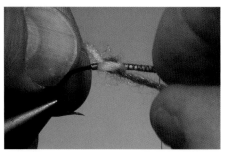

Step 2: Select two four-inch sections of knitting yarn, one orange and the other pink. Separate the segments into four individual strands. Bind one orange strand to the off side of the hook and a pink strand to the near side. Form an overhand knot with the orange strand on top and slip it over the hook shank. Pull the ends to tighten the knot.

Step 3: Continue placing overhand knots on the hook shank, making certain to keep the orange yarn strand on top. It will take several of these knots to form the body.

Step 4: Tie the yarn strands off at the start of the looped-eye platform. We like to tie off the orange on the off side and the pink on the near side, but that is nothing more than personal preference. Trim and remove the waste ends.

Step 5: Tie on a short fur wing, we use rabbit, artic fox or craft fur. Use four strands of Krystal Flash to top and accent the wing. Trim the Krystal Flash so it's a bit longer than the wing material.

Step 6: Attach the red chickabou feather to the hook and wrap a one-turn application. Tie it off and trim the excess material. Tie on the orange chickabou feather directly in front of the red and apply one turn of hackle. Tie it off and trim any excess feather. Fold the red guinea feather and bind it to the bottom of the hook by its tip in front of the mixed chickabou collar.

Step 7: Wrap two turns of the red guinea feather to provide a hackle collar accent. Be sure to tie it off to the bottom of the hook.

Step 8: Cut the excess feather, form a thread head, whip finish, and trim. Apply a coating of head cement; we used Aqua Tuff in this illustration.

Muddle May

The Muddle May is a fly Al developed in 1985 to satisfy a need, and compensate for a lack of materials. His goal was to develop a pattern that floated as well as a Humpy, but still had the slender profile of a natural mayfly. After several failed attempts the answer came from a fly-fishing friend, Ray Miles of Coeur d'Alene, Idaho.

Ray was watching Al finish an order of Muddler Minnows when he happened to look in a box sitting on a side shelf next to the tying area. In the box was a bunch of standard Adams' minus the hackle. When he asked Al about them, he learned they were waiting for a spring shipment of hackle so they could be completed. Ray made a comment something like, "Too bad you can't put a Muddler head on them." The light-bulb flashed on and the first Muddle May came off the vise in short order; an Adams body with a Muddler head and collar.

Over the next couple of years the Muddle May morphed its way through a couple changes until the final version you see here. As the final version evolved Al learned that things like tail length and wing placement were very important to the overall balance of the fly. If the tail was too long/short or the wing wasn't positioned right the fly just did not land right on the water.

As you tie this pattern, pay close attention to quantity, length, and position of materials. Remember, the goal is a fly that has the slender silhouette of a natural mayfly not the more robust appearance of a standard hair fly. The Muddle May is definitely worth the trouble to tie it. It's an awesome mayfly imitation whether used in rough or glassy, smooth water.

Muddle May

Hook:	Dry fly, size 10-22
Thread:	Color to match the body
Tail:	Moose, natural or bleached
Wings:	Looped wonder wings, color of choice
Body:	Dubbing to match the insect
Collar:	Deer hair to match the body
Head:	Deer hair, trimmed to shape

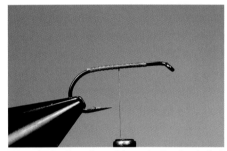

Step 1: Apply a thread base to the hook that starts at about the one-quarter point. Wrap to the end of the hook shank and back about half way. Leave the thread in the center of the shank in preparation for the next step.

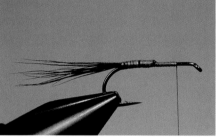

Step 2: Select a clump of moose hair for the tail, clean out the under fur, and even the tips in a hair stacker. Al uses natural moose on darker flies and bleached on lighter flies. Also it's very important to keep the quantity of fibers in the tail very sparse; less than half of what you would normally put in a hair tail. Because the tail is sparse it must then be a bit longer than normal—about one and one-quarter times the length of the shank. Tie a tail using these dimensions, trim the excess fibers, and wrap the thread forward to the one-quarter position.

Step 3: Select, clean, and stack a clump of deer body hair. Al uses a color that closely matches the insect he is trying to imitate; in the illustration, the hair is natural deer to closely match the gray body he will dub in a future step. Tie the stacked fibers on top of the hook at the one-quarter position. Make sure they are as long as the complete hook. Trim the excess fibers at a severe angle to taper the collar and tail fibers together to form the underbody. Also note the loop of thread that keeps those collar fibers on top of the hook.

Step 4: The wing is the looped-wonder wing described on the Quick 'N EZY fly and is constructed the same way. What is critical on this fly is the wing's position, it's not placed directly behind the hair collar fibers as might be expected. It is moved back slightly as illustrated. Do not trim the excess wing material because it makes a great handle when trimming the head in a future step.

Step 5: Dub a body making certain to include the part between the wings and the collar fibers.

Step 6: Stand up the collar hair by wrapping a cone-shaped thread dam directly in front of the fibers. Leave the thread hanging at the front of this thread dam.

Step 7: Spin deer hair to form the head. Use as many clumps as it takes to fill the area between the front of the collar and the eye. Whip finish and trim off the thread.

Step 8: Trim the head to shape. Split the wings, trim the excess feathers, and place them in a clothespin for use on another fly. Spread the collar fibers so they are fanned 180 degrees across the top of the hook. Apply head cement to the trimmed head to increase its durability.

Para Glen

Unlike other flies Al has developed, slightly modified, or kidded himself into believing he actually invented, the Para-Glen did not happen due to a specific need either on the water or from a customer's request. This fly came tumbling out of a bottle of twelve-year-old Glenlivet Scotch whiskey one evening while Al was tying and creating flies with Lars-Ake Olsson, a Swedish fly-fishing friend.

After an inch of that Scotch disappeared, the Para-Glen just magically appeared. With such an unfortunate start in life you would think the Para-Glen would have died a quick and merciful death, but because

the thing actually worked it has quickly become a favorite parachute-style fly. It is particularly effective when fished as an indicator with a smaller submerged nymph on a dropper. With the bulk of the shank bare it fishes like a parachute even though the hackle is wrapped around the hook; in essence, a parachute that's not.

In addition to producing a quick, easy and effective fly, tying the Para-Glen will teach a technique called furling. It's a method of quickly making perfect extended-body flies. Once the furling technique is perfected, the fly tier can modify the pattern to match almost any size or color of mayfly.

Para Glen

Hook:	Scud or dry fly, size 12-20
Thread:	Color to match body
Body/Wing:	Poly, color to match insect
Hackle:	Grizzly or match the insect

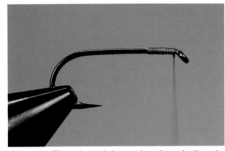

Step 1: The thread base is placed directly behind the hook eye and only covers the front one-fourth of the hook shank. Be certain to leave the back part of the hook bare so it will readily sink into the water.

Step 2: Bind the poly yarn to the hook so a short tuft sticks out over the hook eye and the rest extends toward the back.

Step 3: Twist the section of poly extending to the rear very tight. It should be twisted so tight it starts to "bundle" upon its self.

Step 4: Fold the tightly twisted poly over and allow it to wrap around itself to form an extended body. Bind furled body in place and trim excess even with the poly remaining from Step 2. We find using a bodkin at the fold-over point helpful with this step.

When the bodkin is removed after folding the twisted material, the furled body is formed.

Step 5: Take a couple of loops of thread around the extended body and anchor it to the hook shank. It should stick straight up in the air for the time being. Tie on the hackle directly behind the extended body. Also bind the excess stem to the area just in front of the body.

Step 6: Wrap the hackle one or two turns behind the body and several in front of the body. Tie it off directly behind the wings.

Step 7: Whip finish and trim the thread. Flip the fly in the vise so you can observe the position it takes in the water. It fishes like a parachute but ties like a regularly hackled pattern.

Quick N'EZY

It's peculiar how desperation is often the catalyst of creation. Al had hiked five miles into a favorite area of the Coeur d'Alene River in north Idaho one day, and was having a great day fishing. The fish were hitting an Adams and the day was shaping up to be spectacular when disaster struck; he dropped the box of flies in the river and helplessly watched as all his Adams' floated downstream.

Not relishing the idea of a 10-mile hike to get more flies, Al turned to the small packet of tying materials he carries in his vest. Designed just to tie a few nymphs on the river his supplies were not much, just a couple of hackle feathers, some dubbing, a small plastic zip-lock bag

of assorted hooks, and thread. Using his hemostats as a vise and his tippet nippers as a cutting tool, he set to work tying a makeshift Adams out of a bunch of materials intended for tying wet flies. The Quick 'N EZY was the result and it saved the day.

Besides being a very effective dry fly, the Quick 'N EZY allows you to use "leftovers;" those big neck feathers on the upper end of a dry-fly cape. Once you see how easy this fly is to tie and how good it looks, you'll never use hackle points for wings again. Remember, almost any mayfly dun can be imitated using the Quick 'N EZY method, all it takes is the right color combinations and sizes.

Quick N'EZY

Hook:	Dry fly, size 12-22
Thread:	Color to match insect
Tail:	Hackle fibers left over from the wings
Rib:	Optional
Body:	Dubbing to match the insect
Wings:	Swept-back hackle, Wonder Wings
Hackle:	Ginger or color to match the insect
Head:	Thread

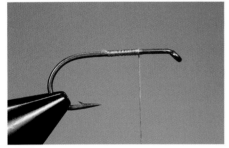

Step 1: Apply a base wrap of thread starting about 1/4 of the way back from the eye of the hook, wrap part way to the end of the shank, and then back to the starting point. Leave the bobbin at this location.

Step 2: The wings and tail are formed out of the feather fibers. To accomplish this, select two feathers that have fibers about the same length. We find using the large hackles on the big end of a cape works really well for this purpose. Place the two feathers together so their natural curves oppose each other. Trim off the large ends of the stems. The wings/tail are formed from the swept-back fibers. The fibers are swept back on a length of stem that is shorter than the hook shank. Measure the hackle stems (shorter) comparing them to the hook shank. Sweep back the fibers and tie them on the hook (very short capturing stem and fibers) with three snug thread turns as illustrated.

Step 3: Now, pull forward on the feathers with enough pressure to slip them part way from under the thread. (Not all the way or you'll have to start over). Pull the feathers out so they are equal in length to the hook shank. Slipping the fibers forward keeps the swept-back fibers aligned with each other. The newly-formed wings should be as long as the hook shank and the hackle stems should be short enough so they are not tied to the shank, in essence they are a looped wing. This makes the wings flexible so the fly will not spin while you are casting. Secure the wings with four or five more turns of thread to anchor them in place.

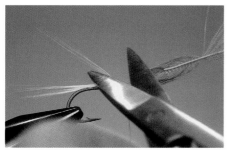

Step 4: To form the tail we trim out the fibers that are either too long or too short. Whether you eliminate short or long fibers is determined by the size of hook on which you are tying your fly. We like a tail that is slightly longer than the hook shank.

Step 5: Wind the thread to the back of the hook while binding the tail into position, then wrap forward to the wings. Place several turns of thread directly in front of the wings to force them to stand up. Divide the wings with a couple of criss-cross thread wraps then trim the excess feathers. (We usually place them in a clothespin where they will be ready for the next fly. You can usually construct several sets of wings from the two feathers.)

Step 6: Apply dubbing wax to your thread and then touch the clump of dubbing to the waxed thread to evenly distribute the material along the thread. Twist your thumb and forefinger in one direction only around the fur-covered thread. This single-direction motion will form a short section of natural fur yarn that you then apply to the hook to form the body. Attach the hackle behind wings. We like dubbing under our hackle to represent a thorax and have done so with the illustration.

Step 7: Wrap the hackle, whip finish and trim the thread/feathers as needed. The completed fly should look similar to the one illustrated. Remember, you can make the Quick 'N EZY any color combination you wish.

Squirrel Spruce (BH)

One of our favorite streamers has long been the Spruce Fly and it was only natural to eventually add a bead head to it when that craze hit the USA several years ago. We tied this version commercially for several shops and it gained a local following. It was especially effective in the fall on Montana, Wyoming, and Idaho waters.

The fly had one little (really pretty major) problem; getting good quality furnace hackle for the wings was a hit-or-miss proposition. We usually buy strung furnace hackle by the pound and matching four well-marked feathers for a standard wing often required extensive searching. In an average length of strung hackle we often would have to discard as many as twenty feathers to get a matched-wing assembly. We even tried putting the black center in a brown feather with a felt-tip pen, but that was a lengthy process and the marking usually faded in the water in a very short time.

Gretchen's father, Dub Evans, is an avid squirrel hunter and over the years he has given us the tails from his harvest, and in time we had more tails than we could ever use for our own tying. We accumulated so many we even scripted and produced a video on using the hair from that harvest in an effort to share our bounty with others. In time it was only natural to notice the similarities in the color of fox squirrel tails and furnace hackle feathers.

At first we married the two materials by using the squirrel tail as an under wing with two furnace hackle feathers as an over wing. The patterns were marginally successful because the squirrel tail provided little or no action in the water. When we fanned the squirrel hair using techniques described in our second book *Tying Hair Wing Flies* (Chapter 19, Bullet Head Mayfly) the under wing came alive and the success rate of the pattern went straight up.

Al often used the fly with clients on various Montana rivers. One afternoon while fishing with dear friends Dale and Doris Shelton he noticed the pattern continued to produce a steady stream of fish even after the feather part of the wings had been ripped off. That afternoon the Bead Head Spruce Fly was modified by several very aggressive brown trout and the Squirrel Spruce (BH) was born. From that day forward we tied the fly with a fanned squirrel-hair wing leaving off the furnace over wing. Try it, we think you will be impressed with its action in the water, and the fish will agree with your assessment.

Squirrel Spruce (BH)

Hook:	Streamer, size 4 -12
Thread:	Black
Tail:	Three peacock herls
Body:	Red floss and peacock herl
Wing:	Fox squirrel tail, fanned
Head:	Brass bead

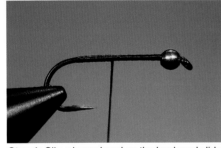

Step 1: Slip a brass bead on the hook and slide it up to the eye. Place a hook in the vise and apply a base wrap over the part of the hook behind the brass bead using red single-strand floss. Note we have found un-waxed size "A" thread is a great substitute for single-strand floss. Leave the thread hanging near the center of the base wrap slightly forward of the hook point.

Step 2: Tie three peacock herls for the tail. In so doing you are also constructing the back part of the body. This part of the body should equal about one-third of the hook shank. Trim the tail so it's as long as the hook gape is wide. Advance the floss forward to a point one-third back on the shank from the eye.

Step 3: Wrap the peacock forward to form the next part of the body. This section should also equal one-third of the shank length. Tie off the peacock and trim the excess. Whip finish the floss and trim it from the hook. Tie on the black thread and trim the waste end.

Step 4: Tie on the squirrel tail wing and trim the waste ends. A drop of head cement applied to the trimmed ends increases its durability. Leave the thread hanging directly behind the bead and be certain the bead is tight against the hook eye.

Step 5: The thread is positioned tight against the bead leaving a distance between it and the tie-in point of the wing. We call this forward thread position in relation to the wing's tie-in point the "pull point." Pull the top two-thirds of the wing up, separating it from the bottom one-third and place a loop of thread between them and anchor it back at the "pull point" with several thread wraps.

Step 6: Again divide the top wing section into thirds. Pull the top two-thirds up and take another loop through to divide them. Again anchor the thread back at the "pull point."

Step 7: Once again pull up the top part of the wing. Divide it in half and place a loop of thread between the two sections. Anchor the thread back at the "pull point" and trim any fibers not in line with the general profile of the wing. Steps 5 through 7 divide the wing fibers into four different segments using three loops of thread. The process fans the wing material. In turn it provides incredible action in the water during a strip/pause retrieve.

Step 8: Fold a furnace hackle feather, tie it on by the tip, and wrap a wet-style, hackle collar. Whip finish, trim off the thread, and apply a coating of head cement.

Tarpon Deceiver

A series of unrelated events was the idea behind this fly. It all started one spring day when friend Bob Lay called us from his home in Florida. He was preparing for a tarpon-fishing trip and wanted us to tie him some appropriate flies. During the course of that call the mail arrived and one of the items was a Deceiver from Lefty Kreh for the book we were working on at that time, the *Fly Pattern Encyclopedia.*

Al ended the call with Bob promising to send a couple dozen standard tarpon flies and returned to the fly-tying room to resume the day's work. Gretchen finished an order of Clouser Minnows for a shop in Texas while Al prepared to tie the flies for Bob. As the two worked side-by-side Al told Gretchen about the Deceiver that arrived in the day's mail. One thing led to another and the two ended up tying several flies for Bob that were a combination Deceiver and Clouser Minnow. They dubbed the fly the Tarpon Deceiver and sent them to Bob along with the standard tarpon flies.

On the second day of Bob's tarpon trip the fish just didn't seem to be interested in the standard patterns. Often the tarpon would inspect the fly and turn away. Changing colors did not seem to improve the situation either. Finally in desperation Bob tied on the Tarpon Deceiver and hooked the first of several fish that day; the pattern had worked when others did not.

You might think the story ended there but it doesn't. We tied several of the patterns in a down-sized version on freshwater hooks to try in local waters and found a size 8 worked really well on crappie, smallmouth bass, and trout. We named this version the Clouser Deceiver and it maintains a permanent position today in our freshwater fly boxes. To tie the smaller version, we suggest substituting calf tail for the bucktail but the tying steps remain the same.

Tarpon Deceiver

Hook:	Saltwater, size 2/0-4
Thread:	White
Tail:	Four white feathers, pearl Krystal Flash
Body:	Diamond Braid, color of choice
Wing:	Peacock herl over yellow & green bucktail
Wing Flank:	Grizzly dyed insect green
Throat:	White bucktail
Eyes:	Dumbbell, white & black
Head:	Thread coated with Aqua Tuff

Step 1: Place the hook in the vise and apply a thread base to the back two-thirds of the hook shank. Match four white feathers (saddle or cape) and tie them to the shank to form a tail that is slightly longer than the complete hook. Accent the tail with four strands of Krystal Flash or any bright material of choice.

Step 2: Tie the eyes on the shank slightly forward of the one-third point with several crisscross thread wraps. Apply a drop of head cement to anchor them in place.

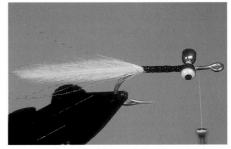

Step 3: Bind the Diamond Braid to the hook and wrap a body over the back part of the shank. Tie it off directly behind the eyes and trim any excess material. Leave the bobbin hanging in front of the eyes.

Step 4: Select a sparse clump of bucktail and remove any short fibers. Bind them to the top of the hook shank (do not stack) both in front and behind the eyes. Trim any excess buck tail. This application forms the throat of the fly.

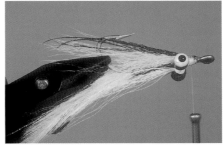

Step 5: Turn the hook over in the vise or rotate the vise one-half turn to complete the rest of the steps. The fly tier who has a true rotary vise will quickly appreciate this feature. Tie on a wing of peacock herl over green over yellow buck tail. Trim any excess fibers.

Step 6: Attach grizzly dyed green feathers to the sides of the wing and trim any excess material. Wrap a thread head, whip finish, and trim. Apply a coating of Aqua Tuff, Aqua Flex, or Dave's Flex Cement.

Triple Lace

It's very common in our business to receive sample materials. They all end up in an airtight plastic container in our fly-tying room until we have the chance to try them out. For a long time we simply called this pattern the Sample Fly because it just kind of crawled out of that box of samples.

Truth be known, it didn't crawl out of the box but was created using Gretchen's artistic eye for color and Al's comment, "That Tiewell flash and the Whiting Laced Hackle would sure make a wild-looking saltwater fly." Gretchen immediately sat down at her vise and tied the fly you see here. It looked so wild they decided to include it in the *Fly Pattern Encyclopedia*.

We never really thought much about it again until the *Fly Pattern Encyclopedia* was published and we started getting reports from readers who were having very good success using it. The interesting thing is the reports were coming from both warm- and saltwater fly-fishers. The wild color combination seemed to be very attractive to fish, especially bass.

We had to try it and decided to test it on pike in a lake near our home, at that time located in western Colorado. The results were explosive as the pike aggressively attached it. Today it is one of our go-to patterns for pike, bass, and panfish in the warmwater lakes near our home in Boise, Idaho. Try it, you'll like it!

Triple Lace

Hook:	Saltwater, size 3/0-1/0
Thread:	Fluorescent orange or pink single-strand floss
Under Tail:	Magenta Tiewell flash
Tail:	Pink and purple hackle feathers
Wings:	Laced magenta hen cape, three per side
Hackle:	Silver badger, tied as a collar
Head & Snout:	Tying thread, Aqua Tuff

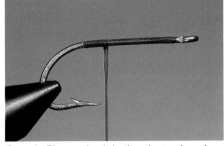

Step 1: Place a hook in the vise and apply a thread base that covers the complete hook shank. Wrap forward from the end of the shank so the bobbin is left hanging directly in front of the hook point.

Step 2: The Tiewell flash material is about eight inches long so select only about six strands of it. Fold them over and cut this section in the middle. Repeat the process again then tie this clump of twenty-four strands on the hook as a tail accent.

Step 3: Select two purple hackle feathers that are reasonably close in size and long enough to make a tail a hook gape longer than the accent. Trim the excess feathers and bind them to the hook (one on each side) flat against each other with the accent sandwiched between them. Next select two pink hackle feathers that are a bit smaller than the purple feathers just tied to the hook. Measure them so they are shorter than the purple feathers and yet longer than the accent. Bind them to the sides of the tail so the previous materials are sandwiched between them as well. Note: The purple and pink feathers together form a tail similar in color to magenta and because the purple feathers are slightly larger than the pink, they provide the illusion of a halo.

Step 4: Select six Whiting Laced hen cape feathers that have been dyed magenta. Match them to form curved wings that sweep away from each other with three feathers per side. The feathers are placed on top of the other so each is a bit shorter than the previous. This allows the natural black points on the tip of each feather to form a triple arrow effect. Bind the two multiple-feather applications to each side of the tail. Trim any excess material. Note: This is a good point to wrap part of the way to the hook eye and then back near the end of the shank; it starts forming the taper to the snout.

Step 5: The original pattern called for a badger hackle collar. In the illustrated fly the authors used a white feather colored with a black felt-tip marker. The effect is very similar to a silver badger feather. Fold this feather and tie it on the underside of the hook shank by the tip.

Step 6: Wrap a hackle collar making certain the fibers are swept back. Tie off the feather, trim the excess, advance the floss forward to the hook eye, and whip finish. Apply a coating of Aqua Tuff to finish the fly. Note: The extra wraps at the end of Step 4 make shaping the snout much easier.

Waker Wulff

We assembled this pattern on a request from a commercial fly customer who gave us a straight-forward directive, "I don't care what it is, just tie me a steelhead dry fly that will float like crazy and really skip across the water's surface."

This fly didn't just happen, it evolved over the next couple of years. We tried heavily hackling it, putting a moose-hair skipping beard on it, and a short, stiff plastic sliding spoon on it. Nothing seemed to work like the customer really wanted. Finally one day we decided to go back to the days Al tied small hair-hackle dry flies. Those flies had floated great we just needed to find out if hair hackle would also make them skip over the water's surface. They did! The customer was happy, and so were we!

You might think the story would end there and it certainly could have, we tie a lot of custom flies and don't always fish with them. There is just not the time to fish with everything we tie on a commercial basis. However, the Waker Wulff did find its way into one of our fly boxes we keep in the drift boat, but remained unused for a couple of years. One fall afternoon we were drifting the Yellowstone River and even though the fishing was great, the catching was real slow. Out of desperation Al tied it on his tippet, punched a cast to the bank, let it set for a moment, and then gave it two hard strips. The water exploded as a heavy brown trout grabbed it and headed to the middle of the river. A sleepy afternoon quickly changed into an adrenaline charged super day.

Does this fly always work this well? No, it does not, but it has saved more than one trout-fishing day for us. It may do the same for you as well. We also consider it an important addition to our steelhead fly box. There is nothing like catching a steelhead on a dry fly as it skitters across the water's surface.

Waker Wulff

Hook:	Salmon, size 2-8
Thread:	Red floss
Tail:	Moose body hair
Body:	Red floss
Wing:	Calf-tail hair
Hackle:	Spun deer hair
Head:	Floss

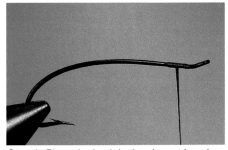

Step 1: Place the hook in the vise and apply a short base wrap of floss, directly behind the hook eye, that is long enough to tighten the looped-eye end against the hook shank. Wrap half way back to the eye leaving the bobbin hanging in the center of the floss application.

Step 2: Select a clump of deer hair, remove the under fur, and align the tips in a hair stacker. Spin the hair just behind hook eye with the tips pointed forward. We find it is much easier to accomplish this if you anchor the hair with three snug (but not tight) thread turns, then trim the excess hair butts before applying the extra pressure required to spin the hair around the hook. After spinning the hair cover wrap the trimmed butt ends. Lastly place a short section of masking tape over the spun hair. Its purpose is to keep the calf-tail wings separated from the deer-hair hackle during the next step.

Step 3: Cut a section of calf-tail hair, clean out the under fur, and even the tips in a hair stacker. Tie the wings on with the tips pointing forward and trim the waste butt ends at a very steep angle that tapers toward the back of the hook. Divide the wings, post each clump, and stand them up as you would when constructing any hair-wing fly. You will quickly appreciate the strip of tape placed in the previous step. Once the wings are divided and posted remove the tape.

Step 4: In this step we will apply the back part of the hackle. It goes on much more easily if you apply it in two sections; first on the near side and second on the off side. Flare each in place with a couple of snug but not tight wraps. It's very important to trim the waste hair butts before pulling on the single-strand floss to apply the extra pressure to spin the hair around the hook. Also, the wings tend to get in the way during this operation; use the fingers of your left hand to brush the hair fibers on past the wings as they spin around the hook.

Step 5: Select, clean, and stack a clump of moose hair for the tail. Tie on a tail that is equal in length to the hook shank. Bind it to the hook with close smooth wraps because you are forming the body as you wind first to the rear and then back to the hackle. Notice that we trimmed the waste hair ends tight against the hair hackle with a blunt rather than tapered cut. Those waste ends will be hidden in the hackle when we stand it up in the next step.

Step 6: Work the floss forward through the hackle/wing assembly until it is hanging in front of it. Wrap a tapered head tight against the front hackle fibers to force them to stand up straight. Whip finish, trim the floss, and apply a coating of Aqua Tuff to finish the head. God gave us fly tiers scissors so we could trim any fibers that aren't "getting with the program." Do so if your fly has any stray fibers heading in the wrong direction.

TOM BERRY

Tom lives near the Gulf of Mexico in Bay Saint Louis, Mississippi with this wife Irene and daughter Rosie. There he serves as Chief Public Defender for Hancock County. At only four years of age, Tom started fishing when his dad gave him a cane pole and tied him to a tree so he wouldn't fall in the water. Since then Tom has evolved from bait, to lures, and finally to fly-fishing.

Fishing the sparkling salt water of the Gulf of Mexico, Tom made his own lead jigs and dyed plastic coca hoe minnows. His fishing skills grew, Tom started fishing in local tournaments eventually becoming King Fisherman at one event four different years. Also his name is familiar to many in the area who read Tom's articles in *Gulf Coast Fishing News* and *Fishing along the Gulf Coast.*

After becoming interested in tying flies through a local fly-tying club, Tom joined the Federation of Fly Fishers when he learned about the magical information available at their regional and national conclaves. He attended his first International FFF Conclave when it was in Grand Rapids, Michigan. Tom attended classes taught by fly-fishing and fly-tying masters all day every day.

From this beginning he progressed to the Exposition in Idaho Falls, Idaho where he first tested his demonstration fly-tying skills. Since then he has demonstrated fly tying at the Sowbug and regional shows like the Southern and Southeastern Conclaves. Tom first shared his skills at the International Conclave when your authors invited him after observing him demonstrate at the Idaho Falls Expo.

Tom was a first-place winner in the *Fly Fishing & Tying Journal*'s Patent Paterns fly-tying contest and has had his fly-tying ideas pub-

lished in the English magazine, *Fly Fishing and Fly Tying.* Other flies by Tom have been published in *Patterns of the Masters, Vol. 6, FFF Fly Pattern Encyclopedia,* and the *FFF Flyfisher* magazine.

Tom Berry

At a recent Federation of Fly Fishers Conclave, Tom got tired of people asking to buy his flies. When a four-year-old girl overheard Tom tell a person the flies sold for a thousand dollar each, she looked him in the eye and said, "Mister, if you would lower your price you might sell some." At another conclave, Tom was tying large saltwater flies and a small boy was waiting to get one. A bluewater fly-fisher was also waiting for one. The boy asked what kind of fish it caught and Tom replied, "Bull croaker." Then he offered the boy a smaller fly and he took it. The blue water fisher laughed and said to the little boy, "I guess I got your fly." The little boy replied, "That's all right, the fly won't catch anything but bull croaker."

With the flashy, gaudy saltwater fish to imitate, its no wonder the flies Tom produces are also objects of beauty. Besides creating his own innovative flies, Tom now typifies the growth many of us in the Federation of Fly Fishers enjoy when we started as students learning from the masters only to become a master ourselves. Many students have learned to weave the magic of thread, hook, fur, and feather from master fly tier Tom Berry.

Big Skinny

Tom developed this fly based on an admiration of the many colorful saltwater minnow species in Gulf of Mexico waters near his home. It features a light belly with a gradual progression to the dark blue so prevalent on many natural fish. He cuts the tail in a "V" to represent the many forked-tail species.

The plastic necklace tape was selected to give the fly more color as well as protect it from the voracious teeth of the predator fish. The stacked tail and wing provide more action as the fly moves in the water. The red chenille collar represents gills and the plastic bead covers the

lead wire wraps, adds dimension, and a jigging movement in the water. Tom feels the eyes are important strike stimulators on all subsurface patterns. He coats the two colors with a think epoxy or Aqua Tuff coating.

He fishes it fast in a feeding school and slows the retrieve when presenting the fly to a solitary fish allowing the jigging action to stimulate a strike. Tom advises, "Since speckled trout are sometimes fickle about the colors they prefer, keep on hand blue (illustrated here), chartreuse, or purple based flies. It has caught speckled trout, red fish, blue fish, and even a jack crevalle."

Big Skinny

Hook:	Mustad 34011, size 1/0 -2/0,
Thread:	Clear mono, green thread
Tail:	White, light green, light blue, and dark blue FisHair
Weight:	Lead wire
Body:	Blue plastic necklace tape
Gills:	Red crystal chenille
Head/Thorax:	Blue bead, blue chenille
Eyes:	Painted, yellow and black
Wing:	Blue over white FisHair
Head:	Green thread

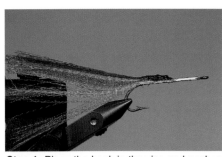

Step 1: Place the hook in the vise and apply a coating of white paint to the complete shank to avoid future material slip. Allow this coating to dry then apply a clear mono thread base to the back half of the shank. Tie on a four-part tail starting with white FisHair. Top it with light green, light blue, and finally place dark blue on the top. Trim any excess materials then coat it with super glue. The tail should be twice as long as the hook.

Step 2: Apply a double layer of twenty-thousandths lead wire in the center of the front part of the hook. Place several thread wraps over the wire, then super glue it as well.

Step 3: Take a section of plastic necklace tape and trim one end at a very severe angle. Tie this end to the back of the hook, advance the thread forward to the lead wire, and wrap the body forward to the same position. Tie it off and trim any excess material. Note: Tom purposely didn't trim the tape at a severe enough angle to demonstrate what happens if this part of the step is not properly completed. Tie on a section of red crystal chenille and wrap two turns. Tie it off and trim the waste end. Whip finish the thread and cut it from the hook. Apply super glue to the lead wraps and slip the blue bead in place. Paint a two-part eye on each side of the bead then allow the assembly to dry.

Step 4: Attach a bobbin of green thread in front of the bead. Tie on a section of light blue chenille and wrap two turns tight against the front of the bead. Anchor it in place with a couple of thread wraps then trim off the waste end. Tie on a clump of white FisHair, top it with dark blue, and cut off any excess material. Trim the wing on a curved angle so it's shorter than the tail then cut a fork in the tail. Whip finish the thread, trim it from the hook, and apply a coating of head cement or Aqua Tuff.

Brackish Water Shrimp

Tom tells us, "Of all the flies I have created, this one is the closest to a freshwater pattern on the Mississippi Gulf Coast. Our bayous, bays, and inlets are made up of a mixture of fresh water pouring in from the rivers and streams and salt water backing up from the Gulf of Mexico. This mixture is considered brackish." Therefore, he ties the fly on a saltwater hook, a standard freshwater hook would only last one trip.

Sometimes the layers of water produce bass, crappie, and bluegill in the freshwater section and speckled trout, flounder, and redfish in the salty stratum. The brackish-water shrimp flourish in this environment.

In warmwater environments, such as around power plants, the shrimp grow fairly large. The resident fish literally fight over these locations to catch the prized morsels. This fly's design was influenced by several crayfish patterns, particularly by Lenny Moffo's shrimp. The bead is used for both weight and to help define the hackle collar. Tom first demonstrated this fly in March 2000 at the Sow Bug Roundup in Mountain Home, Arkansas. He later entered it in the "Patent Patterns" fly-tying contest in *Fly Fishing & Tying Journal* where the Brackish Water Shrimp took first place in the Spring 2001 issue of the magazine.

Brackish Water Shrimp

Hook:	Size 6, Mustad 3302
Thread:	White and green
Mouthparts:	Badger guard hairs & under fur
Body:	Bead, green chenille, ostrich herl
Wing:	Pheasant
Hackle:	Olive chickabou
Eyes:	Melted mono
Optional Eyes:	Painted black

Step 1: Slip a chartreuse bead on the shank then place the hook in the vise. Slide the bead forward to the eye. Apply a thread base from the center of the hook to the end of the shank and back to the starting point. Select a sparse clump of badger fur and guard hairs and tie them on the hook extending to the rear to form the mouthparts. The bead will eventually be positioned at the end of the shank as illustrated, but for now allow it to slip around until we anchor it in position in a future step.

Step 2: Pluck two pheasant breast feathers and strip the webbed fibers from the base of the stem. Apply head cement to both sides of each feather then pull them between your thumb and forefinger to tighten their profile. Lay them aside to dry. We find preparing several of the feathers to be a good idea because we use rubber gloves to avoid messing up our fingers with the glue. After the feathers are dry, tie them on the hook extending to the rear with the natural curve sweeping away from each other. Again the bead is illustrated at its future position.

Step 3: Attach an olive dyed chickabou feather at the end of the shank and wrap a wet-style hackle collar. Tie it off and trim the waste end. Whip finish and cut off the thread. Coat the thread with super glue, slip the bead into position, and allow it to dry.

Step 4: Tie on the green thread directly in front of the bead. Bind a chartreuse-dyed ostrich herl and a section of green micro chenille in front of the bead. Advance the thread forward to the eye and follow that with the green micro chenille to form the body. Trim off the excess chenille. Palmer the ostrich herl over the body, tie it off at the eye, and trim the excess material.

Step 5: Choose two strands of twenty-pound monofilament that are twice as long as the complete hook. Melt one end of each to form the eyes. Bind them to the shank near the hook eye extending to the rear so they end near the feather tips placed in Step 2. The way Tom ties them to the hook they act as a weed guard as well.

Step 6: This is an optional step. Here Tom leaves the monofilament eyes off and replaces them with black painted eyes on the bead.

Diving Tarpon Fly

We find it interesting how 'simple' and 'effective' are two words that often go together; this fly fits both to a "T" as you will see as we tie the Diving Tarpon Fly. It evolved from other tarpon flies with the narrow pointed snout. For several years Tom has used plastic craft beads to cover the non-lead wire wraps used to sink the pattern and give it the "diving" part of its name. He ties it in a range of colors only limited by the shade of the craft bead and related materials. Even though

we illustrated the pink/white pattern here, Tom tells us purple/white and chartreuse/white are also very effective.

He likes to fish it with a slow retrieve using the weight to provide an up-and-down action in the water. When using short, hard strips, the bulk of the bead causes the fly to dart erratically from side to side. Even though the pattern was developed for tarpon, Tom tells us it is very effective for speckled trout as well.

Diving Tarpon Fly

Hook:	Mustad 34011, size 1/0-4
Thread:	Clear monofilament, red
Tail:	Pink over white craft fur
Hackle:	Red, tied as a collar
Weight:	Non-lead wire
Fly Head:	Plastic craft bead
Eyes:	Yellow with black pupils, stick-on or painted
Snout:	Red micro chenille, clear epoxy or Aqua Tuff
Head:	Red thread

Step 1: Pinch down the barb of the hook and place it in the vise. Apply a thread base that covers the back half of the hook shank. Bind a section of white craft fur to the end of the shank and trim any waste ends. Top it with a clump of pink craft fur also trimming any extra material. The length of each should be about twice the length of the hook shank. Coat the trimmed ends with super glue and allow the assembly to dry.

Step 2: Apply a double layer of non-lead wire directly in front of the trimmed tail ends. Coat them with super glue. Make sure the thread is hanging at the end of the hook shank in preparation for the next step.

Step 3: Do not let the super glue dry from Step 2. Immediately slip a plastic craft bead over the hook eye and seat it on top of the wire wraps. While the glue, wire, and bead are drying to form a single unit, position the stick-on eyes or paint them, whichever you prefer. Coat the head and eyes with clear epoxy or Aqua Tuff and allow it to dry. Select a red hackle feather and tie it on the hook by the tip near the end of the shank. Wrap a hackle collar that covers the area behind the bead and in front of the tail. Trim the excess material, whip finish the thread, and clip it temporarily from the hook. Reattach it directly in front of the bead.

Step 4: Tie on a section of red micro chenille directly in front of the bead. Wrap forward about half way to the eye, whip finish the clear thread, and trim it from the hook. Attach the red thread and advance it forward almost to the hook eye. Wrap on several more turns of lead if you want a heavier fly. Coat the whole area in front of the bead then go immediately to the next step.

Step 5: Wrap the chenille forward to the hook eye. Tie it off and trim the waste end. Apply a thread head, whip finish, and trim it from the hook.

Step 6: Place clear epoxy on the front half of the snout, sprinkle on a bit of glitter, and allow the fly to dry. Tom concludes in his instructions to us, "If you like, epoxy the whole snout. It's your option."

D.W. Special

Tom Berry writes, "This fly is a tribute to the great Dave Whitlock—hence the name the D.W. Special. It is a modification of the Bend Back Sheep Minnow he created. Instead of using Icelandic sheep hair, the poly duster material is used. It too is colorful and durable with lots of action. It is also cheaper and more readily available. Also the gill plate at the head is prismatic die-cut material. Tom tells us, "I like to coat the head with Soft Tex and then cover that with Hard As Nails polish."

Tom likes to fish it like a streamer working it slowly allowing it to flutter and sink to represent a wounded baitfish. Since it looks like a baitfish, it can be fished just about anywhere and in all types of water—lakes, streams, canals, and salt water. Bass strike them as well as steelhead, large trout, and in salt water the list is almost endless, including cobia, bluefish, redfish, and mackerel just to name a few. Tom notes, "In salt water it has to be speeded up in the summer and fished slower in the winter."

Tom offers this tying tip, "The poly material used on dusters is about four inches long and very durable. In shaping it, I like to spray it with hair spray before cutting it."

D.W. Special

Hook:	Saltwater, size 2/0-4, bent
Thread:	Clear nylon
Wing Separator:	Red dubbing
Wings:	White & orange poly duster
Over Wing:	Black poly duster over peacock Krystal Flash
Wing Sides:	Grizzly hackle feathers, pearl Flashabou
Gill Plate:	Prismatic material, cut to shape
Eyes:	Stick-on, coated with Soft Tex
Final Coating:	Clear nail polish or Aqua Tuff

Step 1: About two eye-lengths back on the hook shank place a ten-degree upward angle bend. Place the hook in the vise and apply a thread base over the part of the hook between the bend and the eye. Apply a ball of red dubbing just forward of the bent angle.

Step 2: Tie the white poly duster wing on the top of the shank just forward of the ball of dubbing. Do the same with the orange poly duster material, but place on the underside of the hook. Trim any excess material. Tom suggests applying super glue to each application.

Step 3: Turn the hook over in the vise so the orange poly duster wing is on top. Be careful of the hook point, it's easy to snag your fingers on it. Tie the peacock Krystal Flash on top of the orange duster material, then top it with black poly duster fibers. Add three or four strands of pearl Flashabou to each side of the fly and trim any waste ends.

Step 4: Select two grizzly feathers similar in size and long enough to reach about a hook gape behind the wing assembly. Tie one on each side of the fly on top of the Flashabou from the previous step. Cut a strip of prismatic material that is as wide as the hook gape. Fold it in half and trim it to shape. Then unfold it and cut it into two pieces at the foldover mark. Tie one on each side of the fly over the grizzly hackle feather to form the gill plates.

Step 5: Place the stick-on eyes on each gill plate, then coat both units with Soft Tex. Allow this application to dry before coating the complete head, eye, and gill plate assembly with clear nail polish. Hard As Nails is one choice, Aqua Tuff is another clear coating option.

Ever Green Streamer

The mother of invention is often nothing more than the environment of the moment and this is the case for the Ever Green Streamer. Tom was demonstrating fly tying at the Gulf Coast Boat Show in Biloxi, Mississippi where he was experimenting with pearl Flashabou as a translucent application over different-colored base materials. Someone suggested adding dyed ostrich herl to the mix and this pattern's body evolved from that idea. Isn't it amazing the synergy that can flow when like-minded people get creative? The result is a good-look-ing, translucent body with a hint of green (or whatever color of ostrich herl you select).

At the same time, Tom was looking for a real colorful streamer and selected the tail assembly you see here. All he needed to do to finish the pattern was add the "V" cut to the tail; a profile that already proved successful for Tom. The bead-chain eyes added the frontal weight that causes the fly to dip during the stop part of a strip/pause retrieve. A smooth, steady retrieve causes the tail to undulate in the water.

Ever Green Streamer

Hook:	Mustad 33960, Size 6
Thread:	Clear, fluorescent green
Tail:	Red, green, and yellow poly duster material
Body:	Pearl Flashabou
Rib:	Green ostrich herl
Eyes:	Silver bead chain
Head:	Thread

Step 1: Pinch the hook barb and place in the vise. Apply a clear thread base that starts in the center of the hook, goes to the end of the shank and back to the middle. Tie on a clump of yellow poly duster material that extends to the rear and is twice as long as the hook. Trim the excess material and cover wrap the cut ends. Repeat the process with a clump of green poly duster material then follow with a bundle of orange. Note: Each time you trim the waste ends and cover wrap them you are moving forward on the hook shank. When the three-clump application is complete you have moved forward on the hook to a point one-fourth back on the shank.

Step 2: Attach a green ostrich herl at the back of the hook then follow with a section of pearl Flashabou. Wrap the Flashabou forward and tie it off slightly forward of the one-fourth point. Trim any excess material. Palmer the ostrich herl forward, tie it off, and trim any waste end. Whip finish the clear thread and clip it from the hook.

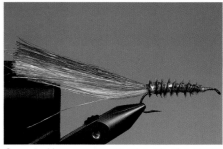

Step 3: Here we exercised a bit of author's privilege and changed the size, spacing, and color of the ostrich herl. The difference is dramatic. What if we added a hackle or another color ostrich with longer fibers? What if...?

Step 4: Tie on the green thread and bind the silver bead-chain eyes to the front of the hook. Notice Tom attached them to the bottom of the shank so the hook will travel point down in water. Wrap a thread head, whip finish, and trim off the excess. Apply a coating of head cement or Aqua Tuff. To cut the "V" shaped tail, Tom suggests giving it a quick shot of hair spray, it makes the trimming process much easier. After trimming the tail, run a comb through it to remove the hair spray.

BILL BLACK

We've know Bill Black for a number of years and find him to be one of the fly-fishing industry's real pioneers. Bill and his brother Dennis were instrumental in shaping much of the way the industry looks today: imported goods, fly-tying factories, modern-day fly-fishing merchandizing, etc. Bill's story is so interesting we decided to let him tell it in his own words.

Bill writes in recent correspondence with us, "I started tying flies at the tender age of twelve. At thirteen, and under the influence of my older brother Dennis who was already an expert professional tier, I took a basic tying class at the famous Long Beach Casting Club. Towards the end of the six-lesson course I entered and won a contest for the best Royal Coachman of the class. This showed me there was something I was good at and enjoyed doing.

By the age of fourteen I was visiting Dennis and his family in Oregon and tying flies every chance I had. Dennis, not being all that happy with my tying material consumption, suggested I'd be better off tying flies for him and getting paid for it. Under his watchful eye I was soon tying two plus dozen flies per hour and making $5.00 for every hour spent. I loved it, considering I still spent the winter in high school working at McDonalds for $1.35 per hour. It's not all bad because based on that experience I can still make one heck of a good shake and fries.

Spending every summer on the North Umpqua River in Oregon tying flies with my brother, along with our friends Lance and Randall Kaufmann, are some of my fondest memories. There are numerous tales of the Blacks and the Kaufmanns I could expand on, but not in this book.

In 1971, my brother Dennis, my other brother Mike, his wife Patty, and my parents set up Umpqua Feather Merchants, a business still active today. The year 1976 found me processing 20,000 rooster necks we imported from Calcutta, India; many of these I personally selected while there. I had debugged the necks by submerging them in formaldehyde for several hours. Then I had to rinse them with a garden hose. It was a cold evening and getting late when I had a great idea. I would wait until the wee hours then go to the local all-night laundromat and run the rinsed feathers through their extractor, thereby eliminating most of the water/formaldehyde. I entered the laundromat about midnight and was happy to find no one around. Then I noticed the line of thirty or more Maytag washing machines. Perhaps I could fill all of them with the necks and put them on the rinse cycle thus eliminating a lot of work. Heck, the more I thought about it, the better the idea seemed so I loaded up every machine in the place. Once the rinse cycle was done I loaded the necks in gunnysacks, stuffed a couple them into the extractor, and gave them the spin of their life. Quickly the entire building filled with the fumes from the formaldehyde and I was forced to spend the wait times outside the building and up wind of the open door; it was really bad. It was all I could do to empty the extractor and place the next two bags inside before beating a hasty retreat. Soon I was watching the sunrise and anticipating a long-needed sleep when the mothers showed up. They marched in with baskets of laundry while I kept my face turned away, but they did observe me put my last two sacks in the extractor. I stepped outside to let the machine do its job. Soon one of the women ran outside to advise me that whatever I had in the extractor was blowing up. I looked inside and the thing was billowing smoke. Being hard-wired, I had to just watch as it almost flew off

Bill Black

the floor it was bolted to. Eventually it stopped, I grabbed my gunnysacks, and made a dash for it. Finally I got to bed about 7:00 a.m., but was not to stay there for long. I was awakened by close friend Frank Silagy who informed me the State police were looking for me. To make a long story short, my feathers had clogged all the pumps on the washing machines closing down the business. The bright spot was the Maytag washing machines were new and still under warrantee. They were all fixed for free while I was left to pay for the lost business and the plumber.

In the mid 70s, Dennis and I would usually spend at least part of the summer tying flies in Yellowstone National Park. I have some great memories of tying flies every morning, catching huge cutthroat trout in the afternoon, and spending time with the many female park employees in the evening. For me, the Park was like Disneyland in the woods!

In 1974, I started a business making jewelry using the art of fly tying and a lot of pheasant feathers. I was making a modest living doing this while learning the silversmith trade, carving (learned from an old Indian friend Jim Van Vranken), and scrimshaw. I still have a local newspaper with the headline that read, 'Bill Black, the happiest man in the world.' And I was! At the time, my retriever and I lived in a $50.00 per month cabin in the woods on Susan Creek in the middle of the fly-fishing waters on the Umpqua River. A quarter-mile hike into the cabin gave me freedom and time to create my unique line of jewelry.

My small business was providing me a modest income when my brother Dennis convinced me to move to Sri Lanka and setup a fly-tying factory for Umpqua Feather Merchants. That move from the cabin in the woods to an island the size of our local county with a population of sixteen million people was a major step for me. I had my work cut out for me. Working with an amazing partner, Mr. Nihal DeMel, I grew the factory and matured into a man. Thanks Nihal. I lived in Columbo, Sri Lanka for four years experiencing their civil war and extreme droughts. I believe the factory remains the premier fly-tying facility in the world today. While living there I also went back and forth to India helping with our friend's fly factory and grading/buying feathers.

Eventually I returned to Oregon and became Vice President of a much-bigger business than I had left four years earlier. I ran much of the day-to-day operations, and in 1980 helped Dennis's son Craig set up a tying operation in Chang Mia, Thailand. My prior experience really paid off and that factory continues today to produce great numbers of high-quality flies. Over the years I personally trained over 400 production tiers who in turn have trained another 1500 tiers. Because of this I can say with confidence that I have been directly responsible for the current overall proportions, look, and feel of most commercial flies now produced worldwide.

In 1990 I started my own company called Spirit River Inc. with the goal to provide top-of-the-line flies, materials, and service; hoping I could mix in my creative spirit as well. I then added as many synthetics to my material line as I could. I feel synthetics offer an advantage because they are fairly inexpensive, readily available, easy to work with, consistent, and no animal is killed in the process. I continue to steer the company towards synthetics as much I can. We have originated such products as our patented counter-drilled Brite Beads, Real Eyes, Dazl-Eyes, Cross-Eyed Cones, Dubbing Dispensers, Fine & Dry Dubbing, Lite Brite, and the Pro 20 Hook Box. These products, along with a large series of innovative and effective fly patterns, have allowed our company to grow and prosper.

In hindsight, my departure from Umpqua and the creation of Spirit River turned out to be a huge blessing. I have been able to take many of my dreams/ideas and turn them into reality. Hopefully I leave a legacy of spirit and innovation. Obviously I did not do all this on my own and owe an enormous amount of gratitude to my wife Jean who puts up with me, my kids Megan and John, all my brothers, personal friends, my former partner Ken Ferguson, my staff, and associates to include the dealers, fly tiers and fly-fishers who buy our products."

Mr. Bill's Flying Ant (Brown)

Bill designed this fly in 1993 to utilize Spirit River's unique wing material patented under the name Wing & Things. As the pattern evolved, he added Crystal Splash for the antenna and legs, which we think really added to the fly's attraction.

Bill talks about fishing the pattern, "I fish it on Camas Creek, a very small stream full of native cutthroat trout. The pattern sits flush

in the surface film and these little guys gobble it up. Though these fish are not particular about their meals I have found it works just as well subsurface as it does on top. I sent three dozen to my buddy Lefty Kreh and a couple months later he wrote me a letter saying it was the best spring-creek ant he had ever used. That's quite an endorsement!

Mr. Bill's Flying Ant (Brown)

Hook:	Size 10-20, dry fly
Antenna:	Gold Crystal Splash
Body:	Antron dubbing, brown
Legs:	Gold Crystal Splash
Wing:	Mottled brown Wings & Things

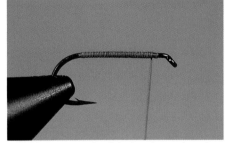

Step 1: Place the hook in the vise and apply a thread base to the complete hook shank. Leave the thread hanging at the front of the hook.

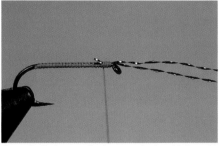

Step 2: Select a single strand of gold Crystal Splash and fold it in half. Tie it on the hook directly behind the hook eye to form the antenna. Trim away the excess material.

Step 3: Apply dubbing to the thread and form the front part of the body. Wrap the thread to the center of the hook, again apply dubbing to the thread, and construct the back segment of the body. Note it is much larger than the front. Be certain to leave a space between the two applications equal to one-eighth of the hook shank.

Step 4: Tie two segments of gold Crystal Splash on the hook at the front of the back body segment. They should sweep toward the back of the hook.

Step 5: Tie two segments of gold Crystal Splash on the hook at the back of the front body segment. They should sweep forward. Trim the legs so they are all the same length.

Step 6: Cut a section of Wings & Things that is almost as wide as the distance of the hook gape. Use a pair of scissors to shape a wing and tie it to the hook between the two body segments. Whip finish and remove the thread from the hook. Use a pair of scissors pressed against a finger to shape a foot at the end of each leg. Apply a coating of Aqua Head to finish the fly.

Bunny Crayfish

Bill wanted to design a crayfish pattern for the smallmouth bass in the Umpqua River near his home. He had two goals. The pattern would maintain its claw shape and also be durable enough to hold up to fifty-fish days when he was lucky enough to encounter them. Unlike marabou that becomes too slender in the water or feathers that have little life, the rabbit-strip claws were the answer to the first part of the equation and Bodi Stretch provided the required durability. Bill added several turns of lead wire tight against the eyes so the fly would sink in the water column hook-point up and postured similar to a natural crayfish.

He fishes the pattern on a dead drift over weed beds often allowing it to sink to the bottom then stripping it with a short, quick retrieve. Bill comments, "I have found my Lite Brite Minnow will catch more fish, but the Bunny Crayfish catches bigger fish." We've found this pattern to be one of our best producers in any water with a population of crayfish. This is a must-have pattern.

Bunny Crayfish

Hook:	Size 4-10, 4XL streamer
Thread:	Black
Antenna:	Brown rubber leg material
Eyes:	Spirit River Mono Eyes
Mouth Parts:	Brown ostrich herl
Rib:	Copper wire
Carapace:	Brown Bodi Stretch
Weight:	Lead wire (Mini Bulk)
Claws:	Brown Zonker strips
Body:	Brown rabbit dubbing
Crayfish Tail:	Trimmed brown Bodi Stretch

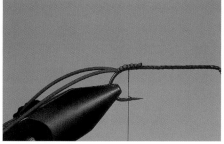

Step 1: Place the hook in the vise and apply a thread base that covers the complete shank. Select two segments of brown rubber leg material and attach them at the end of the shank to form the antenna. Be sure to bind them part of the way into the hook bend. Trim any excess material and leave the thread at the back of the hook in preparation for the next step.

Step 2: Tie on a brown ostrich herl by its tip and trim off the waste end. Cut a section of Bodi Stretch so it's as wide as the hook gape and tie it to the underside of the hook shank. Note that both materials are attached to the hook past the end of the shank and down into the bend. Select a medium pair of mono eyes and tie them on the hook at the end of the shank.

Step 3: Apply several wraps of lead wire in front and in back of the eyes. Apply rabbit dubbing to the tying thread and cover the lead wire turns. Wrap the ostrich herl over the covered lead application. The thread should be hanging even with the hook point.

Step 4: Tie on a section of copper wire to use later as the rib. Tie on two rabbit strips with the hide side touching the hook shank, one on the far side and the other on the near. Trim off any waste ends. Apply dubbing to the thread and wrap it forward to the hook eye. Notice the profile of the body that is larger toward the back of the hook and more slender near the front.

Step 5: Pull the Bodi Stretch forward and tie it to the underside of the hook directly behind the eye. Wrap the copper wire forward forming the segmentation in the carapace.

Step 6: Tie off the copper wire and trim away the excess. Clip the excess Bodi Stretch long enough to form the crayfish's tail. Cut the rabbit strips to length, forming the claws. Whip finish and remove the thread. Apply a coating of cement or Aqua Head to anchor the whip finish. Notice we've photographed the fly in the hook-up position.

Crystal Wing Para Hopper

Bill designed this fly as part of his Crystal Wing fly series. This idea can transcend into other patterns like Wulffs or Stimulators. He tells us, "I use our Crystal Splash as a parachute wing post because it almost glows in low-light situations. As I slip into the fifties, I find any pattern I can see in low light a real plus. I also like the ever-so-slight twinkle that can be more realistic than natural calf hair. The only drawback to the Crystal Splash as a wing post is it tends to be heavy and you need to be somewhat conservative when using it."

Bill fishes it tight to the bank on a dead drift. It has taken a number of local trout on the North Umpqua River and the cutthroat in Yellowstone Park just love it. We find the improved visibility has moved this fly to a permanent place in our fly boxes, it's our go-to pattern during hopper season here in Idaho.

Crystal Wing Para Hopper

Hook:	Dry fly, size 4-12, 2XL
Wing:	Pearl Crystal Splash
Body:	Olive Fine & Dry dubbing
Legs:	Yellow rubber leg material
Wing:	Mottle turkey quill
Hackle:	Grizzly
Head/Thorax:	Olive Fine & Dry dubbing

Step 1: Place the hook in the vise and apply a thread base that covers the back three-fourths of the shank. Select a clump of pearl Crystal Splash and tie it on the hook at the one-fourth point on the shank. Trim the waste ends at a severe angle and cover them with thread. Leave the bobbin hanging at the back of the wing material.

Step 2: Pull the wing Crystal Splash up and wrap a parachute hackle platform at the base of the material. Anchor the wing post so it stands up straight. Apply dubbing to the thread and construct a body on the back three-fourths of the hook shank. Leave the thread hanging at the base of the wing post.

Step 3: Select two sections of yellow rubber leg material. Tie them on the hook at the post making certain they are anchored both behind and in front of the wing. Trim any waste ends and leave the thread to the front of the post.

Step 4: Select a slip of mottled turkey quill that is as wide as the gape of the hook. Trim one end so it has a rounded profile; this will be the end of the wing. Tie on the wing behind the post and trim off any waste material. We treat our turkey quills with Aqua Flex to improve their durability. You may wish to do so as well.

Step 5: Prepare a grizzly hackle feather by removing the fuzzy material at the base of the stem. Tie it on the hook in front of the post and trim away the waste end. Apply dubbing to the thread and wrap a head/thorax. Leave the thread hanging at the hook eye.

Step 6: Wrap the feather around the platform post to form a parachute hackle. Tie the feather off at the hook eye and trim away the excess. Whip finish and remove the thread from the hook. Apply Aqua Head to finish the fly.

Irresistible Temptation

Bill designed this fly to splat on the water like an adult stonefly often does. He wanted a pattern that sat in the surface film for a realistic silhouette and would remain floating throughout the day. Bill is convinced the antennas are an important aspect to this pattern's silhouette, making it more attractive to selective fish.

Besides presenting it to trout, Bill likes to use it on a local bass pond as well. The fly is big and splats the water hard enough to really grab their attention. Bill tells us, "For best results I usually fish it about a foot off the weed line. With that said I must admit this pattern is a bear to tie. Having access to my own offshore tying facility allows me the opportunity to create some interesting and time-consuming patterns; ones that I would not normally want to produce in any real volume on my own." We agree and usually tie the body on our version of Bill's pattern with a strip of foam rather than the trimmed deer hair.

Irresistible Temptation

Hook:	Size 4-12, TMC 200R
Thread:	Orange
Tail:	Black deer hair
Body:	Black deer hair
Wing:	Black Wing & Things
Over Wing:	Black deer hair
Antenna:	Black monofilament
Legs:	Black rubber leg material
Eye:	Black mono eyes
Hackle:	Black
Head:	Orange Fine & Dry dubbing

Step 1: Place the hook in the vise and attach the thread at the back of the hook directly over the barb. Select, clean, and stack a small clump of black deer hair. Tie it on the hook as a short tail that is no longer than the width of the gape of the hook. At this point we usually place a small section of Scotch tape over the tail to isolate it from the body hair. Trim off the waste ends. Select a clump of black deer hair and remove the under fur. Spin it around the hook shank just forward of the trimmed tail ends. Spin several more clumps of hair each in front of the previous until you reach a point on the shank that is one-third of the way back from the hook eye. Whip finish and remove the thread from the hook. Remove the hook from the vise and trim the body to shape. Remove the Scotch tape to expose the tail. Place the hook back in the vise and reattach the thread.

Step 2: Select a piece of Wings & Things that is as wide as the distance of the hook gape. Round one end to form the end of the wing, tie it in place, and trim away the waste end. It should end evenly with the tail fibers. Select two segments of black monofilament and tie them to the sides of the hook to form the antennas. Trim off the excess material.

Step 3: Select, clean, and stack a clump of black deer hair. Tie it on the hook as an over wing that is equal in length to its counterpart. Trim the waste ends and cover them with a thread base.

Step 4: Select four sections of black rubber leg material and bind two to each side of the hook. Trim off the waste ends then cut the legs to length. They should be as long as the overwing. Cover wrap the waste ends with a thread base. Bind the eyes to the hook in the center of the thread base with several figure-eight wraps.

Step 5: Prepare a black feather by removing the fuzzy fibers at the base end of the stem. Tie it to the hook directly in front of the wing and trim off excess stem. Apply orange dubbing to thread and cover the head behind and in front of the eyes. Leave the bobbin hanging at the hook eye.

Step 6: Palmer the hackle forward to the hook eye, tie off the feather, and trim away the excess. Whip finish and remove the thread from the hook. Apply a coating of Aqua Head to finish the fly.

Lite Brite Zonker (BH)

We are really impressed with this pattern and hope you will be as well. In a recent email Bill told us about it, "I came up with this pattern in 1994 and ever since then it has been my 'last resort' fly. It is fast and easy to tie plus it can take a real pounding. I had always liked fishing regular Byford Zonkers for steelhead here on the North Umpqua River. Early in 1994 I discovered a magical material called Lite Brite and soon there after Spirit River introduced it to the fly-fishing industry. It is a very fine shredded Mylar I started using on many of my favorite patterns including the Zonker. I have fished it extensively for trout, bass, crappie, and even shad. However, it is particularly effective on steelhead. I also tie a white version with rubber legs on each side and the smallmouth bass cannot resist it."

Lite Brite Zonker (BH)

Hook:	Size 4-12, 4XL streamer
Thread:	Brown
Weight:	Brass bead
Body:	Copper Lite Brite dubbing
Gills:	Ruby red Lite Brite dubbing
Wing:	Brown Zonker strip
Head:	Copper Lite Brite dubbing

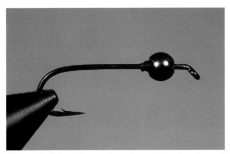

Step 1: Slip a brass bead on the shank and place the hook in the vise jaws. Slide the bead all the way forward to the hook eye. At the one-fourth point on the shank wrap a large enough thread dam to keep the bead from slipping over it. Whip finish and remove the thread from the hook. Apply a drop of Krazy Glue to the thread then slip the bead on it. Set it aside to dry.

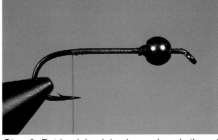

Step 2: Put hook back in vise and apply thread base that covers complete hook shank. Leave bobbin hanging at the end of the shank.

Step 3: Select a Zonker strip and trim the end to a point. Tie it on the top of the hook at the end of the shank with several tight thread wraps.

Step 4: Apply copper Lite Brite dubbing to the thread and wrap it forward forming the body. Stop just short of the brass bead. Dub on a small section of ruby red Lite Brite dubbing to complete the body. Whip finish and remove thread. Reattach thread in front of the bead.

Step 5: Tie down the wing in front of the bead then trim off the waste end. Wrap thread base over the trimmed material.

Step 6: Apply a small amount of copper Lite Brite dubbing to thread and wrap the head. Whip finish and remove thread. Apply a coating of Aqua Head to finish fly.

TOM BRODERIDGE

Tom Broderidge

One of the hundreds of stories that Tom Broderidge has had published during the last two decades was a piece of humorous fiction about a fly-fisherman's quest for "the perfect fly." The protagonist didn't find it in the story, just as none of us find it in real life, but that doesn't stop us from trying. We look to modern materials with the continued hope that the newest space-age plastic might have just the right reflectivity to be irresistible to fish, or that the next generation of genetic hackle might float a dry fly better than ever before. Every Federation of Fly Fishers' conclave offers the promise of learning something new, or at least some old information viewed in a new light. This attitude that fly-fishing is a dynamic puzzle to be solved is one thrust of Tom's interest in the sport.

Another is the search for understanding that comes from learning about the history of fly-fishing. The idea that we have a 500-year written record of human effort to catch trout on a fly is both intriguing and enlightening and gives us a reference point for understanding more about ourselves and our sport. Tom notes that successful flies, with seeming disregard for their separation by time or space, often share many characteristics of proportion, shape, and color. Some of the flies in Dame Juliana Berners' fifteenth century volume *Treatyse of Fysshynge Wyth an Angle*, for example, are still tied and fished today. That historical connection also partly explains Tom's interest in traditional salmon flies, as well as his fascination with old patterns from Britain and Ireland.

Tom found fly-fishing at the age of fourteen. As a kid, his strategy for approaching new information was always the same: he went to the public library and read all the books he could find on the subject. Fly-fishing offered a rich literature and described a discipline that was surely worthy of a life's work. Slightly more than forty years have passed, and Tom is a Master fly-casting instructor, writer, author, and fly-tying teacher. He grew up as a fly-fisher hunting trout in the hallowed Catskill Mountains of New York state, and now finds himself living near the Gulf of Mexico where he usually manages to fish about 150 days a year for anything from six-inch sunfish to 200-pound tarpon.

At this point, Tom wonders (often out loud) just how his lifetime involvement in a pastime as bucolic as fly-fishing has affected his attitudes and worldview. In a newspaper column, Tom once wrote that he was more influenced by Huckleberry Finn than by Donald Trump; more admiring of the Dalai Lama than of Vince Lombardi; more inspired by Groucho Marx than by Karl Marx. In fly-fishing terms, he would quickly admit that his heroes are really more likely to be anti-heroes, such as the reclusive Theodore Gordon or the hard-fishing but introspective Gus in David James Duncan's classic novel *The River Why*. And while it's a safe bet that Tom wishes he and not John Gierach had come up with the term "Trout Bum," it is a safer bet that nothing would make Tom happier than for that term to apply to himself for the rest of his life.

Beaded Wobbler

Saltwater fly-tiers are constantly searching for a spoon fly that has flash and motion and imitates the size and shape of baitfish eaten by game fish such as spotted seatrout, redfish, bluefish, Spanish mackerel, snook, and cobia. The Beaded Wobbler is just that. By using two strings of plastic beads lashed to the sides of the hook to form the body, which is then filled in with a clear hardening agent such as epoxy or Loon Hard Head, the fly is easy to tie and easy to duplicate. To make tying even easier, the beads don't have to be placed symmetrically along the hook. In fact, a slight unevenness in bead placement usually helps the fly wobble better.

Another adjustment to increase this fly's wobble (and most other spoon flies as well) is to shorten the tail. A tail on a fly acts like the tail on a kite and stabilizes the fly, this means less wobble. The tail shown here adds billowing movement and sparkle to the fly, but at the slight sacrifice of some wobble. Don't make the tail any longer than it is here, and if the fly doesn't wobble enough to suit you or the fish, consider shortening the tail or cutting it off entirely.

In clear water or on bright days, the translucent Beaded Wobbler sparkles and flashes and can be seen from a long distance. In dark conditions, the fly's wide cross section and flat-sided beads push a lot of water while its wobbling sends out vibrations to attract fish that feel the fly's presence long before they see it.

Faceted beads come in a wide range of colors and sizes and are available in national craft store chains such as Michaels, Ben Franklin, and also in the craft sections of Wal-Mart. The beads used here fit well on a size 1 Mustad 3407, which is a slightly short-shanked hook. For other hooks, use beads that produce a similar body shape.

Beaded Wobbler

Hook:	Mustad 3407, size 1
Thread:	3/0 Monocord, white
Thread for stringing beads:	Monobond Super Strength
Tail:	White rabbit strip, silver Flashabou
Body:	Strung beads, on the sides

Step 1: At the rear tie-in point, bind in a strip of rabbit skin on top of the hook for a tail. It should be 1/8-inch wide and about as long as the hook shank.

Step 2: Also at the end of the hook shank, tie in four strands of Flashabou on each side of the tail. Trim any excess fibers and cut the Flashabou so it is even with the end of the tail

Step 3: Again at the end of the hook shank, tie in a six-inch-long piece of heavy thread for stringing the beads. Lay the heavy thread across the top of the hook, and use two or three figure-eight wraps with the tying thread to secure the heavier thread in place. Move the tying thread forward to the front of the hook just behind the eye. Leave it at this position.

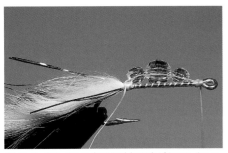

Step 4: Slip three faceted beads (4mm, 9mm, 4mm) on the heavy thread on the far side of the hook. Bring the beaded thread forward, pull it moderately tight, and secure it just behind the hook eye with tying thread. Trim any excess.

Step 5: String three beads onto thread on the near side of the hook in the same manner as outlined in Step 4, tie the heavy string off near the hook eye, and trim any excess. Wrap the tying thread between the beads several times, pulling them tightly against the hook shank. Tie off the tying thread, trim, and whip finish.

Step 6: Apply a coat of epoxy or any thick, clear filler, such as Aqua Tuff, to fill in the gaps between the beads thus completing the body. Apply additional coats if needed.

Foam Crab

To be a successful redfish fly, a crab pattern must look like a crab and also act like one when the fly is presented to a fish. The shape of the foam material and the proper placement of the weight from lead eyes in the form make the Foam Crab plop on the water, move downward at steep angle, and then scuttle across the bottom just as a real crab does. The porous foam is also a perfect canvas for coloring the fly to match the local crabs in the area. Choose a light foam of the same color as the bottom of the natural crabs in your area. That way you only have to color the top of the fly.

Many of the ideas for new flies aren't really new, but are adaptations of ideas that have been used successfully on other flies. This is the case with the Foam Crab. Several years ago, Tom watched Tony Spezio, the fine fly tier and bamboo-rod maker from Flippin, Arkansas; use a similar foam technique to make his freshwater frog. The major difference is that Tony's frog is a top-water fly and the foam lays flat along the hook to produce a two-dimensional outline and silhouette that looks like a frog when viewed from below. The Foam Crab's lead eyes make the fly sink, and curling the foam creates a three-dimensional body that looks like a crab from any angle.

Note that the lead eyes are placed on top of the hook, this turns the fly over and makes the hook point ride up, which is a handy way of keeping the Foam Crab weedless as it scoots across sand or oyster bars or tiptoes across the tops of sunken grass beds. The rubber legs provide constant movement, and the curling of the foam body ensures that the legs are pushed downward and outward so their movement appears lifelike at any speed of retrieve.

The best foam for this fly comes from the 1/8-inch-thick sheets sold through fly-tying suppliers and appears softer and more open-celled than the denser foam available in craft stores. That denser craft-shop foam tends to be cut by the tying thread more easily, is thinner, and does not work as well for tying the Foam Crab.

Your choice of tying thread is very important. Even with the right kind of foam, you need a thread that flattens to increase its surface area and lessen the chance of cutting through the foam. Danville Flat Waxed Nylon works superbly, and comes in a wide enough range of colors to help imitate virtually any crab. Felt-tip markers are available in any crab color. A final tip to help preserve the color on marked foam flies also comes from Tony Spezio: when the fly is done, coat the foam with Rain-X automobile windshield treatment, and the colors will stay bright and vivid for a long time.

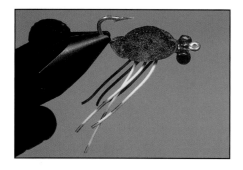

Foam Crab

Hook:	Mustad 3407, size 2
Thread:	Brown (or color to match local crabs)
Legs:	Rubber legs, size small, tan (or color to match local crabs)
Eyes:	Lead dumbbell eyes
Body:	1/8-inch-thick foam, cut into 1/4-inch-wide, three-inch-long pieces, with one long edge beveled at a 45-degree angle; tan (or color to match the bottom of local crabs)
Markers:	Felt-tip marker, color to match local crabs

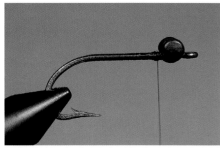

Step 1: Tie the lead dumbbell eyes on top of the hook about one eye width back on the shank. For the most secure eyes, instead of using multiple figure-eight wraps, make about 30 wraps in one direction diagonally across the eyes, then 30 wraps across the other diagonal. Finally, make about a dozen horizontal wraps that go under the eyes but over the hook to pull together the 60 diagonal wraps, tightening them. Wrap the hook with tying thread back to the end of the shank to provide a less slippery surface for tying in legs and foam.

Step 2: At the three mid tie-in points, bind the rubber legs on top of the hook shank, one leg at a time. Use two or three figure eight wraps for each leg. Be sure to leave the tying thread just behind the eyes.

Step 3: Turn the hook over in the vise. From the 1/8-inch-thick foam sheet, cut a 1/8-inch-wide, three-inch-long foam strip. Bevel one long edge at a 45-degree angle. Place the foam just behind the dumbbell eyes (remember, the eyes are on the opposite side of the hook). The bevel is up and points toward the hook bend. Secure the foam with two or three tight figure-eight wraps. Wrap the tying thread back to the end of the hook shank, being careful to avoid the rubber legs in the process.

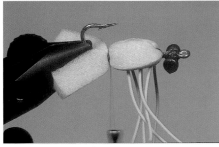

Step 4: Fold both foam ends back toward the hook bend and bind them down with two or three wraps of tying thread at the rear tie-in point. Note: The 45-degree beveled edges are touching each other creating a dimensional, rounded body.

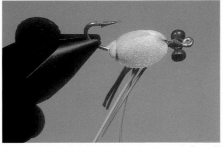

Step 5: Whip finish and trim the thread. Cut off the waste foam at the hook bend.

Step 6: Turn the crab over in the vise or remove it from the vise and prop the fly so the underside of the body is exposed. Spread the legs, and apply a coat of epoxy or clear filler such as Aqua Tuff to the concave underbody and exposed thread.

Step 7: Use felt-tip marking pens to color the top of the body and legs. Coat the body with Rain-X to preserve the colors.

Painted Caddis

Tom grew up as a fly-fisherman in the Catskill Mountain streams of New York State, where cased caddis were common in the streams—and in the stomachs of trout. These caddis nymphs make their cases by cementing together grains of sand from the river bottom, and because the colors of the sand vary from stream to stream, so do the colors of the caddis cases. The Painted Caddis allows you to match the size, shape and especially the color of local cases, so you wind up with patterns that are stream-specific, and sometimes even specific to one part of a stream.

The Painted Caddis has essentially no buoyant material and so sinks quickly and stays deep, even in moderately fast currents. It's worth noting that the strongly weighted body with its clean lines makes the fly look and behave much like the Czech nymphs that have done so well in international fly-fishing competitions in recent years.

The 3X-long 9672 hook gives the fly about the right proportions. Select a hook-shank length to match the size of the case caddis in your stream. Wire comes in environmentally-friendly non-lead versions in the same range of sizes as lead, so you should have no problem finding a wire size that builds the right diameter case with very little extra work, other than flattening the end of the wire to produce the rear taper that is almost always present in the real caddis case.

The colors of natural caddis cases are usually more subdued than the flies that imitate them. But don't worry; your flies will get better with age. The abrasive wear and tear from fishing dulls the sheen on the paint and makes the fly more understated, and often more effective. You can shortcut that process by rubbing the finished fly lightly with a scouring pad or a piece of fine steel wool. When on the stream, before making the first cast it never hurts to turn over an underwater rock and rub the Painted Caddis in the slime to help remove any human smell and make the fly seem more like a natural element in the stream. Adding slime also tends to slightly darken the Painted Caddis, making it look even more realistic.

Painted Caddis

Hook:	Mustad 9672, usually sizes 12-16
Thread:	Black
Body:	Wraps of lead wire, acrylic paint over
Paint:	Acrylic, colors to match local caddis cases
Head:	Ostrich herl, black

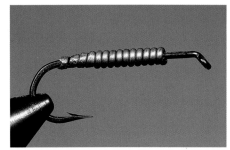

Step 1: Taper the last one-fourth inch of lead wire by squeezing it with long-nose pliers. Begin with the tapered end of the body and wrap the wire around the hook shank up to the front, leaving room for the ostrich herl head. Wrap wire tightly, butting each wrap up against the previous one.

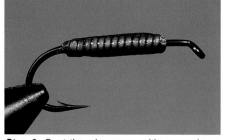

Step 2: Coat the wire wraps with epoxy, Loon Hard Head, or Aqua Tuff to secure the wraps and smooth the surface for painting. Apply a second coat if needed.

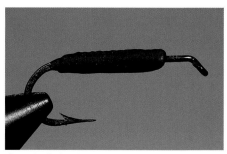

Step 3: Paint the body with acrylic paint. The first coat covers the whole wire body and should closely match the general color of the local caddis cases or the sand on the stream bottom. Let it dry in preparation for the next step.

Step 4: Paint dabs of whatever color matches the cases in your local stream. White, cream, and black are common, and even red and blue are sometimes found. Rather than using a paintbrush, use the sharp end of a toothpick to dab color on, as these specks represent grains of sand that the caddis has cemented together to make the case. Let it dry.

Step 5: Paint more toothpick dabs of the appropriate colors. Again, let it dry in preparation for the last step.

Step 6: Attach the tying thread in front of the body and tie in a piece of ostrich herl. Wrap the herl forward to form the head and tie it off at the hook eye. Trim any excess material and whip finish. Apply a coating of head cement.

MIKE BUTLER

Innovative fly tier Mike Butler lives in Jefferson City, Missouri with his lovely wife Beth. Born deaf without an auditory nerve, he has learned to speak very well when among "hearing people." Mike communicates in many different ways, such as writing notes, speaking, lip reading, and sign language. This multi-faceted ability is referred to as "total communication."

He is a self-taught fly tier learning the basic skills as a little boy after his father bought him a fly-tying kit. Mike didn't tie a lot when at home, but really improved his skills when he left his parents' home to attend a school for the deaf, first in Iowa and then later in Missouri. By 1994 he was an adult and full-time fly tier. Today he makes his living as a full-time video photographer and a part-time still photographer.

Mike's partner, Cecil Scantlin was also born deaf. Together they love to tie flies and fish the streams close to their home in Missouri and even south into Arkansas where the White River calls to them. Often in the summer they travel north to Minnesota to fish area streams and lakes. Another hearing-impaired friend, George McNece, has also helped Mike progress with his fly-tying and photography skills.

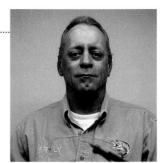

Mike Butler

He especially wants to thank fellow Federation of Fly Fishers members who have helped develop his fly-tying and fishing skills. Mike refers to them as "hearing people" and they include Mark Van Patten, Ed Strzelczyk, Royce Dam, Jack McGee, John Lincoln, Sue Halblom, and Pat Smith. He especially wants to thank Mark Van Patten for getting him started as a demonstration fly tier at shows in Mountain Home, Arkansas. Mike is a member of the Federation of Fly Fishers, Capital City Fly Fishers, and the Missouri Deaf Fly Fishers. His dedication and hard work have not gone unnoticed. Mike was the proud recipient of the Capital City Fly Fishers 1997 Fly Tier of the Year.

When he is not demonstrating fly tying, Mike can be found with his wife Beth canoeing, fishing, riding into backcountry streams and traveling gravel roads searching for new fishing locations. Their love of photography dovetails nicely with the other outdoor activities they pursue.

Double Shell Back Damsel

The damsel is an important food source to many stillwater fish species and this pattern does an excellent job representing it. The beadchain eyes are positioned on the under side of the hook so the fly travels through the water in the hook-down position. Should you want the fly to ride hook-point up, all you need do is place the chain eyes on top of the shank. The great design of the DSB Damsel creates a similar profile no matter which way it is suspended in the water—hook point up or down.

It's best fished on a floating line in shallower water conditions not much deeper than eight or ten feet. You can easily adjust your tippet length to get it to the depth you need. Should you need to go deeper, a ten-foot sink-tip will quickly get you to the desired depth.

With a slight modification you can change the whole action of the fly and we present this as only an idea should you want to pursue it.

Change the eyes from bead chain to melted mono and use a narrow strip of foam as an under body. Even though the fly looks the same this formula changes it into a floating damsel nymph.

Our purpose here is not to fish it as a floating damsel, but to use Gary LaFontaine's yo-yo technique to fish it. Use a fast-sink fly line with a short leader/tippet combination and the floating damsel on the end. When you cast into a weed bed the fly line sinks straight to the bottom but the nymph floats just above the weeds (given an appropriate leader length). During the retrieve, the fly line will disturb insects in the weeds making them accessible to cruising fish and of course your fly is mixed in with the naturals. It's a deadly technique whenever damsel nymphs are present. Try it; you will be amazed at the results!

Double Shell Back Damsel

Hook:	Size 8-12, 2X long
Thread:	Olive
Tail:	Green goose biots
Rib:	Fine gold or copper wire
Under body:	Non-lead wire or foam
Body:	Turkey tail fibers, felt-tip marker
Thorax:	Peacock and hackle
Shell backs:	Turkey tail, coated with epoxy
Eyes:	Bead chain or melted mono
Head:	Thread

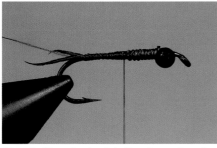

Step 1: Place the hook in the vise and apply a thread base covering the complete hook shank. Bind a pair of beadchain eyes on the hook directly behind the eyes—top or bottom of the shank; it's your option. Place several non-lead wire wraps directly behind the eyes and anchor them in place with the tying thread. Tie on a tail of olive biots. Then bind the wire rib material to the hook as well.

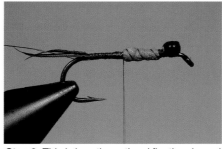

Step 2: This is how the optional floating damsel is constructed. The eyes are melted mono and the lead wire is replaced with a thin strip of foam wrapped around the hook directly behind the eyes.

Step 3: From this point, the fly is constructed the same whether it is to be a sinking or floating damsel. Tie on several strands of turkey tail by the tips at the end of the hook shank. Wrap the thread forward to the eyes. Follow it with the body and rib material. Trim any waste ends.

Step 4: Use a green felt-tip marker to color the body material. Select two sections of turkey tail fibers for the shell backs and attach one to the top and the other to the bottom of the shank. Tie on several peacock herls by the tips. Stroke out the fibers on a brown hackle feather and also tie it on the hook by the tip. Twist the peacock and hackle together in preparation for wrapping the thorax.

Step 5: Wrap the twisted unit forward to form the thorax while dressing the hackle fibers back after each turn to avoid trapping them under the herl. Tie it off behind the eyes and trim any waste ends. Pull the under side shell back forward and tie it off in front of the eyes. Trim the excess material.

Step 6: Pull the top shell back over and tie it off in front of the eyes. Trim any waste ends and whip finish. Remove the thread and apply a liberal coating of epoxy or Aqua Tuff to the shell backs and head. Apply a second coat if needed.

DSB Nymph

Mike developed the DSB Nymph (Double Shell Back) as an all-purpose nymph that looked the same to the fish no matter which way it traveled through the water—hook up or hook down. The solid bead head with the extra lead in the body causes the fly to quickly sink and is particularly effective when, "It slides down along the drop-offs where there are rocks and nymphs usually hide under rocks."

He also points out the shell backs are very durable because Mike coats them with at least two applications of Gloss-Clear Lure and Jig Epoxy. The DSB Nymph is certainly attractive and durable in appearance.

Mike likes to fish it on a floating line with a strike indicator. He lengthens the drift by dropping his rod tip as the fly drifts past and below him. Then at the end of the drift, Mike twitches the rod tip as the

nymph rises through the water column toward the surface. Let the fly rise all the way to the top, then let it hang in the surface film for a few seconds before recasting it up stream.

It has served him well in Minnesota lakes and streams, where it has scored perch, bluegill, bass, trout, and even a "surprised walleye." He well remembers a trip to the Root River at Forestville State Park where many brown trout near the Old Iron Bridge fell for the DSB Nymph. Mike states, "All fish were released back to the water after testing the DSB." Mike advises it's equally effective back in his Missouri home waters.

Your authors have tested this fly and are very impressed with its results and appearance. You will see real soon just how impressed we really are.

DSB Nymph

Hook:	Size 4-16, 2X long
Thread:	Brown
Weight:	Non-lead wire
Tail:	Brown biots
Under Body:	Gold High Voltage tinsel
Over Body:	Larva Lace, brown
Thorax:	Peacock herl and brown hackle
Shell Backs:	Turkey tail, coated with epoxy
Head:	Copper bead

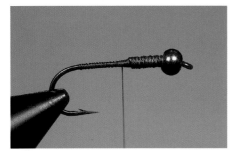

Step 1: Straighten the TDE if you prefer a ring-type eye. Slip on the bead so the small hole is to the front and the larger faces the rear. Wrap six to eight turns of .025 non-lead wire on the hook shank and trim any excess. Push the wraps forward so they are tight against and slightly inside the larger hole on the bead. Apply a thread base that covers the wire and the hook shank. Leave the bobbin hanging in the center of the hook.

Step 2: Select two brown biots and bind them to the hook to form a split tail. Trim a three- or four-inch section of brown Larva Lace and trim one end at a 45-degree angle. Tie it on the hook at the end of the shank; the 45-degree angle sets the material in place ready to wrap. Last attach the gold High Voltage or Holographic tinsel in place and wrap it forward to the start of the wire wraps. Tie it off and trim any excess material. Advance the thread forward to the bead head.

Step 3: Wrap the body material all the way forward to the bead, tie it off, and trim the waste end. Select two turkey tail quill strips that are as wide as the gape on a hook one size smaller than the subject one in the vise. Tie them on the top and bottom of the shank to eventually form the double shell back. Leave the thread hanging near the center of the hook.

Step 4: Bind several peacock herls on the hook by the tips and trim any waste ends. Stroke out the fibers on a brown hackle feather and tie it to the center of the hook on top of the peacock herls. Twist the peacock herl and hackle together in preparation for wrapping the thorax.

Step 5: Wrap the thorax making certain to stroke back on the hackle fibers as each turn is applied to the hook. Tie it off just behind the bead and trim any excess material. Fold the top shell back over, bind it to the hook at the bead, and trim any excess.

Step 6: Pull the bottom shell back over and tie it off at the bottom of the hook. Trim any excess, whip finish, and trim the thread. Apply a liberal coating of epoxy or Aqua Tuff that coats both shell backs, extends out onto the bead, and covers the thread wraps as well. Apply a second coat if needed. A fly turner will ensure the coating dries evenly.

DSB Stone

We have long looked for a good, all-around stonefly nymph pattern and the goal always seemed just a bit out of reach. Though many patterns worked well enough they didn't "tweak" our fancy. That was until we saw Mike's fly and were immediately impressed with it. The profile is great from either direction: hook up or down.

Like most fly tiers/fly-fishers we apply any good idea to our fishing situations. The DSB Stone is a good example of this; several people's ideas influenced the pattern you see here. Of course Mike's double shellback design was a major influence in the overall appearance of the DSB Stone. We are not sure of whom to credit for the rubber leg influence, but Al first learned about them from one of Jack Dennis's books so that's as good a source as any for this discussion. Besides, we'll state again, "There is very little invented in fly tying. If you think you have a new design, check with your grandfather's generation, chances are good that anything you dream up was probably thought of long ago."

The last influence came from Gary LaFontaine. Much of his study of the sport of fly-fishing focused on triggering mechanisms. What was it that caused a fish to strike? His Natural Drift Stonefly nymph was constructed so it would have the same posture in the water as the natural stoneflies he observed during scuba-diving sessions. Those stoneflies floated in the current tail down and head up. To get his Natural Drift Stonefly to maintain this posture in the water he put lead wire on the back of the hook and spun deer hair on the front.

Gary also was convinced that eyes on a fly were a major triggering factor, and we agree they are important on subsurface flies. So let's put the ideas listed here together in a fly that looks similar when viewed from above or below, has action in the legs, drifts in the water column like a natural insect, and has the predominant eyes we feel are important to the fish. Does the DSB Stone work? You bet it does, but don't take our word for it, try it for yourself.

DSB Stone

Hook:	Size 2-12, 2X long
Thread:	Orange
Tail:	Black biots, black bead, Krazy Glue
Rib:	Fine gold or copper wire
Under body:	Foam cylinder
Body:	Black Brazilian velour
Thorax:	Peacock herl
Legs:	Montana Fly Co. Centipede Legs, black
Gills:	Gray ostrich
Shell backs:	Turkey tail, coated with epoxy
Eyes:	Fake flower stamens
Head:	Thread

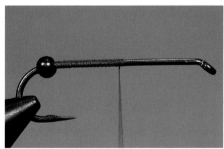

Step 1: Place the hook in the vise after slipping a black bead on the hook and leave it positioned down around the hook bend. Apply a thread base that starts in the middle of the hook, goes past the end of the shank into the bend a short way, and then back to the end of the hook shank. Place a drop of Krazy Glue on the short thread base located on the hook bend then slip the black bead onto this position.

Step 2: Tie on the black biots for the tail using the black bead to separate them. Slip a foam cylinder on the hook and bind it in place on the forward part of the shank. Tie the flower-stamen eyes in place and trim any excess material. Anchor three sections of the Centipede Leg material on top of the foam cylinder leaving the thread hanging in the center of the hook.

Step 3: Bind a section of black chenille or Brazilian velour to the back part of the hook then anchor a piece of wire for the rib. Wrap the velour forward to form the body then follow with the rib material. Trim any waste ends and leave the bobbin hanging in the center of the hook.

Step 4: Select two sections of turkey tail fibers and bind them to the hook (top and bottom) to form the double shell back. Next tie on a gray ostrich herl then anchor the peacock herls by the tips. Wrap the peacock herl forward to the eyes and tie them off there. Trim the waste ends leaving the thread in front of the eyes.

Step 5: Wrap the ostrich forward making one turn in front of each leg segment to form the gills. Bring the underside turkey shell back forward and anchor it in front of the eyes. Trim the waste ends from the gills and shell back.

Step 6: Fold the top shell back over and bind it to the hook in front of the eyes. Trim the waste end, whip finish, and clip the thread. Coat each shell back with epoxy or Aqua Tuff and place the fly in a turner to dry. Apply a second coat if needed.

JERRY CARUSO

Jerry's signature line on all of his e-mails simply states, "All things considered, I'd rather be in Philadelphia." Many people ask him why he would want to be there. The fact that it's a quote from W. C. Fields is a consideration, but also of equal importance, Jerry was born, raised, and has lived in the same house for most of his fifty-five years.

More importantly, forty-plus years ago he learned to fish nearby when his father took him to the Schuylkill River to catch sunfish and bass. Unfortunately the river was quite polluted and Jerry tells us, "I remember the fish we brought home for my grandfather to cook never tasted very good, and the red/white bobbers we used often had a coal tar ring around them at the end of a day on the water. I continued to fish through high school and when I enlisted in the Navy in 1967, a spinning rod went with me when I was assigned to a submarine rescue ship based in New London, Connecticut."

After his tour of duty, Jerry eventually went to college in Tennessee and of course a couple of spinning rods went with him. The fish he caught were not released, but instead became table fare along with rabbits and squirrels he was able to hunt. Roger Peacock introduced him to fly-fishing on a nearby farm pond. During the day, Roger tried to show him how to fly-fish, but "it just didn't take." However the seed was planted and lay dormant for several years until Jerry happened to join a local club, the Mainline Fly Tyers. The group often made an annual pilgrimage to a bed and breakfast, Maple Hill Farm, near the Delaware River for the spring shad run. The owner, Bill Horvath, eventually convinced Jerry to lay aside his spinning rod in favor of fly-fishing equipment.

Jerry Caruso

The Mainline Fly Tyers introduced Jerry to fly tying via a beginner's class where he learned to tie his first fly, a Delaware Flymph. After the class, a more experienced club member gave him a fly-tying book with notes scribbled in the margins from previous owners. He had given Jerry the book because the person who gave it to him told him to use it and pass it along when he no longer needed it. Jerry received it with the same expectation. Four years ago he passed it along with the same instructions. With help from Bill Horvath and classes from the club, Jerry became an accomplished fly-tier. Internet fly swaps gave him the much-needed practice and motivation to really excel at his new-found avocation.

Jerry writes us, "I'm currently single and share the house I grew up in with my eighty-year-old mom who tolerates my fishing and tying as long as I can spare her a day or two each month to take her to Atlantic City and don't neglect the house and yard too much. I've worked for the Federal Government for the past twenty years and I'm currently the account manager for the Subsistence Prime Vendor Program in Guam. I may be one of the few people who have ever fly-fished in Guam. Other than fly-fishing and tying, I enjoy the occasional micro-brew, my bi-weekly poker game, and trips to the range to do a bit of target, trap, or skeet shooting."

Baby-S

When Jerry initially started tying the pattern he spent a lot of time searching for the right colors. He tells us, "What I do now with any material that takes permanent markers well is I tie the pattern in white leaving me a blank canvas with which to work. Depending on the color, this fly can be tied to mimic a shad, herring, golden shiner, perch or sunfish." Jerry normally ties the pattern so it is about three inches long, but has constructed flies as long as six inches. He uses the Bob Popovics technique employing Photo Flo (photography dark-room wetting agent) to shape and smooth clear silicone over the head and eyes.

It is fished like a streamer on either a sink-tip or regular floating fly line. On the sink-tip, Jerry likes to treat the fly with Water Shed so it will rise in the water column during the pause part of the retrieve. When he uses the floating line he crawls it along the surface in an effort to simulate a wounded minnow. He normally fishes it for bass but it has also taken trout, pike, perch, and crappie.

Baby-S

Hook:	Size 1, worm hook
Thread:	White
Weight:	Optional rattle
Flash:	Sparkle Flash
Body:	White Polar Fiber
Eyes:	Doll eyes
Color:	Felt-tip markers, green, yellow, red, and black
Coating:	Clear silicone

Step 1: Apply an 1/8-inch-long thread base directly behind the hook eye. If you plan on adding a rattle, bind it to the center and bottom of the hook shank. Select a clump of Sparkle Flash or Flashabou that is twice as long as the shank. Tie it on the hook about 1/8 inch back from the eye using about three snug but not tight wraps. Pressing down on the clump with a thumbnail will cause it to disperse around the shank then bind it in place with several tight anchor wraps. Trim any waste ends.

Step 2: Select a clump of white Polar Fiber or similar synthetic hair and tie it to the off side of the hook. Repeat the process with another bundle and bind it to the near side of the hook. Trim any excess material and cover-wrap the clipped ends. Notice Jerry used a razor blade to shape a taper to each clump.

Step 3: Bind a third clump of fiber to the top of the hook and then to the bottom. Trim the excess, cover-wrap the clipped ends, whip finish, and cut the thread from the hook. Shape the taper on the top and bottom bundles just like you did on the side clumps in the previous step. Apply super glue to the head and allow it to dry before continuing.

Step 4: Use a comb or toothbrush to blend the fibers, then use a toothpick to apply Flex-Loc from the head to the bend of the hook. Be sure to apply the glue to both sides of the fly. Squeeze the glued area between your thumb and forefinger to create and hold the shape after it's dry. Allow the Flex-Loc to dry then use felt-tip markers to color the body. Here Jerry used red, yellowish chartreuse, fluorescent green, and black. Don't forget to color the head as well.

Step 5: Apply a thin coat of clear silicone over the front of the fly. When it's tacky, press the dull surface of foil to each side to transfer additional sparkle to the fly. Jerry used Delta Renaissance foil. Also while still tacky, press the eyes into position.

Step 6: Apply a second coating of silicone thicker in the front to cover the eyes and thinner towards the back. Dip your fingers in Photo Flo to smooth the wet silicone. Set the fly aside to dry.

Emu Nymph

This pattern grew from a common situation many fly tiers face; getting a new material then figuring out what to do with it. For Jerry the material came from a fellow fly tier who received a large quantity of emu feathers as the result of a road-killed bird.

At the time he received the feathers, Jerry was preparing to demonstrate at his first North East Council Conclave near the Ausable River in New York. He wanted to demonstrate a dark nymph in size 10 or 12 to imitate the Hendrickson and March Brown nymphs and sought something a bit different from the standard Pheasant Tail or Gold Ribbed Hare's Ear. Jerry's last goal was to keep the pattern simple and this fly definitely meets that expectation.

Jerry fishes it in both moving and still waters. On streams and rivers he lets it dead drift, then swing across current, and last, strips it back part way before repeating the cast. Does the fly work? Jerry tells us in his own words, "Over the last four years, I've caught brown, rainbow, and brook trout with it. Other species I've caught include smallmouth bass, pan fish, rock bass, perch, and some large golden shiners." It sure looks "buggy" to us!

Emu Nymph

Hook:	Size 8-12, TMC 2488
Thread:	Black
Weight:	Non-lead wire
Tail:	Stripped emu fibers
Body/legs/thorax:	Emu feather, trimmed
Wing case:	Dark gray emu feather, epoxy or Aqua Tuff

Step 1: Place the hook in the vise and attach the thread about one eye width back on the hook shank. Wrap to the end of the shank and back about half way. Wind several turns of non-lead wire on the front part of the hook. Place a drop of head cement on the wire wrap then cover-wrap this area with the thread. Leave the bobbin hanging in the center of the hook. Flatten the wire wraps with a pair of pliers.

Step 2: Strip three or four fibers from a feather, even the tips, and tie them on the back part of the hook to form a tail that is as long as the hook shank. Trim the waste ends then wrap the thread to the end of the hook shank. Leave it there for the next step.

Step 3: Select a fairly long, light-gray feather and tie it on the end of the shank by the tip. Wrap the thread forward to the center of the hook and tie on a dark-gray feather to use later for the wing case. It is also tied to the hook by its tip. Advance the tying thread forward and leave it hanging just behind the hook eye.

Step 4: Wrap the light-gray feather forward all the way to the eye, tie if off there, and trim any excess material. Be sure the wraps are close together because the trimmed feather creates the body in a future step.

Step 5: Pull the wing case feather over the top of the thorax area, tie it off just behind the eye, and trim the excess material. Whip finish the thread, cut it off, and apply a drop of head cement to finish the head. Jerry suggests that any dark feather will make a great wing case if you don't have the shade of emu he used here.

Step 6: Trim the under side of the fly as close to the shank as possible without cutting the wrapped feather stem. Also trim the back part to represent the abdomen as illustrated. Be careful, it's easy to cut off the tail in the process. Leave the fibers on the front sides as legs. Coat the wing case with epoxy or Aqua Tuff and let it dry. Apply a second coat if needed.

SJB Shiner

Jerry explains about the pattern, "I spent about forty-five years using spin-fishing gear and I've only switched over to fly-fishing for all species in the last five years. Toward the end of my career on the dark side, soft plastic baits with names like Slug-go and Fin-S were hot items and excellent fish catchers that imitated injured or dying baitfish. When I moved over to fly-fishing I found there weren't any flies that imitated the action of those spinner baits. After much experimenting, I found this pattern is the closest I've been able to come to matching their action or shape."

In trying to imitate spinner baits, Jerry soon discovered there were no standard fly-tying hooks that fit his need and had to resort to a light-wire, worm hook. E-Z Body or Corsair Tubing provided a body with dimension that was light enough to fly cast. He jokingly admits, "There may be one advantage of coming up from the spin-fishing ranks. To tie this pattern, it sure helps to know how to rig a plastic worm or other plastic bait on a worm hook."

Jerry uses the SJB Shiner in streams, lakes, and salt water preferring to present the fly and as soon as it hits the water begin a quick strip-pause retrieve. A good alternate method is to let the fly sink in the water column a couple of feet and employ a longer (twelve- to eighteen-inch) retrieve with an extended pause, thus allowing the fly to re-sink again.

SJB Shiner

Hook:	Size 1, wide-gape worm hook
Thread:	Clear mono
Tail:	Pearl Sparkle Flash
Body:	Pearl E-Z Body
Eyes:	Stick-on, yellow with black pupils
Head & back:	Felt-tip markers, epoxy coating

Step 1: Cut a piece of tubing about three to six inches long. Use a lighter to singe the end that will eventually be the front of the fly. To prevent it from corning unraveled during the tying process. Color one side of the tubing with a dark green felt-tip marker. Pinch the barb on the hook then insert the point through the bottom of the tube about 1/8 inch from the singed end. Note: Even though we illustrate the first three steps using a vise, it's much easier to accomplish them without it.

Step 2: Push the hook through the tube until the bend behind the hook eye comes through the bottom. Rotate hook so the point is up and prepare to push it through the tubing.

Step 3: Push hook point through the bottom of tube and then straight out the top, making certain the entry and exit holes are in line with each other. When this is complete the hook shank should be parallel with the bottom of the tube and the eye should be the only part sticking out the front. This measurement is critical and may take more than one attempt. Just be certain your unfinished fly looks like the illustration.

Step 4: Adjust the hook in the vise so the eye is tilted up slightly. Mix a small batch of five-minute epoxy and fill the first quarter inch of the tube to anchor the hook eye in place. Place the unit in a fly turner to dry it.

Step 5: Once the unit is dry, use a red felt-tip marker to color the front. Place it in the vise the reverse of normal. Take a three-inch section of Sparkle Flash and fold it in half. Insert the material into the rear end of the tube (now pointing to the right, assuming a right-handed tier) holding the tube and material inside of it in place with the thumb and fore-finger of the left hand. Wrap several tight turns of thread around the end of the tube collapsing it, and thus holding the Sparkle Flash in place as a tail. We've found using a dental floss threading loop (available at any drug store) is helpful in forming a whip finish. Place a drop of super glue to the whip finish to ensure durability.

Step 6: Turn the fly back around in the vise and stick on the eyes. Use the green and red-felt tip markers to touch up the body colors. Mix a small amount of five-minute epoxy to coat the eyes and front of the head. Place the fly in a turner to dry.

BILL CHANDLER

Bill currently works as an administrative assistant at a senior living community in northern Vermont. In addition to those duties he is a professional fly tier, guide, and casting instructor. Currently Bill is single and enjoys spending time with his friends dancing, working out, playing golf, and of course, fly tying and fly fishing.

His fascination with fly tying started over twenty years ago when he saw a gentleman tying flies on an outdoor TV program, and also observing Ed Schirmer, a local fly shop owner, tie flies at a local outdoor show. Since that time, Bill has spent much time studying the history of fly tying including current tiers as well as those from history. Today he is known by some of his angling associates as the "Professor of Tying." He is often asked for information about flies, techniques, or tiers from the past.

Bill started tying flies long before he learned to fly-fish. Even though he loves to catch anything that swims, his first love and addiction is tying flies. Bill tells us, "I would describe myself as a fly-tier first and a fly-fisher second. I remember when I first started tying flies I used my father's old work-bench vise, spools of sewing thread, old pieces of yarn, and a squirrel tail. The first fly I created was the Red Dog because it had a red wool body and a wing using hair from my dog."

After struggling with this crude set of tools, he decided to upgrade and was pleased to find that Farrell Allen, a very respected fly-angler and tier, owned a fly shop in downtown Burlington. With Farrell's help then and through the years, Bill was on his way to a

Bill Chandler

lifetime of enjoyment.

Bill Chandler's flies have appeared in *American Angler* and *Fly Tyer* magazines, as well as books such as *Patterns of the Masters, Smelt Flies* by Don Wilson, and the *Encyclopedia of Fly Patterns* by your authors, Al & Gretchen Beatty. Over his 25-year tying career, Bill has demonstrated his tying skills at regional and national Federation of Fly Fishers' Conclaves, the International Fly Tyers' Symposium, the American Museum of Fly Fishing, the Fuller Museum of Art, local angling clubs, and the first Fly Fair USA. He was named the Northeastern Fly Tying Champion in 1988 and twice has placed in the top ten in the Mustad Fly Tying Championships. In 1995 the Fly Tyers Guild of the North Atlantic Salmon Federation honored Bill with the title of Master Salmon Fly Tier.

Bill talks about the FFF, "The Federation of Fly Fishers is an organization, amongst many, that I support. I feel that they bring many new people to the sport and pastime of fly-fishing. That can only help fly-fishing grow and bring more support to conserving our waters. Beside the reasons just stated, I like the FFF because it helps me do the things I love, meeting others who share my interests and teaching the skills and techniques of tying flies and fly-casting. I learned those things because of the FFF and I can share them for the same reason. Please support the Federation of Fly Fishers, they can use your help."

Break Water Smelt

Bill is not sure when he created this pattern but remembers it was around 1990. At the time he was experimenting with color combinations for streamers he used on Lake Champlain for land-locked salmon. This pattern is the result of those experiments.

The first day he used this pattern he landed six fish on the fly. Bill considered it a success and named the fly for the area he was fishing, inside the breakwater in the Burlington, Vermont harbor. He recalls, "It was a cloudy, windy, over cast day with 1 1/2-foot swells;

a perfect day for catching salmon. My technique is to troll with two rods using a different pattern on each, one off the stern and the other off one side or the other. I prefer using an 8-weight rod, a 25-foot sink-tip, a straight piece of 8-pound monofilament leader, and steer an 'S' pattern while trolling about two miles per hour." He prefers the sink-tip because it gets the fly down to the fish quickly and keeps it away from the "pesky seagulls."

Break Water Smelt

Hook:	Size 1, 8 XL Rangeley streamer hook
Thread:	White & black
Body:	Silver Mylar tinsel
Under wing:	Several peacock herls
Belly:	White bucktail
Under shoulder one:	Red hackle fibers
Under shoulder two:	Yellow hackle fibers
Wing:	Light blue & gray saddle hackles
Shoulder:	Lavender guinea fowl feathers
Cheek:	Jungle fowl nails
Head:	Black thread

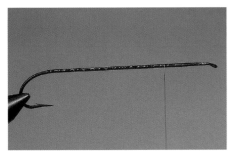

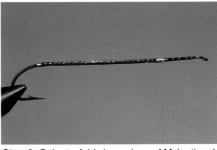

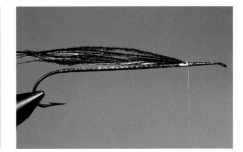

Step 1: Select two light blue and two dark gray saddle hackle feathers. Place the two blue feathers together with the dull side touching each other and the tips even. Sandwich them between the two dark gray feathers. The gray feathers should be shiny side out as well. Even the tips of all four, measure them for length, and trim the excess feathers at the base of the stem. Place a drop of glue on the trimmed ends and allow the ends to dry. We find a clothespin holds them in position quite well while they dry. Once they are dry, place a guinea feather and a jungle cock feather to each side of the assembly and glue them in place as well. Return the unit to the clothespin to dry. Place the hook securely in the vise jaws. Using white thread, start a thread base near the hook eye and wrap to the end of the shank. Wind the thread back forward stopping at a point about one-fourth of the shank back from the hook eye. Leave the bobbin hanging there. Coat the thread with head cement and before it dries go immediately to next step.

Step 2: Select a fairly long piece of Mylar tinsel; trim one end at a severe angle and tie that end to the underside of the hook at the one-fourth point. Wrap the tinsel to the end of the shank then reverse direction and return to the starting point. Tie off the tinsel and trim any excess material. At the turn-around point at the end of the shank, Bill suggests allowing one turn of tinsel to extend beyond the last turn of thread before reversing directions and returning to the front part of the hook.

Step 3: Tie on an under wing of eight or ten peacock herls. They should be long enough so they extend slightly beyond the end of the hook. Trim the excess herl and cover-wrap the cut ends. Leave the thread hanging slightly forward from the underwing tie-in point.

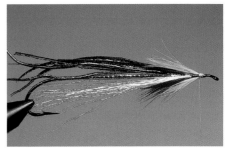

Step 4: Select a sparse clump of white bucktail, clean out the short fibers, and even the tips in a hair stacker. Tie them to the bottom of the shank as a belly allowing them to extend even with the inside of the hook bend. Trim the waste ends and leave the bobbin slightly forward of the tie-in point.

Step 5: Strip a clump of red hackle fibers from a feather stem. Bind them to the top of the hook so they are about one-half inch long and trim an excess material. Select a second clump and tie it to the bottom of the shank so it's as long as the first application. Notice the staggered tie-in points. Leave the thread slightly forward of the second clump. Trim any waste ends.

Step 6: Select a clump of yellow hackle fibers and tie them to the top of the hook so they are slightly shorter than the red fibers. Trim any excess material. Repeat the process on the under side of the shank and trim any waste ends.

Step 7: Whip finish the white thread, trim it from the hook, and attach the black thread for this last step. Remove the glued wing assembly from the clothes pin constructed in Step One and bind it in position directly in front of the yellow fibers. Cover-wrap the head area with black tying thread, whip finish, and trim off the thread. Apply a coating of head cement or Aqua Tuff and allow it to dry. Place a second coat if needed.

GEORGE "CHAPPY" CHAPMAN

George Chapman is a retired navy commander with thirty years of service to his credit. He feels he has "beat the system" because he's been retired for more than thirty years as well.

Chappy writes, "I was lucky to have been born in a family that took camping and fishing very seriously. I have fished on and off all of my life. By the time I was six I was an expert at catching crawfish with a bacon rind at the end of a piece of string. Enough so that years later when I saw my first Gold Ribbed Hare's Ear I attributed its attraction to fish was that it looked more like a baby crawfish than a nymph. I still think so."

The valley where he grew up had many small creeks that were bluegill hatcheries. He quickly graduated from dapping worms, crawfish and other bait to fishing small poppers and sponge rubber spiders. The only problem he had with the artificial bait was it cost money. George jokingly tells us, "I swiped my sisters sponge rubber ball and cut it up into spider bodies that, equipped with rubber band legs, worked as well as the store-bought ones. I was sternly reprimanded by my mother and got a licking from dad, but wow! I had a whole summer's worth of spiders."

From this beginning it was an easy transition to conventional bait, plug casting, and spinning gear. His navy career afforded him the opportunity to fish many exotic places. He remained an enthusiastic spin fisherman until one day Chappy and his son Tom were canoeing on the Potomac River working the pocket water for bass and bluegill. Because the water was moving quite fast they were missing some of the pockets because it took so long to reel in the lure and recast. Fishing

right behind them were two fly-fishers. They were hitting all the pockets because they could execute a quick pickup, back cast, and then place the forward cast in the next spot. He advises, "I became an instant and permanent convert to fly-fishing."

George "Chappy" Chapman

He got his hands on a Herter's catalog and purchased equipment, tying tools, materials, and his first book, *Professional Fly Tying and Tackle Making Manual*. In short order his wood-working skills helped him produce some pretty decent looking poppers, but his deer-hair bugs were atrocious. Their only saving grace was they caught fish. As you will soon see, George's tying skills have come a long way since those early years.

Chappy closes with this bit of information, "My last tour of duty was Officer-in-Charge of the Navy Motion Picture Office in Hollywood where I was liaison with the contractors who produced training films. A part of the job was being the duty gold braid at premieres, studio screenings, and a few parties. It was a tough job, but someone had to do it." We are certain our friend Chappy did a great job!

Since retiring, George joined the Federation of Fly Fishers where he shares his fly-tying skills at shows like the Southwest Council's Conclaves. For a number of years he published the newsletter for his home club, the Sierra Pacific Flyfishers. He followed that with several years as an education and conservation chairperson.

The Dorado Fly

The Dorado Fly is the premiere pattern in Chappy's Cortez Series and is a streamer designed to represent a small baitfish. Early in his research Chappy discovered a small baitfish whose only defense against predators was a large false eye at the wrist of the tail. The predator zeroing in on the eye expected the baitfish to flee in one direction while it went in the opposite to safety. Chapman tells us, "I resolved that all my streamers thereafter would have to accommodate the largest eye possible located near the point of the hook. I developed a unique system of stacking the wings to maintain the fish head profile with a flat area for the big eye."

It is primarily a blue-water fly that Chappy presents on a ten-weight rod with a fast-sink shooting head, fishing it just as you would

a lip-hooked live bait. Cast just beyond schooling fish then strip as quickly as possible, if necessary holding the rod between your legs or under your arm as you double-hand strip. When fish are not visible, troll it at a medium speed with the fly trailing just behind the roll of the wake. When fishing with a partner, the first to hook a Dorado reels in close to the boat and holds the fish on a short line. The school will usually follow the hooked fish and the partner can present a fly to them. On hook up, the first fish is released giving that person the opportunity to cast again to the schooling fish. Alternating in this manner, with a little chum tossed overboard, this orgy can last for thirty minutes and be some of the most exciting fly-fishing in the world for one of its most active and beautiful fish.

The Dorado Fly

Hook:	Mustad 9175, size 3/0
Thread:	White
Tail:	Gold Mylar braid, picked out
Wing:	FisHair, green/chartreuse/white
Wing accent:	Krystal Flash, black marker
Gills:	Red thread
Head:	Epoxy mixed with green glitter
Eyes:	Painted large, yellow with black pupils

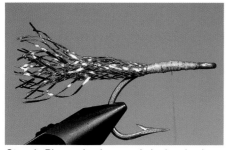

Step 1: Place a hook securely in the vise jaws then using a medium file or stone, scar the front half of the shank. Apply a light coat of Super Glue, lock the thread near the eye, and wrap a thread base to a location just above the hook barb. Wrap the thread back to the middle of the shank and tie on a one and one-fourth section of gold Mylar braid extending to the rear of the hook as a tail. Return the thread to the center of the hook and unravel the section of braid extending behind the hook using a bodkin.

Step 2: Tie on a 3 1/2-inch section of pearl Krystal Flash as a wing accent extending beyond the back of the hook. Leave the thread hanging in the end of the shank. Select a 3 1/2-inch section of white FisHair and trim the front of this segment on an angle. Hold it slightly above the shank with the angle-trim end near the hook eye. Take a loop of tying thread around the FisHair bundle near the hook's center but not around the hook. After placing the "lock loop" around the FisHair, position the bobbin on the opposite side of the hook. Pull down on the bobbin while sliding the FisHair down to meet the shank. Wrap forward on the hook toward the eye binding the FisHair to the hook. Wrap to the eye and back to the end of the shank. Tie on another segment of pearl Krystal Flash as another wing accent. Leave the thread hanging at the end of the hook shank.

Step 3: Prepare a four-inch section of chartreuse FisHair by trimming the front end at an angle and tie it on the hook on top of the white wing from the previous step. Be sure to use the "lock loop" explained in Step 2. Top this material with several strand of chartreuse Krystal Flash. Whip finish and trim the thread. Flatten the unfinished head with duckbill pliers then soak it with thin head cement. Place the partially finished pattern in a fly turner until it is completely dry.

Step 4: Place the unfinished unit in the vise and attach the tying thread near the end of the hook shank. Tie on a 4 1/2-inch section of chartreuse FisHair using the same techniques explained in Step 3. Top this with a 4 1/2-inch segment of dark green FisHair mixed with a similar colored Krystal Flash. Trim it on an angle before applying it to the hook with the same "lock loop" already described. Whip finish and remove the white thread. Attach red tying thread near the end of the shank and wrap several turns to simulate gills. Whip finish and remove this thread. Wrap a strip of paper around the wing to keep it from flaring; hold the paper in place with a short section of tape. Flatten the head again with the pliers, dip it in head cement, and dry it on a fly turner. When it is dry, apply a coat of epoxy sprinkled with green glitter on top and multi-colored on the sides. Again, place the fly in a turner to dry.

Step 5: Use yellow and black acrylic latex enamel to form the eyes. Use a nail head to place a circle of yellow paint on each side of the head and dry it in a fly turner. When it is dry, remove it from the turner and apply a black pupil using a smaller nail head. Again dry the unit in a fly turner. When it is dry, dip it one more time in clear lacquer to protect the eyes. Dry it one last time in the turner.

Step 6: Remove it from the turner and slip off the paper non-flare loop. Use the pliers to flatten the wing behind the gills. Trim the underside of the wings on an upward curve to the dark green FisHair. Use a black felt-tip marker to apply the vertical par markings.

DOUG CHRISTIAN

Doug Christian

Doug was born in May 1940 to two mathematics teachers in Saint Louis, Missouri and still makes his home there today. He got started in fly-fishing with his grandfather and uncle at the age of ten and became hooked on fly tying after receiving a Thompson vise as a gift. Doug still has that vise today.

In his early years, materials and instruction were not readily available, but he did find information in books. Doug became an avid reader and improvised with whatever materials came to hand. Much of his early fishing and tying focused on bluegills and he still considers them a favorite today.

After graduating from Grinnell College in 1962, Doug started teaching high school mathematics. He earned a MS degree in mathematics and continued teaching at the same high school until retiring thirty-four years later. Doug was married to Carol in December 1965 and soon after bought his home in Florissant. He still lives there today.

By contrast, his daughter Laurie has lived all over the country managing a career in engineering and raising their first grandchild, Justin.

Doug joined the Ozark Fly Fishers soon after it was organized in the 1970s. Like many who experience a Federation of Fly Fishers organization, he was first a student but soon became the teacher.

Doug has demonstrated his skills at Southern Council events for the past twenty years. Those events include the Southern Council Conclave, the Sow Bug Roundup, and the Federation of Fly Fishers International Conclave. The Ozark Fly Fishers named Doug the Fly Tier of the Year in 1988 and the Southern Council honored him twice with that title: first in 1993 and then again in 2001.

Doug's Spider

This simple and effective pattern had its start as a bluegill and bass fly, but it has also gained success as a trout fly. Tying it in gray or yellow produces a really good hopper imitation while a mix of orange and black imitates a salmonfly really well. The rubber legs provide the illusion of life in all waters for all species.

The design is simple but still needs a bit of explanation on the fold-over process. Doug uses a strip of craft foam to construct his spider and the bright chartreuse wing makes it highly visible in many different fishing conditions. Whether you use dubbing over the foam body is totally a matter of esthetics, it fishes equally well whether the body is plane foam or dubbing.

Doug's Spider

Hook:	Size 4-10, dry-fly style
Thread:	Black single-strand floss or to match the body
Body:	Black foam or color of choice
Wing:	Chartreuse deer hair or color of choice
Legs:	Black rubber leg material
Head:	Black foam

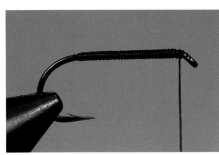

Step 1: Place a hook in the vise and apply a thread base that covers the complete hook shank. Start and stop this base directly behind the hook eye.

Step 2: Cut a strip of craft foam that is as wide as the hook gap and at least three inches long. Bind the foam strip to the hook anchoring it to the complete shank. Make certain there is excess foam extending both to the front and rear of the hook. Apply dubbing to the back two-thirds of the hook shank. Leave the thread hanging one-third back from the hook eye.

Step 3: Fold the back section of foam over, bind it there at the one-third point, and trim the excess. Cover wrap over the trimmed foam to anchor it in place.

Step 4: Select a clump of dyed chartreuse deer hair and remove the underfur. Even the tips in a hair stacker and tie them on the hook as a Trude-style wing that extends slightly past the hook bend.

Step 5: Tie on four strands of black rubber leg material in the center of the front one-third part of the hook. Apply black dubbing over this section leaving the bobbin hanging at the one-third point.

Step 6: Fold over the front section of foam to form the head. Bind it in place, whip finish, and trim off the thread. Trim any excess foam remaining from the head so it looks similar to the illustration. Leave the legs long, you can adjust their length on the water should you feel it necessary.

Fun Foam Popper

Doug Christian writes, "I started tying with foam after reading an article in *Fly Tyer Magazine* about tying popper heads shaped from shower togs. I've lamented the limitations imposed by the colors I was able to find and fortunately discovered Fun Foam, a children's craft item available from craft stores and craft departments of discount stores like Wal-Mart. This material is a closed-cell foam sheet two millimeters thick, which comes in twenty or so colors."

Doug says he likes to tie and fish small poppers for bass and bluegill. He laminates the foam into a long block he later cuts into square blocks. The squares are then mounted on the hook with Super Glue and shaped with a sander. Many of his poppers incorporate a multitude of colors however, this pattern features a single color augmented with felt-tip markers. The doll eyes are available in the same craft areas as the foam, and certainly provide an attractive addition to the popper heads.

Fun Foam Popper

Hook:	Mustad 33903, size 6
Thread:	Yellow
Head:	Six sections of foam, laminated
Head colors:	Black, olive, and red felt-tip markers
Coating:	Glitter and polyurethane varnish
Eyes:	Doll eyes
Tail:	Yellow marabou, dyed grizzly feathers, Krystal Flash, deer hair
Hackle:	Grizzly dyed olive
Legs:	Yellow rubber leg material

Step 1: First create the foam block by laminating two-by-six-inch strips of fun foam. A paper cutter is the easiest method to produce the strips. Glue the strips together using rubber cement. Coat each strip and allow the rubber cement to dry for about ten minutes before pressing them together. Doug recommends seven strips for a size 4 hook, six for a 6, and five or a size 8. After the large block is complete, cut it into one-half inch sections on a sixty-degree angle. Each large block will produce three or four popper heads.

Step 2: Place a hook in the vise and apply a thread base to the front three-fourths of the hook shank. Whip finish and trim the thread. Use a razor blade to cut a slit in the bottom of the popper head and mount it to the hook using Super Glue over the thread base.

Step 3: Use a fine sandpaper block on a variable speed drill to shape the head. After shaping the head, color it using olive and black mottled markings. Add a red slash to the bottom of each side about three-fourths of the way back on the head. Mount the doll eyes using Super Glue. Coat the markings with clear head cement or finger nail polish and sprinkle on a bit of gold glitter. After this is dry coat the entire head with polyurethane varnish. Doug usually applies three to six coats to get the right finish. Dry the heads in a fly turner to keep the varnish from running to one side.

Step 4: Tie on a section of marabou to form a tail that is as long as the complete hook. Accent it with gold Krystal Flash then flank the tail with two grizzly dyed olive hackle feathers.

Step 5: Select a clump of dyed olive deer hair and remove the short fibers and underfur. Even the tips in a hair stacker, then apply them to the hook as a topping that reaches the center of the tail. Attach a grizzly dyed olive hackle feather and wrap it as a collar directly behind the popper head. Tie it off, trim the waste end, whip finish, and clip off the thread. Apply head cement as needed.

Step 6: Use a narrow needle to insert legs that form an "X" pattern. Medium round rubber leg material seems to work the best.

Jig Crayfish

Doug tells us, "As a member of the Southern Council of the FFF for a number of years and living in a state with limited and crowded trout fishing, smallmouth bass fishing is the top sport." He believes that smallmouth bass have a "craving for crayfish" and many good patterns have been developed, most providing good results when presented properly.

Doug finds weight distribution important to a crayfish's design. The naturals tend to swim backwards and horizontal instead of diving. To solve the weight distribution problem, Doug went to a jig hook and the hook up design avoided much of the possibility of snagging the bottom.

He ties this pattern in two sizes, 1/64 ounce and 1/32 ounce. He uses a mold from Hilts for the 1/64 and a mold manufactured by Do It for the 1/32.

When Doug is encountering active feeding conditions on a stream, he likes to dead drift the fly at the edge of the current along a seam line. In ponds or slow-water conditions, he likes to use an erratic retrieve to simulate a swimming crayfish.

Jig Crayfish

Hook:	Eagle Claw 630, size 6-8
Weight:	1/32-ounce jig head, painted tan
Thread:	Tan
Mouth parts:	Deer hair, dyed tan
Antenna:	Krystal Flash
Rib:	Copper wire
Over body:	Tan furry foam
Body:	Tan furry foam, tan dubbing
Claws:	Two rabbit fur clumps
Hackle:	Ginger
Crayfish tail:	Excess over body material
Head:	Thread

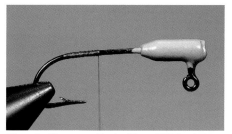

Step 1: Place an Eagle Claw 630 hook in a 1/32-ounce Do It jig mold and pour a lead head. Coat the head with tan acrylic paint then when it's dry, coat it with polyurethane gloss varnish; both are water based. Place a prepared hook in the vise and apply a thread base to the back one-third of the hook shank. Leave the thread hanging slightly forward of the hook point.

Step 2: Tie on two sections of dark Krystal Flash to form antennae that are as long as the complete hook. Select a clump of dyed tan deer hair and remove the underfur and short fibers. Even the tips in a hair stacker, and tie them to the hook so the tips extend beyond the hook about one-fourth inch and the butts are trimmed slightly forward of the hook point. The deer hair performs three functions: The tips act as mouth parts, the anchored hair is a base for the crayfish head, and the trimmed butts separate the rabbit hair claws.

Step 3: Turn the hook over in the vise. Cut a strip of tan furry foam that is about five-eighths inch wide and three inches long. Cut one end to a point and anchor this end over the deer hair, binding all the way to the end of the shank. Cover this tie-down area with tan dubbing mixed with Antron. Leave the thread hanging slightly forward of the trimmed deer hair.

Step 4: Tie on a section of copper wire for the rib then tie on a ginger hackle feather by the tip. Cut a clump of natural rabbit fur and tie it on the off side of the fly so the tips extend to the rear end. Make them even with the deer hair from Step 2. Cut a second clump of rabbit fur and tie it to the near side of the hook with the same proportions in the previous sentence. The two clumps of rabbit fur are the crayfish's claws. Cover the middle section of the hook with the tan dubbing mixed with Antron used in Step 3. Leave the thread hanging just behind the jig head.

Step 5: Wrap the hackle forward over the body, anchor it at the jig head, and trim the excess feather. Wrap the thread forward on to the jig head and leave it hanging at the eye. Pull the furry foam over the body, puncture a hole in it with the jig eye, and anchor it there with thread wraps both in front of and behind the hook eye. Wind the rib forward and secure it on the jig head at the hook eye. Trim the excess copper wire, whip finish, and cut off the thread. Apply a coating of head cement to the jig/thread application. Trim the excess furry foam to shape the crayfish's tail.

Step 6: Use a black felt-tip marker to make the eyes and to place two horizontal strips in the middle of the fly. Then mottle the body with a brown or olive marker. Lastly, color the tip of the tail and the tips of the claws with an orange felt-tip marker. Note: We turned the fly over in the vise and used the rotary function to better display the fly.

JIM CRAMER

Jim is a retired engineer living in Bodega Bay, a small fishing and tourist village on the Northern California coast. Fly-fishing and fly tying have always been an important part of his life. He tied his first flies over fifty years ago after seeing his great-uncle's fly box. Stored between two felt pads in round aluminum boxes were a couple dozen size 10 wet flies with gut snells. The felt pads were used to keep the gut wet so a fly-fisher could change flies while fishing without having to wait for them to soak. Jim advises, "Needless to say this storage method did little for the long-term appearance of the flies. The fish, however, weren't as educated as those of today, so we all managed to catch more than were ever needed. It is a shame that mankind wastes so much before they wise up."

Living on a wheat farm in the Oklahoma panhandle, Jim was about as far from the fly-fishing scene as a small boy could be. His first flies were tied on bait hooks with his mother's cotton sewing thread and feathers from the hen house. Having never seen a fly tied, a book on the subject, or even a tying vise, Jim's first attempts were a bit wild. It was a mystery to him how all those little hairs (the hackle) were tied in place.

But the Fish Gods and a loving uncle took pity on Jim and he received a fly-tying kit for Christmas that included a copy of George Herter's book *Professional Fly Tying and Tackle Making Manual*. Jim tells us, "A whole new world opened up and I was hooked for life. My high school days were spent in Albuquerque where I peddled my flies

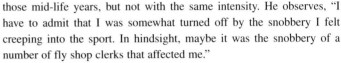

Jim Cramer

to local tackle shops to support my addiction. After all, hooks were $.85 per box, silk floss was $.20 per spool, and jungle cock necks were out of sight at $16.50 each." Tying continued through high school and college and then took a back seat to family, career, and making a living for the next few decades. Jim did keep tying during those mid-life years, but not with the same intensity. He observes, "I have to admit that I was somewhat turned off by the snobbery I felt creeping into the sport. In hindsight, maybe it was the snobbery of a number of fly shop clerks that affected me."

Jim retired twelve years ago and once again is tying flies, fly-fishing, and writing about his experiences. In 1995, he purchased two furled leaders in a shop in Vienna. They were quite expensive by American standards. After arriving home and giving them close inspection he was certain he could build a better leader and set out to do so. Several hundred leaders later Jim has developed one of the best furled-leaders constructed from tying thread. The word has spread and today he gets orders for them from all around the world. He admits, "I consider my leader making more of a service to my fellow anglers as I really don't need another business to interfere with my fly-fishing time." Of course, fly-fishing is a great way to share the virtues of the furled leader.

Parachute Midge Cluster

The Parachute Midge Cluster is a pattern with a long heritage. In fact, Jim prefers to think of it more as an early evolutionary step and is waiting to see what its offspring may produce.

Jim writes, "Often when I am not stocking my fly boxes in preparation for a trip, my sessions at the vise are experimental ventures in the manipulation of materials and tying methods. It was during such a session a couple of years ago that the pattern came into being. At the time I was thinking of how one might easily create a spot on the water that would represent a collection of midges, i.e., a midge cluster. This fly was the result. It meets many of the criterion that I strive for when developing a new pattern; a simple, quick, easy tie utilizing common materials while producing the image I desire."

Two of the many patterns Jim's fertile mind has produced are

illustrated here, the Parachute Midge Cluster and the Parachute Crab. Now don't do a "double-take" like we did when first reviewing Jim's information for this book. Yes, we said "parachute" when referring to the crab. In referring to his style of parachute flies Jim advises, "All of them use the same basic construction method, but the Parachute Crab is the most advanced in the evolutionary chain. Tied for bonefish and permit, it features hackle tips tied a bit down on the bend so they will extend upward when the hook is inverted." The fly's posture is hook point up due to the dumbbell eyes at the hook bend, the ram's wool body tied on the underside mid shank, and the soft parachute hackle. The body is trimmed to shape and spotted with a felt-tip marking pen. We think Jim's parachute design is one of the most innovative we've seen in some time.

Parachute Midge Cluster

Hook:	Size 14-16, dry fly
Thread:	Black
Body:	Thread and clump of Antron yarn
Wings:	Body yarn, trimmed
Hackle:	Grizzly
Head:	Thread

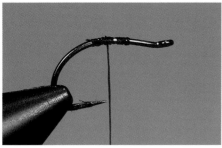

Step 1: Place a hook in the vise and apply a thread base that covers the center part of the hook shank. Leave the bobbin hanging in the center of this base.

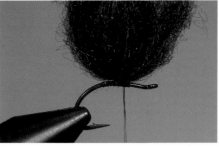

Step 2: Tie on a clump of Antron dubbing or combed-out yarn at the center of the hook with three or four tight thread wraps. Pull up on the clump while tightening the turns of thread because it's important to keep it on top of the shank. Post this clump with three or four turns of thread as close to the hook shank as possible. Follow with two turns around the shank to the front of the post.

Step 3: Select a grizzly hackle feather and strip off the webbed material at the base of the stem. Bind the feather to the hook shank directly in front of the parachute post material.

Step 4: Wrap three or four turns of hackle around the post as close to the shank as possible. Tie the feather off in front of the post and trim the waste end. Whip finish and cut off the thread in front of the post. Apply a coating of head cement to thread wraps from the bottom of the hook. If necessary, press with your thumb to spread out the post.

Step 5: Here is an illustration of the bottom of Jim's Parachute Crab. Note the dubbing around the eyes and on the hook shank.

Step 6: This is a view of the top of the crab with the mottled markings from brown and black felt-tip markers. Jim's Parachute Crab is really a thought-provoking design. We've already started calling it Cramer's Crab and look forward to giving it a thorough test.

GALE DOUDY

Gale Doudy

"I was raised in western Colorado and as long as I can remember, I loved to fish," Gale says. At a young age he fished the East Portal of the Gunnison River with his uncles in the early 1950s. They fished with bamboo rods and live stonefly nymphs, or hellgrammites as they referred to them. It was Gale's job to help collect a coffee can full of nymphs before they would start fishing. He recalls, "They would wade out into the river and drift the riffles with the live nymphs, normally only making a cast or two before they would either catch a fish or lose the nymph. This fishing was very difficult for me and it was several years before I caught a fish on my own." Gale must have learned those lessons well because we've had the pleasure of fishing with him and he is one of the best nymph fishers we know. His family also spent a lot of time fishing the many lakes on the Grand Mesa near Delta, Colorado.

After graduating from high school, Gale spent four years in the US Navy. In 1967 he returned to Colorado and married Donna. He went to work for an airline in Denver as an electronic technician. While employed with that company Gale was responsible for the electronics equipment in Montana and spent much of his time traveling and working (fishing) in the state. He tells us, "At that time I loved fishing in Montana and Wyoming as it seemed so easy compared to the tough fishing on the South Platte River near my home in Denver."

In 1986 the company went bankrupt and the Doudy family decided to move home to Colorado's Western Slope. The move was a family decision based on the agreement that Donna would join Gale on his trips to the field to hunt or fish; this woman was no longer staying at home waiting for her man. During the next ten years Gale guided on the Gunnison River and introduced Donna to the sport, first via spin rod and in time she graduated to the fly rod. She learned her lessons well because she is the second-best nymph fisher we know.

Your authors introduced them to the Federation of Fly Fishers where they immediately found a home with people who believed as they do. Gale comments, "I feel strongly that education is the strongest conservation tool that we have. If we convert one young man or woman into a fly-fisher it is worth more to the conservation movement than any stream section we can adopt. If we do not pass on our knowledge, we do a severe injustice to those who have taught us." Gale is presently employed by the Colorado Department of Corrections. He reflects, "I see many young men whose lives are in despair. I wonder how many would be there (in prison) if someone had taken the time to teach them the values of fly-fishing at a young age." We certainly agree. The Federation of Fly Fishers is an organization focused on fly-fishing education, and Gale and Donna are part of what makes it work.

Black Two Way

Frustration is the driving force behind the Black Two Way. We were so impressed with it when Gale submitted it for the *Fly Pattern Encyclopedia* we just had to ask him about it. Gale recalled a day several years prior when he and Donna were fishing a BWO hatch on the Frying Pan River. The fish were in a feeding frenzy and could not see their small Parachute Adams'. Yes, they did land several fish, but missed many more due to the visibility problem. In desperation they finally resorted to small strike indicators about a foot from the fly.

Gale recounts his thoughts as he developed the two-way concept, "On the way back home I was totally frustrated by our inability to see the fly. So much so that I got to thinking about a fly that wouldn't sink so easily in ripple water and was also visible during the kind of midday darkness we had encountered. The two-way series was a brainstorm that eventually proved quite successful. Now I tie all my smaller parachutes this way. If needed, I could always trim the bottom off one hackle, but to date I never have."

Black Two Way

Hook:	Size 14-20, dry fly
Thread:	Black
Tail:	Whiting tailing fibers
Body:	Stripped hackle stem, black
Thorax:	Black dubbing
Wing:	White turkey flat
First Hackle:	Grizzly
Second Hackle:	Silver badger
Head:	Thread

Step 1: Attach the tying thread to the hook about one-third back on the shank from the eye, wrap to the end of the shank and back to the starting point. Select a clump of Whiting coq de leon tailing fibers and bind them to the hook to form a tail as long as the complete hook. Trim the excess fibers and leave the thread hanging at the one-third point.

Step 2: Prepare a turkey flat feather by clipping out the tip as illustrated. Also strip the fibers from a black hackle stem and place it in a small container of water to soak in preparation for use in a future step.

Step 3: Bind the prepared turkey flat to the hook at the one-third point. Gale likes the wing to be slightly longer than the hook shank to help improve the visibility.

Step 4: Trim the excess turkey flat and wrap over the cut ends. Wind several turns of thread around the wing to construct a parachute hackle platform. Wrap the thread to the back of the hook and tie on the stripped hackle stem by its tip. Advance the thread forward and leave it hanging in front of the wing post.

Step 5: Wind the stem forward, forming a segmented body that ends two turns to the front of the wing post. Tie it off and trim the waste end. Notice that the natural shape of the stem creates an evenly tapered body. Leave the thread hanging at the front side of the post.

Step 6: Select a grizzly hackle one size larger than normally used on the hook and tie it to the hook in front of the post. Also bind it to the post in preparation for a parachute application. Pick a hackle one or two sizes smaller than normally used on this hook. Tie it to the hook in front of the post in preparation for a standard hackle placement. Dub a small thorax leaving the bobbin hanging at the hook eye.

Step 7: Wrap the grizzly hackle to the parachute platform starting at the top and place each subsequent turn closer to the body. Tie hackle off at the eye and trim the waste end. It's a good idea to place a half hitch at the hook eye in preparation for the next step.

Step 8: Gently raise the parachute hackle and wrap the badger hackle forward around the hook constructing a standard, dry-fly hackle application. Trim the excess feather, whip finish, and clip the thread from the hook. Apply a coating of cement to the head and also at the top of the parachute post.

Orange Bead

Gale started tying this fly because he often had success fishing a simple Partridge and Orange soft-hackle fly. He wanted a fly that would sink quickly in the water without having to use additional weight on his leader. Gale tells us, "I wanted to capitalize on the magical translucent qualities of floss once it is wet." This pattern certainly takes advantage of that quality in a rather unique way.

Gale uses the fly as a searching pattern when fish do not seem to be keying on any particular insect. He fishes it on a dead drift, a downstream swing, or stripped like a Woolly Bugger. Gale advises, "The fish on the Gunnison River seem to be especially attracted to the color orange." If you follow Gary LaFontaine's theory of attraction, Gale's belief falls right in line with that concept; the canyon walls along the Gunnison River are a dirty orange color.

Orange Bead

Hook:	Mustad 9671, size 10-18
Thread:	Orange & black
Body:	Orange floss
Rib:	Body floss, twisted
Thorax:	Brass bead
Hackle:	Furnace
Head:	Black ostrich

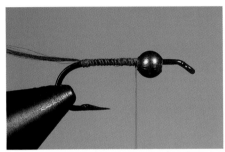

Step 1: Slip a bead on the hook, place it in the vise jaws and slide the bead forward on the shank. Apply a thread base that covers the back one-half of the hook, then tie on a fairly long strand of floss.

Step 2: Wrap the floss forward to the center of the hook then back to the end of the shank. Twist the floss into a tight rope.

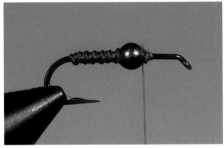

Step 3: Wrap the twisted floss forward to form the rib. Tie it off, trim away the excess, whip finish, and remove the thread from the hook. Place a drop of Krazy Glue on the body at the center of the hook and slip the bead onto it. Allow the glue to dry then attach the tying thread to the front of the bead.

Step 4: Select a furnace soft-hackle feather and prepare it by removing the fuzzy fibers near the base of the stem. Spread out the fibers and tie the feather to the hook shank by the tip.

Step 5: Trim off the tip of the feather and whip finish the orange thread. Attach black tying thread tight against the trimmed feather tip. Wrap a two-turn soft-hackle collar, tie off the feather, and trim away the waste end.

Step 6: Tie on a section of ostrich herl while advancing the thread to the hook eye. Wrap the herl to form a head, tie it off, and trim away the excess. Whip finish and remove the thread from the hook. Apply a coating of Aqua Head to finish the fly. Note: We suggest paying attention to the segmented translucence of the body when it is wet.

Woven Caddis

One afternoon we were fishing Colorado's Gunnison River with Gale during a sporadic caddis hatch. We all caught fish, but it was evident Gale was enjoying much better results than our Elk Hair Caddis provided us. Finally we could no longer stand it and wandered over to find out his secret. He showed us one of his woven caddis flies. "It's the lateral line created by the weaving process that makes the difference," he advised as he shared a couple of the flies with us. We are not sure about the lateral line, but those flies sure made a difference that day and many days thereafter. Today it has a permanent spot in our fly boxes and continues to produce fish here in Idaho.

Gale likes to offer it on a quartering up-stream presentation. When the fly is across from him he throws an up-current mend, raises his rod tip, and skitters the fly across the water as it continues down stream. The strikes tend to be savage so be prepared to lose a few flies.

Woven Caddis

Hook:	Size 6-20, dry fly
Thread:	Brown
Tail:	Krystal Flash
Body:	Light & dark Antron yarn
Body coloring:	Red felt-tip marker
Wings:	Turkey under elk
Hackle:	Brown
Head:	Thread

Step 1: Place the hook in the vise and apply a thread base to the back two-thirds of the hook shank. Tie on four strands of Krystal Flash to be trimmed as a short tail in Step 3. Bind a light and dark strand of Antron yarn to the near and off sides of the hook shank. Wrap them onto the tail strands so they can form a short extended body in the next step. Leave the thread hanging at the one-third point.

Step 2: Apply two overhand knots to the Krystal Flash behind the hook. Be certain to keep the dark color on top and the light on the bottom. Then apply more overhand knots to the hook, forming a body that covers the back two-thirds of the shank plus the small extension. Tie off the waste ends of the yarn on top of the hook shank then trim away the excess. It's very important the yarn is tied off on the top of the hook to provide a base for the wing in the next step.

Step 3: Color the end of body with a red felt-tip marker and trim the tail so it is quite short. Select a turkey quill slip and tie it to the hook tent style. Be sure the wing is a little shorter than the body. Apply a coating of Aqua Flex to the end of the body and the turkey quill wing. Allow this to dry before continuing to the next step.

Step 4: Select, clean, and stack a clump of elk hair. Tie it to the hook as a Trude-style over wing and trim away the waste ends. It should be a little longer than the under wing.

Step 5: Cover the trimmed elk hair ends with a layer of tying thread. Prepare a hackle feather by removing the fuzzy fibers near the base of the stem. Tie it to the hook at the one-third point. Leave the thread hanging at the hook eye.

Step 6: Wrap the hackle, tie it off behind the hook eye, and trim away the excess. Whip finish and remove the thread from the hook. Apply a coating of Aqua Head to complete the fly. Gale ties this fly in a range of sizes and colors. We highly recommend you do so as well; we do!

CHUCK ECHER

Chuck began his fly-tying career in 1948 at the age of seven. Since then he has been actively teaching fly-fishing and fly-tying classes and seminars in San Francisco, Sacramento, and other Northern California areas. Chuck has literally taught thousands of students the art of fly-tying and fly-fishing.

Since 1988 he has been a featured fly-tier at the International Sportsmen's Exposition Fly Tying Video Theater at both the Sacramento and San Mateo shows. Chuck has also been a featured fly-tier at many Federation of Fly Fishers' International Conclaves. He has demonstrated internationally at Fly Fair in Holland, the Chatsworth Angling Fair in England, and the FFF Conclave in Calgary, Canada.

Chuck has demonstrated at so many shows here in the United States that it's impossible to name them all. Some of them include the International Fly Tying Symposium in New Jersey, the New England Fly Tying Conclave in Massachusetts, and Northwest Fly Tiers Exposition in Oregon. In his native California, some demonstrations include the Northern California Council Conclave, the Southwest Council Conclave, Fort Mason fly-tying functions, the Dutch Fly Dressers Guild, and the Golden Gate Angling & Casting Club. He has been a fly-tying judge at several functions, including the United Fly Tyers in Boston.

Chuck was the 1993 recipient of the prestigious FFF Buz Buszek Memorial Fly Tying Award.

Chuck Echer

Chuck's flies have been featured in *Patterns of the Masters, Fly Pattern Encyclopedia* and several videos produced through the Federation of Fly Fishers. He is presently a Certified Casting Instructor, on the Casting Instructor Advisory Committee, an active member of the Diablo Valley Fly Fishermen, and a life member of the Federation of Fly Fishers. His home club recognized him with the DVFF Lifetime Achievement Award for his contribution to fly-fishing.

Chuck has been keynote speaker at many East Coast, Great Lakes, and West Coast fly-fishing functions. He has fly-fished Alaska, Canada, New England, Michigan, western United States, Baja Mexico, Costa Rica, and England. Chuck is a fly-tying veteran with skills for tying fresh- and saltwater patterns. He predominately dresses trout dry flies, but enjoys tying everything from midges to sailfish patterns.

Today he makes his home in Pollock Pines, California with his wife Davina. The Echers moved there after Chuck retired from his position as an Electron Microscopist at Lawrence Berkley Labs at the University of California, Berkley.

Chuck's Fan Tail Cahill

Chuck developed this fly in the spring of 1995 based on a balanced hair-wing stonefly and a fluttering hair-wing caddis originated by Chuck Stranahan from Hamilton, Montana. He tested it for the next couple of years and enjoyed improved fishing success on stillwater fisheries, but found the tail was a bit fragile. Chuck increased the fly's longevity by applying Aqua Seal at the base of the fantail.

Chuck tells us, "Since this pattern takes a little effort to tie, I have only field-tested it on stillwater in typical and extreme flat-water conditions. One can vary the color and size to suit the particular mayfly imitation of choice." When we first saw this pattern while writing the *Fly Pattern Encyclopedia* we knew it had to be included in this book and here it is!

Chuck's Fan Tail Cahill

Hook:	Size 12-16, dry fly
Thread:	Black
Wing:	Woodduck flank
Tail:	Barred ginger hackle
Body:	Barred ginger hackle stem, stripped
Thorax:	Ginger dubbing
Hackle:	Barred ginger hackle
Coating:	Aqua Seal or Aqua Flex

Step 1: Place the hook in the vise and apply a thread base that covers the back two-thirds of the hook. Leave the thread hanging at the one-third position.

Step 2: Select a woodduck flank feather and tie it to the hook to form a wing that is equal to the shank in length. Stand up the wing with several thread wraps directly in front, then wind around the wing to form a parachute platform.

Step 3: Select a saddle hackle long enough to use for the tail and the parachute application. Cut a section from the base end about an inch long and strip the fibers from the right side when observing the feather with the dull side down. Stroke the fibers out on the left side so they stand away from the stem. Trim about one-quarter inch of them off the tip end of the feather leaving short stubs along that part of the stem. Next start trimming at the butt end of the stem and stop when *seven* fibers remain near the center. Tie the prepared feather on the off side of the hook by the *trimmed tip*. We've photographed this step with hackle pliers attached to the butt end of the stem to illustrate the partially fanned fibers. The tool is also helpful when tying the butt end of the stem to the shank in the next step.

Step 4: Complete the fantail by bringing the butt end of the stem around to the shank and binding it to the near side of the hook. Adjust the seven tail fibers so one sticks straight out the back and three are evenly distributed on each side. Select another barred ginger feather and strip all the fibers from the stem. Tie it to the end of the shank by its tip to form the abdomen in the next step. Wrap the thread forward to the wing and leave it there for the moment.

Step 5: Trim off the waste end of the stripped feather, then wrap it forward forming the abdomen. Clip off the leftover part of the stem, then prepare a saddle hackle feather by stripping the fibers from its base. Tie it to the hook in front of the post and trim off any stem waste. Apply ginger dubbing to the thread and construct the thorax behind and in front of the post ending up at the hook eye. Wrap the hackle three turns up and then three turns down the post. Anchor it at the hook eye and trim the waste end. Whip finish and remove the thread.

Step 6: Apply a coat of Aqua Head to the whip finish. Place a drop of Aqua Seal or Aqua Flex to the inside of the tail loop to strengthen it and cement the fibers into position.

Chuck's October Caddis

This fly is one of Chuck's adult insect imitations constructed using his "V hackle down-under" technique developed in 2002. It is an adaptation of a hackling method most recently made popular by the late Ned Long in which the feather is wrapped around super floss and folded over the top of the hook. Chuck is the first person we've seen use a similar technique on the underside of the hook. Also, he accomplishes the feather's application without the use of a gallows tool, not an easy task.

Chuck's October Caddis employs a four-stage wing, which builds a high-floating pattern with a very small head like the natural insect. If tying a smaller fly, just reduce the number of wing applications based on the amount of hook space available for the size of the hook selected. This pattern sits on the water like a natural insect and should prove irresistible to a feeding fish.

Chuck's October Caddis

Hook:	Size 6-12, 2XL dry fly
Thread:	Black
Body:	Dirty amber dubbing
Hackle base:	Olive super floss
Hackle:	Cree or dyed ginger over grizzly
Wing:	Dyed dun elk hair
Head:	Dyed dun elk hair, bullet style

Step 1: Place the hook in the vise and lay down a thread base that covers the shank. Leave the thread at the end of the hook, apply a small amount of dubbing to it, and wrap forward to the center of the hook.

Step 2: Select, clean, and stack a small clump of dyed dun elk hair. Tie it to the hook as a wing segment at the center of the hook allowing it to extend Trude style just past the bend. Trim off the waste ends and tie on a section of olive super floss to the under side of the hook. Prepare a hackle feather by stripping off the fuzzy material at the base of the stem and tie it to the under side of the hook as well.

Step 3: Pull the super floss to the side of the hook, stretch it, and wrap it around your little finger at the joint using a couple of turns; bending that finger anchors the stretchy material in place. Wrap the hackle several turns around the tightly stretched super floss first moving away from the hook then winding back towards the hook. Bind the hackle to the hook and trim off the waste end. Put a small amount of dubbing on the thread and wrap another small section of the body covering the most recent thread turns.

Step 4: Select, clean, and stack another small clump of elk hair. Tie it to the hook as a second wing with the tips even with the first.

Step 5: Trim off the waste end of the wing and apply dubbing to the thread to cover the butts of the hair. Repeat this process, constructing a third body/wing segment. Pull the super floss with the hackle attached forward on the under side of the hook, bind it to the shank, and trim off the waste end.

Step 6: Tie on the last wing segment with the tips pointing forward and cut off the butt ends of the hair. Fold this segment over and tie it down bullet-head style. Whip finish and remove the thread. Trim the bottom of the hackle "V" style then apply a coating of Aqua Head to the whip finish to complete the fly.

FLOYD FRANKE

Floyd Franke

Floyd was born in northwestern Pennsylvania. After fulfilling his military obligation in the Navy, he entered Edinboro State University in Edinboro, Pennsylvania and later the University of Pittsburgh in Pittsburgh, Pennsylvania, where he received his Doctorate Of Philosophy Degree in 1976. His work in higher education administration allowed him to remain in Pennsylvania until 1979, when he accepted a position as Dean of Students at Nichols College, Dudley, Massachusetts In 1985, Floyd and his wife Alberta moved to Roscoe, New York, dubbed Trout Town, USA, where he took a position as the guidance counselor in the local school district. This move was a turning point in Floyd's life. In Roscoe he met Poul Jorgensen, who became his fly-tying mentor and Joan Wulff, who became his fly-casting mentor. Today he works as an instructor at her school in Lew Beach, New York.

Although retired, Floyd continues to teach at the Wulff School and to operate his guide service, *Ephemera.* He is presently writing a book, *Fish On: A Guide To Playing Big Fish,* which is scheduled for publication in 2003 by Derrydale Press. Recently he started a small business to manufacture and sell an innovative new aquatic insect collection net for which he holds a patent. Named Top To Bottom Aquatic Insect Collection Net, sales are to begin in the summer of 2002.

Floyd's dedication to excellence in fly-tying has yielded him 48 national and international awards. In 1993, the Northeastern Council of the Federation of Fly Fishers awarded him the Elsie and Harry Darbee Memorial Fly Tying Award for "…His fine showing in international competition." In June 1997, Floyd accepted the invitation of the Norwegian Forestry Museum to tie at their Annual Fly Fishing Show in Elverum, Norway. In February 1998, Floyd and three other

U.S. fly tiers were recognized in *Fly Fishing* magazine as being… "Truly the best in the world." That same year he was invited to tie at fishing shows in both Holland and England.

A willingness to share is a hallmark of Floyd's thirty years of fly-tying. His skills as a tier, his career experiences in education, and his passion for fly-fishing have made him a respected and sought-after workshop presenter, teacher and guest tier. His two-day intermediate/advanced fly-tier's workshop, which he designed and conducted for six years at the Catskill Fly Fishing Center and Museum, remains their most successful fly-tying program to date.

Floyd has the unique distinction of having co-founded with Mathew "Matty" Vinciguerra the Catskill Fly Tyers Guild. It is a fly-tying organization dedicated to the following purposes:

"Preserve, protect and enhance the Catskill fly tying heritage.
Work cooperatively to promote the work of present Catskill tiers.
Provide a forum for the sharing of information.
Promote the development of future generations of Catskill fly tiers."

Founded in February of 1993 with twenty-four charter members, the Guild has grown to over 200 members who live primarily in NY, NJ, CT and PA.

Floyd is a life member of the Federation of Fly Fishers. He is an active participant in the Federation's Casting Instructor's Certification Program and chairs its Casting Board of Governors.

Foam Stone fr.

The sight of big trout feeding on large stoneflies on the Delaware River in New York and the Madison River in Montana had not gone unnoticed by Floyd. However, developing a realistic fly for these big fish took time and more than a few false starts.

The most troublesome hurdle was the size of the natural insect. Using conventional tying standards seemed to warrant the use of a long-shank hook, but being too rigid and heavy their use was both esthetically and functionally unacceptable. The solution lay in the use of the extended-body concept. In 1999, an adaptation of earlier experiments yielded the pattern you see here which floats better and looks

more realistic than its predecessors. The Foam Stone fr. is an improvement on the earlier Extended Foam Stone published recently in the Federation of Fly Fisher's *Fly Pattern Encyclopedia.*

Floyd tells us about fishing it, "Because this fly sits low in the surface film, it can be difficult to see at a distance. Hence, I do not use it as a searching pattern requiring long drifts. I prefer to target individual risers and cast to them. The soft splat of a not-so-delicate presentation often brings an immediate strike. Although used primarily for trout, the fly has taken smallmouth bass whenever the two inhabit the same water as on the Delaware River."

Foam Stone fr.

Hook:	Size 10, dry fly
Thread:	Brown
Tail:	Brown biots
Body:	Brown craft foam
Rib:	Brown tying thread
Thorax:	Dark brown dubbing brush
Legs:	Knotted turkey tail fibers
Wings:	Natural bucktail

Step 1: Cut a four-inch-long strip from a one-sixteenth piece of craft foam. It should be about 1/4-inch wide. Fold the strip of foam in half, forming a doubled unit and trap the loose end of the tying thread between them. Starting at the fold, wrap two turns of thread as close to the end as possible. Advance the thread forward one-sixteenth inch and wrap two turns to form the next section. Pass it between the two layers to hide the thread when advancing it from one segment to the next. Repeat this process until you have formed seven or eight segments. Whip finish the thread and trim it from the extended body unit. Use a needle to insert the tails into position and anchor them with a drop of Super Glue. Trim the underside of the unit on a taper that is shorter than the hook shank. Insert the point of the hook into the body and bring it out at the second segment.

Step 2: Position the hook in the vise and attach the thread near the center of the shank. Capture the trimmed end of the foam extended body and bind it to the hook shank.

Step 3: Bind the body to the back part of the hook, then wrap the thread forward to the hook eye. Select, clean, and stack a clump of bucktail. Tie it to the hook with the tips pointing forward. The bucktail should be as long as the combined distance of the complete hook, body, tail, and hook gape. Cut any excess fibers then cover wrap over the trimmed butts ending up at the extended body. Make a dubbing brush using fur and fine copper wire or use a commercially prepared unit. Tie it on the hook near the end of the shank.

Step 4: Mentally divide in two the space between the eye and the position where the extended body is anchored to the hook. Reserve the rear half for the legs and thorax. Form three sets of legs by placing an overhand knot in fibers from a turkey tail. Tie on the legs in their reserved location then advance the dubbing brush forward. Tie it off and trim the excess setting it aside for the next fly.

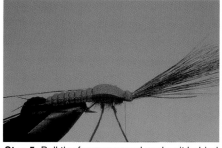

Step 5: Pull the foam over and anchor it behind the hook eye. Cut off the excess foam so the trimmed end will form part of the head as illustrated. Leave the bobbin hanging here.

Step 6: Fold over the bucktail and anchor it behind the hook eye where we left the thread in the last step. Whip finish the thread and trim it from the hook. Move back to a position between the back and middle legs and wrap several turns of thread to press the wings flat against the body. Whip finish and trim off the thread. Apply head cement to the two thread applications.

KEITH FULSHER

Keith Fulsher was born and raised in Tomahawk, Wisconsin, a small town in the north-central heart of that state's greatest fishing area. Wild brook trout, musky, northern pike, bass and many other species seemed to be in endless supply as he was growing up in the 1920s and 1930s. His father and a favorite uncle, who both were avid anglers, introduced Keith to fishing at an early age. Fortunately, his uncle was one of only three or four fly-fishermen in that small town, so Keith was exposed to fly-fishing and the required tackle from his very first days of fishing. Nine-and-a-half-foot, three-piece split bamboo rods, automatic reels, fly lines and gut leaders (that all seemed to need endless care,) snelled wet flies, creels and wading gear were all familiar objects on those long ago, before-dawn trout fishing trips. He still has some of the artifacts.

His first efforts at fly-tying took place at around age ten while visiting a cousin who lived in La Crosse, Wisconsin on the Mississippi River. They would fish for bass and panfish from the walkways that surrounded boathouses tethered along the shores of the Mississippi. In an effort to get the fish to swim out from under the floating homes, Keith and his cousin bought the smallest hooks available; held them in their fingers crudely; and tied on scraps of cloth, yarn and anything else that they thought would attract those fish. Keith claims that once in a while their creations worked.

During Keith's high school years fishing became less important. With the advent of World War II and completion of one year of college in Wisconsin and a vacation in New York City, Keith enlisted in the U.S. Navy and spent three years with the fleet air wing. After his discharge he returned to New York, completed his college education at Brooklyn College, earned a Bachelor of Science degree in accounting and took up commercial banking as a career. It was at a college sorority formal in New York that Keith met his wife Lois who became interested in fly-fishing and often joined him on fishing trips. She became a good fly-fisher. Later their daughter Susan and son, Keith Jr. joined

Keith Fulsher

them on those trips. Both children now have families of their own and have given Lois and Keith four grandchildren.

It was also during his college years in New York that Keith's interest in fly-tying returned. He bought a fly-tying kit and taught himself how to tie from an instruction sheet that was included. During his early days of tying he met and was helped by some great fly-tying personalities: Reub Cross, Herb Howard, Lew Oatman and Alex Rogan all became good friends, answering his fly-tying questions and helping solve fly-tying problems.

Keith continued his banking career, retiring as a senior executive in the U.S. arm of a large English bank, but always remained active in fly-tying and fly-fishing circles. In the late 1940s, he was tying for a prominent fly-fishing shop in Manhattan, usually trading flies for equipment. His interest in streamer flies lead to the development of his Thunder Creek Series of exact Baitfish Imitations in 1962. In 1973, Freshet Press, Inc. published his book on the flies entitled *Tying and Fishing the Thunder Creek Series*, documenting fifteen patterns. There are presently 22 freshwater patterns in the series and six saltwater imitations, each designed after a specific baitfish or young game fish. Keith also tied many Atlantic salmon flies, both classics and hair-wings, and became interested in the development of the hair-wing style of tying. This resulted in the book entitled *Hair-Wing Atlantic Salmon Flies*, published by *Fly Tyer* Magazine in 1981, that Keith authored jointly with his fishing partner, Charles Krom.

In his retirement, Keith has continued his interest in fly-tying and fly-fishing, doing tying demonstrations and slide presentations on various fly-fishing experiences. He only ties for collectors now as he's approaching his octogenarian years.

Swamp Darter

Keith originated this pattern in March, 1968 in connection with a feature article that Al McClane (*Field & Stream* fishing editor) was writing. Ten fly-tiers from across the country were each sent several paintings of different baitfish (34 in all) by artist Richard Younger. McClane's challenge to them was to duplicate each with a fly pattern. One of the paintings sent to Keith was a swamp darter, a species found from Massachusetts to Texas. The article entitled "The *Field & Stream* Match the Minnow Steamer Fly Series" appeared in the July, 1968 issue and included the artist's rendition and the fly-tier's reproduction all illustrated in full color. As a result, the Thunder Creek Swamp

Darter became an established pattern and was added to the original eight Thunder Creek patterns already in existence.

Darters, which are small members of the perch family, usually live among the rocks on the bottom of rivers and lakes. Keith likes to fish it with a sink-tip and short leader working the fly close to the bottom using a quick erratic retrieve. He tells us, "Casting directly across stream or quartering down is the easiest method of fishing the fly. Casting it upstream or quartering upstream and letting it travel along the bottom on the retrieve is another great technique, especially on smaller streams."

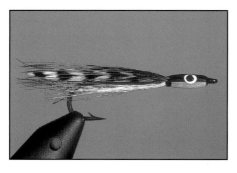

Swamp Darter

Hook:	Mustad 36620 or Partridge CS5 KF Thunder Creek, size 2-10
Thread:	White, 3/0 & 6/0
Wing:	Grizzly hackle, silver Krystal Flash accent
Top & back:	Natural brown bucktail
Bottom & belly:	White bucktail
Eyes:	Black over white lacquer
Gills:	Red lacquer
Coating:	Clear lacquer or Aqua Tuff

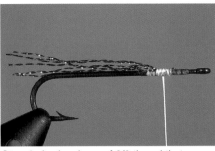

Step 1: Apply a base of 3/0 thread that covers the front one-third of the hook shank. Bind several strands of Krystal Flash to the hook as a wing accent that is slightly longer than the hook. Trim the waste ends and leave the thread hanging at the one-third point on the shank.

Step 2: Select a matched pair of grizzly hackle feathers and place them together with the dull sides touching. Tie them on the top of the shank with several tight thread wraps and trim off the excess material. Advance the tying thread forward almost all the way to the hook eye and leave it there in preparation for the next step.

Step 3: Select a small bundle of brown bucktail (remember to keep it sparse) and tie it on the hook with the tips pointing forward. When folded over, the fibers should be a little longer than the grizzly wings, adjust their length accordingly. Trim the waste ends of the hair with your scissors parallel to the hook shank to provide a smooth base under the head. Cover wrap them with thread leaving the bobbin hanging at the hook eye. Moisten your index finger with water and twist the tip ends of the hair together to keep them from mixing with the belly hair in the next step.

Step 4: Tie on a sparse clump of white bucktail on the underside of the hook shank. Adjust the length so they are slightly shorter than the brown fibers from the previous step. Again trim the waste ends with the scissors parallel to the hook shank to provide a smooth base under the head. Whip finish the 3/0 thread and tie on the 6/0. Cover wrap the trimmed hair butts ending up near the one-third point on the hook shank.

Step 5: Reverse the hair and secure it at the start of the wings with several thread wraps. Whip finish and remove the thread. We find folding over the back and belly hair separately much easier than trying to do both at the same time. The main objective when reversing the hair is keeping the colors evenly separated.

Step 6: Apply a very thin coat of epoxy over the head or use several coats of clear lacquer. We like to use Aqua Tuff because it's water based. No matter which you select, place the fly in a rotator so the coating will dry evenly.

Step 7: When it's dry remove the fly from the rotator and place it back in the vise. Paint a touch of red lacquer on each side of the bottom part of the thread collar to simulate gills. Then paint a white lacquer eye base on each side of the head. Position them slightly higher and forward of center. A small dowel or head of a finishing nail serves as a tool that makes the job much easier. Just dip the tool in the paint then touch it to the head. Place the fly back in the rotator to dry.

Step 8: When step seven is dry return the fly to the vise. Place a black lacquer pupil in the center of each eye base. Return the fly one last time to the rotator to dry before taking it fishing. We've found the key to a well-tied Thunder Creek is using fine, straight bucktail and keeping the bundles very sparse. Until we received instructions from Keith all of our Thunder Creeks were overdressed.

TOM HAWLEY

Tom Hawley

Tom lives near Boulder, Colorado along the Front Range of the Rocky Mountains. When he is not fishing, he enjoys spending time with his parents David and Dorothy, brother David and wife Shannon and newly arrived nephew, Kaden. Tom writes, "I also enjoy exploring the foothills and mountains here, and seeking out new and interesting water every chance I get."

His grandfather, Fred Mett (affectionately know as Bop), was an angler in his spare time, often fishing the shores near his home in Milford, Connecticut. When Tom's family visited, Bop would take him and David fishing at a neighbor's private pond. He still has a photo in which he is holding a bluegill caught there. He believes that to be the first fish he ever caught.

In time, he drifted away from fishing, but by the age of 24 his friend Mark Stevens re-introduced him to the sport. Mark taught him how to cast a fly, how to tie a leader, and eventually how to tie flies. With these newfound skills, Tom began fishing for smallmouth bass on the Potomac and Shenandoah rivers in Virginia. Eventually he discovered the wild brook trout in Shenandoah National Park. From there Tom made many trips to the various spring creeks in Pennsylvania where the fishing was much more technical and very challenging.

Tom tells us, "I moved west to Idaho in 1997, eager to fish the challenging water I had only read about in books. Mark had moved there a couple of years before and we saw a good opportunity to rekindle our fishing relationship. I was introduced to many of the most beautiful places I have ever seen such as Silver Creek in Sun Valley, the various waters of Yellowstone Park, and the Henry's Fork just to name a few."

Two years later Tom moved to his present home in Colorado where he is in John Gierach's backyard. He had expected to find the river and stream banks loaded with fishermen, but was surprised at how much water one can fish during the course of the day and never see another angler. He thinks it depends on where you look.

Tom reflects on his fly-tying skills, "As I said, Mark taught me how to tie flies. I struggled at first, but eventually would come up with flies that resembled something that at least the most stupid trout or bass might actually eat. Now a little over eight years later, I can honestly say that those first few years of frustration at the vise made me a better fly-tier. I've since tied for a fly shop in Boise, and cranked out several custom orders for friends and co-workers."

Tom wants to share a few beliefs he holds in high regard that are outlined in a quote from Robert Fulghum's *All I Really Need to Know I learned in Kindergarten*.

"I believe that Imagination is stronger than Knowledge.
That Myth is more potent than History.
That Dreams are more powerful than Facts.
That Hope always triumphs over Experience.
And I believe that Love is stronger than Death."

Crippled Bandit

Tom originally tied the fly as a spent mosquito imitation, but it has evolved at the vise and on the water into a convertible pattern. It can represent a variety of insects by simply performing "bankside surgery" to turn it into whatever is needed. He has used it as a spent-wing bug, midge emerger, subsurface nymph, and as a *Callibaetis* cripple, just to name a few.

It is not intended to be a dry fly, but rather an "in the surface" pattern. If treated with fly floatant it will definitely float, but the foam-wing case is actually intended to slow the pattern's sink rate and can be removed with a pair of scissors if a faster descent is needed.

Crippled Bandit

Hook:	TMC 200R, size 10-18, natural bend
Thread:	Black
Tail:	White ostrich herls
Abdomen:	White & black moose hairs
Shuck:	Light dun Z-lon
Wing case:	Gray foam
Wings:	Grizzly hackle tips
Legs:	Grizzly hackle
Thorax:	Peacock herl

Step 1: Apply a thread base that starts behind the hook eye and goes to the end of the shank. Tie on three white ostrich herls and two moose hairs (white and black). Wrap the thread forward about two-thirds of the way back to the hook eye and trim off the excess material. Leave the thread hanging there at the one-third point on the hook shank.

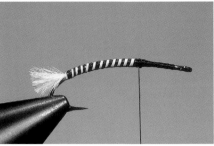

Step 2: Wrap the two moose hairs forward keeping them close together. Bind them to the hook when they reach the thread and trim off the waste ends. Cut off the ostrich herl to form the tail. Coat the abdomen with varnish or Aqua Tuff and allow the application to dry before continuing.

Step 3: Select and tie on a sparse segment of Z-lon. Trim a section of gray foam so it is not quite as wide as the hook gape. Tie it in place and trim away the waste end. Leave the thread directly in front of the tie-in point.

Step 4: Fold the foam over, bind it to the shank, and trim away the excess to form a bubble wing case. Advance the thread forward to the middle of the front one-third of the hook shank. Prepare two grizzly hen feathers, tie them on spent style, and trim off the waste material. Cut off the Z-lon shuck even with the hook point.

Step 5: Tie on several peacock herls and a grizzly hackle feather at the one-third point. Advance the thread forward almost to the hook eye.

Step 6: Pull the hackle feather up straight so the first turn of peacock herl is placed behind it. Advance the peacock herl forward.

Step 7: Tie off the herl and trim the excess material. Palmer the hackle forward and tie it off at the hook eye. Trim away the waste end, whip finish the thread, and cut it off the hook. Apply a coating of cement or Aqua Head. Leave the fly like it is if you plan on fishing it dry or later performing "bankside surgery."

Step 8: If desired, trim the hackle on the bottom of the fly. This creates a much lower profile allowing it to sink into the surface film.

Kaden Jackson

This fly holds a special hope for the future. Tom explains, "It is named for my first and currently only nephew, Kaden Jackson Hawley. The fly came to be through the efforts of myself and fellow fly tier/angler Fred Sackett. It is my dream that one day I will be able to take Kaden fishing and have him land a salmon on this fly. It would be one of the ultimate moments in my fishing life."

The pattern certainly has all of the characteristics of a productive pattern however only time can prove its worth. Never fear though because we'll be helping Tom give it a thorough test here in Idaho on area steelhead. We have confidence it will pass that test with flying colors.

Tom tied the illustrated pattern with polar bear hair as an under wing. Very few of us have this material so we've suggested bucktail as a substitute. Other possible underwing materials are Finnish fox fur or Canadian goat.

Kaden Jackson

Hook:	Size 6-2/0
Thread:	Black
Tag:	Gold oval tinsel, yellow floss
Tail:	Golden pheasant tippets
Butt:	Black ostrich herl
Body hackle:	Brown saddle hackle
Rib:	Fine gold, oval tinsel
Body:	Olive floss, olive brown Seal-EX
Under wing:	Light orange over pale yellow bucktail
Over wing:	Mottled turkey tail quill segments
Head:	Thread

Step 1: Apply a thread base from the eye to a position directly over the hook barb. Tie on a section of gold, oval tinsel and wrap a five-turn tip. Do not trim away the excess tinsel. Tie on a segment of yellow floss and complete the tag. Bind the excess floss and tinsel to the hook shank all the way to the eye platform and back to the tag. Tie a clump of golden pheasant tippets on as a tail that is long enough to extend slightly beyond the hook bend. Trim off the excess tail material, tie on a black ostrich herl, and wrap a butt that covers the trimmed ends. Tie off the ostrich herl and trim the excess.

Step 2: Tie on a length of fine gold, oval tinsel in front of the butt. Prepare a brown saddle hackle by stripping the fibers from one side of the stem and tie it on the hook by its tip also in front of the butt. Advance the tying thread forward to a position about one-third of the shank back from the eye. At that point attach a section of olive floss.

Step 3: Wrap the olive floss back where it meets the ostrich butt and then forward again to the tie-in point forming a double-layered floss body. Advance the tinsel forward forming a five-turn rib and tie it off. Follow with the hackle, placing each turn tight against the rib and tie it off with the floss/rib materials. Trim away the waste ends.

Step 4: Place olive brown Seal-EX in a dubbing loop and construct the last part of the body ending at the start of the looped eye platform. Pick out the dubbing with a bodkin.

Step 5: Select a clump of pale yellow bucktail or polar bear hair and tie it on as an under wing that is almost as long as the tail. Top the yellow with a clump of orange bucktail or polar bear hair. Trim away the excess material and cover the cut ends with a thread layer. Note: Do not stack the hair or be concerned if it flares a bit.

Step 6: Tie on matched turkey quill segments on either side of the hair to form the over wing. The hair will protrude between the quill segments. Cut off the waste ends, cover them with a thread head, whip finish and trim it from the hook. Apply a coating of cement or Aqua Head.

Polar Bunny

This fly evolved through the process of creating an "improved" version of a double bunny pattern with a twist on a Clouser Deep Minnow. It incorporates one of Tom's favorite materials, polar bear hair, however aren't lucky enough to have some legal fur you'll have to settle for bucktail as a substitute.

Tom developed the fly with no particular fish species in mind. He advises, "It is more or less a non-specific pattern in the sense that it could be mistaken for a large minnow, trout or bass fry, a leech, or many other varieties of prey." No matter what the fish think it represents, we've found that like its cousin the Double Bunny, it is a very effective fly with a lot of action in the water. It's what we call a "big-fish fly" and that's just what it produces.

Polar Bunny

Hook:	Mustad 80300BR stinger, size 2-8
Thread:	Olive
Eyes:	Silver dumbbell eyes
Body/Wing:	Two olive rabbit strips
Lateral line:	Olive & Black Krystal Flash
Over wing:	Pale yellow bucktail or polar bear
Collar:	Olive rabbit

Step 1: Mentally divide the hook in half. Apply a thread base that starts at the hook eye, goes to the center of the hook, and is then wrapped half way back to its beginning. Tie the silver dumb bell eyes on the top of the shank with several tight figure-eight wraps. Cut a section of olive rabbit strip that is as long as the complete hook and tie it on the shank first in front and then behind the eyes. Note: The dumbbell eyes will cause the hook point to ride up in the water column.

Step 2: Cut another section of rabbit strip that is one and one-half times as long as the complete hook. Impale the strip on the hook point positioning it so the forward segment of hide is long enough to reach slightly in front of the eyes.

Step 3: Take the hook out of the vise, slip the second rabbit strip around the bend to meet the first, and place it back in the jaws point up. Advance the thread forward and bind the second rabbit strip to the hook both in front and behind the eyes.

Step 4: Add a wing of pale yellow polar bear hair, or bucktail. It should be three-fourths as long as the rabbit-strip body/wing. Trim any waste ends.

Step 5: Select three strands each of olive and black Krystal Flash. Tie them to the sides of the fly to form lateral lines and provide a bit of flash. Apply a generous coat of head cement to the fly to include in front, around, and behind the eyes.

Step 6: Use a dubbing loop to construct a rabbit-fur collar behind the eyes. Tie off the thread, whip finish, and trim it from the hook. Glue the two rabbit strips together behind the hook bend with Shoe Goo. Apply a coating of cement or Aqua Head to finish the pattern.

Step 7: We really like this black/olive version of Tom's Polar Bunny.

Step 8: The gray/grizzly with a black hackle is a very interesting color combination.
Note: We've photographed Step 8 with the vise rotated 180 degrees to illustrate the fly's posture in the water.

Q. D. Caddis

Over the last year Tom has experimented with various caddis larvae patterns looking for one that would quickly sink to desired fishing levels. When he discovered Quick Descent in a local fly shop he hoped this material would fit his needs.

Tom was looking for a way to add weight without a lot of extra bulk and the dubbing did just what he hoped. It also provides a subtle metallic sheen with the Larva Lace adding translucence. Although he has not had a lot of time to test the pattern, initial results are very positive.

Tom shares a thought, "In smaller sizes and other colors, I think the Q. D. Caddis would double as an effective Chironomid imitation." Also, by changing the amount of weight (remove the bead or apply more dubbing), a tier can dress this pattern to suit different water depths and conditions. For our local Idaho waters we like it tied with a bead head in olive, chartreuse, orange, and tan.

Q.D. Caddis

Hook:	Daiichi 1150, any scud hook, size 10-18
Thread:	Black
Head:	Black, gold, or silver bead
Abdomen:	Quick Descent or Spirit River's Depth Advantage, olive
Over body:	Clear Larva Lace
Hackle:	Starling body feather
Thorax:	Peacock Lite Brite dubbing

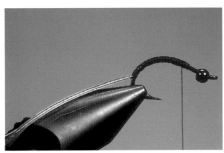

Step 1: Slip the bead on the hook and place it in the vise jaws. Slide the bead forward to the eye and apply a thread base that starts far enough back on the shank to allow room for hackle and thorax in a future step. Wrap the thread down into the bend then attach the clear Larva Lace on the return trip to the front of the hook.

Step 2: Using olive Quick Descent or Spirit River's Depth Advantage dubbing, apply a slightly tapered under body. Be sure to leave enough room between the body and bead for the hackle/thorax application.

Step 3: Wrap the Larva Lace forward using close turns, covering the complete under body. Tie it off and trim away the excess material. Note the sparkle, segmentation, and translucence of the body that makes this fly so effective.

Step 4: Select a feather from the back of a starling skin and prepare it by stroking out the fibers on each side of the stem. Tie the feather on the hook by its tip directly in front of the body.

Step 5: Make two turns of hackle, tie off the stem, and trim away the excess. Build up a thread base to cover the trimmed stem and force the fibers back into a collar.

Step 6: Last, add a thorax of peacock Lite Brite. Whip finish and trim away the thread. Apply a coating of cement or Aqua Head.

Step 7: Al's favorite for local Idaho waters is the tan version of Tom's fly.

Step 8: The red under body certainly produces an attractive fly. It looks almost orange when combined with the clear Larva Lace.

Tree Line Damsel Nymph

For some time Tom has relied on simple damselfly nymphs for his fishing flies, but has always been interested in the more "realistic" style that just looked good to him. This fly is a combination of both with a little extra thrown in. The extra about which we speak is the foam wing case that, along with the bead-chain eyes, causes the fly to travel through the water hook point up. The foam creates a neutral buoyancy pattern or can even be constructed to cause the fly to rise during the pause part of a retrieve. The rising version is a perfect candidate for the LaFontaine yoyo technique. It is a method Gary often used in which he incorporated a full-sinking shooting head, short leader, and a fly tied with foam. We can testify to the fact that it is a deadly fishing method with this fly or other damsel nymphs; just be sure the fly will rise in the water column during the pause part of a retrieve.

Tom tells us, "I think this fly will prove to be an excellent choice for fishing high-mountain lakes or any place where damsel nymphs are abundant. It may be fished solo or as a dropper under a larger fly such as a Woolly Bugger or leech." As an alternative, we suggest tying it in tan or olive brown in addition to the illustrated color.

Tree Line Damsel Nymph

Hook:	TMC 200R, size 12-18, natural bend
Thread:	Olive
Eyes:	Silver bead chain
Tail:	Medium olive marabou
Abdomen:	Olive Antron, light green Krystal Flash
Wing case:	Gray foam
Thorax:	Olive Ice Dub
Legs:	Olive hen saddle feather

Step 1: Apply a short thread base to the front part of the hook covering a distance equal to three eye widths. Mount the bead chain eyes on top of the shank with several figure-eight thread wraps. Select a sparse clump of olive marabou and bind it to the back part of the hook starting directly behind eyes and wrapping to a location directly above the hook barb. For this discussion we'll refer to this position on the hook as the "end of the shank." Don't worry about the tail length; it will be trimmed in a future step. Advance the thread back to the eyes and leave it there for the next step.

Step 2: Select one strand of olive Antron yarn and two strands of light green Krystal Flash each about three or four inches in length. Bind them to the hook, stopping at the end of the shank. Wrap the thread forward stopping almost to the eyes.

Step 3: Twist the Antron and Krystal Flash into a single strand and wrap this unit forward to meet the tying thread. Be sure to leave space enough behind the eyes for the construction of the abdomen in the next steps. Tie off the tag ends and cut off the excess materials.

Step 4: Trim a section of gray foam so it is not quite as wide as the hook gape. Secure it to the bottom of the shank and trim off the waste end.

Step 5: Build a thorax of olive Ice Dub. Make sure to use several figure-eight wraps around the eyes. Leave the thread hanging just to the front of them.

Step 6: Pull the foam strip forward and anchor it in front of the eyes. Trim off any surplus and cover the trimmed end with tying thread.

Step 7: Select an olive hen saddle feather and, in front of the eyes, tie it to the hook by its tip. Wrap a two-turn collar and bind down the stem. Trim off the excess and build a thread head to cover any exposed waste ends. Apply a whip finish and cover the head with cement or Aqua Head.

Step 8: Pick out the material in the thorax with a dubbing needle. Trim the tail so the fly is complete. Don't cut it too short!

Tom's Stonefly

Tom tells us about his pattern, "I'm not one to often make attempts to *invent* new fly patterns. Rather, I view myself as a fly tier that tries to occasionally *improve* an already existing idea. The fly was 'born' through a very kind invitation by Al and Gretchen Beatty to submit a pattern or two for a book they were writing (the *Fly Pattern Encyclopedia*). I was more than pleased to take part and set to the task of trying to come up with a pattern that would not only fish well, but solve a dilemma that had been on my mind for a while: durability and floatation."

The twisted Antron abdomen is durable and heavy enough to allow it to set below the water's surface much like the natural insect. The foam center wing provides the extra floatation needed to keep the pattern in this position and yet quite visible to the angler.

Tom fishes it in any type of water often using it as an "edible strike indicator" on a two-fly rig. Its superb floatation makes it an excellent searching pattern when no hatch is evident. With slight material or size changes it can imitate a range of stoneflies or grasshoppers.

Tom's Stonefly

Hook:	TMC 200R or Daiichi 1270, size 4-10
Thread:	Black and hot orange
Tail:	Gray goose biots
Abdomen underbody:	Closed-cell foam
Abdomen:	Black & burnt orange Antron yarn
Under wing:	Moose body hair
Center wing:	Black closed-cell foam
Bullet head:	Moose body hair
Over wing:	Elk body hair
Thorax underbody:	Black dubbing
Legs:	Round rubber leg material
Thorax:	Orange dubbing

Step 1: Place the hook in the vise and apply a thread base that starts one eye width back on the hook and travels to the end of the shank (we identify this as a point directly above the throat of the barb). Tie on a divided biot tail that is slightly longer than the hook gape is wide. Next tie on the body Antron and the underbody foam. Use the waste ends to form a body base that covers the back two-thirds of the hook shank. Leave the bobbin hanging at the one-third position.

Step 2: Apply tension to the foam strip as you wrap it forward to meet the thread and tie it off there. Twist the black and orange Antron into a rope in preparation for the next step.

Step 3: Wrap the twisted yarn forward to meet the foam strip and tie it off. Trim the waste ends of both materials.

Step 4: Select, clean, and stack a sparse clump of moose body hair. Tie it on the hook as an under wing that ends even with the tip of the tail. Cut a strip of black closed-cell foam that is as wide as the hook gape. Clip off a section that is as long as three-fourths the length of the shank. Trim this piece into a teardrop shape and tie it to the hook by the tip of the teardrop. It should extend evenly with the end of the body and form the center wing. Leave the thread hanging at the one-third point.

Step 5: Clean the under fur from a medium-sized clump of moose hair. Tie it on the hook by the tips making certain it is evenly distributed around the shank. Tom suggests tying it on with two soft loops, then squirm the hair around the hook. Whatever method you use be certain it is bound around the hook all the way to the eye because it will later form the bullet head. Trim off any excess tips.

Step 6: Select, clean, and stack a clump of elk body hair. Tie it on the hook as an over wing that is as long as the moose hair applied in Step 4. Trim away the excess hair then cover the thorax area with black dubbing. Leave the thread hanging at the one-third point.

Step 7: Sweep the moose hair back from the hook eye and secure with a couple of soft thread wraps. Check all sides of the fly to ensure even distribution of the hair. Finish tying off the hair with several very tight wraps. Whip finish the black thread and trim it from the hook. Trim all the waste moose hair ends then attach the hot orange thread and cover wrap over the black.

Step 8: Tie on the black rubber legs material, one per side. Tom likes to leave them a little longer than needed so he can adjust their length in the field. Add a thorax of orange dubbing, whip finish, and trim off the thread. Apply a coating of head cement. We loved this fly and fish it ourselves with one variation; we just use the hot orange thread for the thorax and leave off the dubbing.

Tuxedo

Tom tells us, "I've long been an admirer of steelhead and salmon flies that are not only effective but are also attractive to the angler. To me, there is little better than to fish a pattern that looks good enough to frame and at the same time know it can bring a nice fish to hand." We think this pattern certainly falls into this category.

It is a dark fly with white highlights we find effective in many low-light fishing situations. It's a pattern Tom worked on for several months in his mind's eye before approaching the vise to bring it to fruition. At that point he approached fellow fly tier and mentor, Fred Sackett for further inspiration. The result is a very effective pattern that has found its way into our steelhead fly boxes. Does it work? You bet it does!

Tuxedo

Hook:	Size 6-2/0, salmon fly
Thread:	Black
Tag #1:	Fine silver, oval tinsel
Butt #1:	Black ostrich herl
Tag #2:	White floss
Tail:	Amherst pheasant tippets
Butt #2:	Black ostrich herl
Rib:	Fine silver, oval tinsel
Body:	Black & white floss, black ostrich, black Seal-EX dubbing
Wing:	Gray fox over black bear hair
Collar:	Guinea fowl
Head:	Red dubbing, thread

Step 1: Apply a thread base that starts near the hook eye and ends directly above the barb of the hook. Tie in a section of silver, oval tinsel, wrap a five-turn tag, tie it off, and trim the waste end. Tie on a black ostrich herl, wrap a butt, and tie it off as well. Tie in a section of white floss and advance the thread forward to the start of the looped eye platform and then back to a position directly above the hook point. The excess material from the tags and butt create a smooth under body along the hook shank.

Step 2: Wrap the white floss forward to meet the thread forming the second tag. Tie it off and bind the excess to the bottom of the hook shank for the same reason mentioned in the previous step. Tie on a clump of Amherst pheasant fibers as a tail with the inner black band shrouding at least one-half of the white tag. Trim away the waste ends of the tail then cover them with a second butt formed from black ostrich herl.

Step 3: Tie a section of silver, oval tinsel and a length of black floss to the under side of the hook shank. Advance the thread forward to the one-third point and trim off any excess floss or tinsel. Wrap the floss forward to meet the thread and tie it off. Follow it with a five-turn rib and tie it off as well. Trim away the waste ends of both materials.

Step 4: Tie on a third ostrich herl, wrap it to form a body butt, tie it off, and trim away the excess. Tie on a section of white floss, wrap it to form a short body segment, tie it off, and clip off the waste end.

Step 5: Place black Seal-EX in a dubbing loop and wrap the last segment of the body so it ends at the start of the eye platform. Tie it off and trim away any excess. Pick out the dubbing with a bodkin. Tie on an under wing of black bear hair that is long enough to reach tag #1. Top it with a clump of gray fox hair as an over wing. Trim away the waste ends of the wing materials. Cover the trimmed ends with thread and apply a coating of head cement.

Step 6: Tie on a black-and-white guinea body feather by its tip and wrap a two-turn collar. Tie off the stem and trim away the waste. Construct a small band of red dubbing tight against the hackle to press the collar fibers back. Form a thread head, whip finish and trim it. Apply a coating of cement or Aqua Head.

HOWARD "BUD" HEINTZ

Howard "Bud" Heintz

Born in Oakland and raised in Gustine, Bud Heintz is a native Californian who currently lives in Modesto with his wife Carol. They have raised two daughters: Amy who teaches third grade and is married to Chad, a manager with United Parcel Service and Sara who is a college student and a designer of beaded jewelry. Bud has been employed with the city of Modesto for the past thirty-one years, currently as a Senior Civil Engineering Assistant while wife Carol is an Administrative Secretary to the Dean in the Arts and Humanities Division of Modesto Junior College.

Fly-fishing and fly-tying have been an important part of Bud's recreational enjoyment and a hobby for more than thirty years. He was introduced to the sport by his boss Ed Gish and received his first lessons from Mal Rose. From those first instructions he gained further skills from books by Jack Dennis, Randall Kaufman, Dave Whitlock, and others. His most influential mentors were Federation of Fly Fishers legends Darwin Atkin and Wayne Luallen. Bud feels he has not only learned a great deal from observing and discussing tying techniques with them, but their encouragement has helped him become one of the best demonstration fly tiers your authors have seen. His attention to detail is evident in the flies he presents here today.

Like many good demonstration tiers, Bud paid his dues at the demonstration tables and also as a commercial tier for more than twenty-five years. Today he is well recognized at the international level for both the Federation of Fly Fishers and for the International Sportsmen Expositions. He is a master with spun hair (note his cricket on one of the next pages) and balsa wood poppers. Many people, including your authors, consider his creations works of art. Fly tying, creating his own patterns, and refining his techniques has always been a welcomed challenge to him, but above all he enjoys sharing information and techniques with others (a trait shared by many of the great individuals in the FFF). If you get a chance to attend the class he teaches at Modesto Junior College, take it. You won't be disappointed.

Over the years Bud has developed many patterns. Some of them are marketed through McKenzie Flies. He incorporated Krystal Flash in mayfly wings long before others considered it a potential material for dry flies. He mixes flared and spun deer hair in his hopper and cricket patterns producing a beautifully mottled appearance. Bud's work has been featured in several magazines, *Patterns of the Masters*, the *Fly Pattern Encyclopedia*, and several magazines.

Black Cricket

Here is a perfect example of Bud's attention to detail. Look how evenly he spaces the different colors of deer hair. As you will find out, some of the applications are spun into position and others are flared in position on the bottom with another color flared on top. We call the process stack flaring and it certainly produces a beautiful fly.

The legs are as close to perfect as we've seen in a while. Bud constructs them so he has a right and left with the shiny side of the fibers facing out. Also notice the placement of the knot; he didn't trim the legs to make the last section on each the same length. Bud did it the hard way, by adjusting the position of the knot.

Black Cricket

Hook:	Mustad 94831, size 4-10
Thread:	Black 3/0
Tail:	Trimmed hackle center
Tail flank:	Two stripped hackle stems
Body:	Gray, brown & black deer hair
Hackle:	Deer hair
Head:	Gray, brown & black deer hair
Antenna:	Horse hair

Step 1: Strip the fibers from two hackle feathers and set them aside for a moment. Next strip most of the fibers from a third feather leaving on a few at the very end. Trim them to form a point. Attach the tying thread at the end of the shank with about six thread turns. Trim the waste end and apply a drop of head cement. Tie on the three-part tail starting with the center and then add the stripped stems as a tail flanking, one each per side. Trim any waste ends.

Step 2: Select a clump of natural gray deer hair and clean out the under fur. Position it on the off side and at the end of the shank. Secure it with three snug, but not tight, wraps. Trim off the hair tips then apply pressure to the thread and spin it to the underside of the hook. The hair will spin all the way around the hook so keep it under control and force it to remain on the under side of the hook. Apply a drop of Aqua Flex.

Step 3: Select and clean a clump of dyed brown deer hair then flare it on top of the gray. Make certain it stays on top of the hook so use about three very tight thread wraps to anchor it there.

Step 4: Clean a clump of black deer hair and flare it on top of the brown. Again use several very tight wraps to anchor it in place. Place a drop of Aqua Flex on the junction of the three colors of hair.

Step 5: Use your thumb and forefinger and press back on the clumps of hair to compress them. Advance the thread forward so it's in front of the first three-part application. We often use a hair-compressing tool and suggest you do so as well. Apply another three-part hair assembly with gray on the bottom and black over brown on top. Compress it with your fingers or a tool. Apply a couple more three-part applications so the back two-thirds of the hook is covered. Be sure to place a drop of Aqua Flex on each junction.

Step 6: Whip finish and remove the thread temporarily from the hook. Trim the body to shape using scissors to get a rough cut then provide the finishing touches with a double-edge razor blade. Reattach the thread. Select two sections of pheasant-tail fibers and place an overhand knot in each to form the legs. Bud suggests coating the fibers with Crylon Clear Finish before shaping the legs. Tie them in position in front of the trimmed body. Trim any waste ends and leave bobbin here for the next step. Trim the tail flanks so they are about half as long as the tail.

Step 7: Select, clean, and stack a clump of natural gray deer hair. Tie it to the under side of the hook with the tips pointing to the rear forming half of the collar. Prepare a clump of black deer hair just as you did the natural gray and attach it to the top of the fly to form the top of the collar. The waste ends of both colors form the first part of the head. Use the procedures outlined in Steps 2 & 3 to add a three-part hair application. Tie on two horse-hair fibers to form the antenna. Whip finish and remove the thread.

Step 8: Trim the head to shape using scissors and a double-edge razor blade. Use caution to avoid accidentally cutting off the horse-hair antenna.

Bud's Spinner

Bud shared this fly with us several years ago at a Federation of Fly Fishers Conclave in Livingston, Montana. He assembled it while there to meet a specific need on the area waters. It worked so well we asked him to publish it in the *Fly Pattern Encyclopedia* and in this book as well.

It's not a particularly difficult fly to tie, but according to Bud you do face a couple of challenges, "Since spinners have a tendency to land upside down there are two options you may use to correct this problem. You can dub the thorax and leave off the biots, or use a biot on the top and the bottom. By using either option the fly will land looking the same no matter which way it lands." We've always tied it with one biot on the top and not worried whether the fly looked the same each time we presented it. In fact we felt it was a positive situation to be able to present a different fly on two consecutive casts and not have to tie on another pattern.

Bud's Spinner

Hook:	Size 12-22, dry fly
Thread:	Color to match the insect
Tail:	Micro Fibbets, divided
Abdomen:	Stripped hackle stem
Thorax:	Dubbing
Wing case:	Biot to match the body
Wings:	White Z-lon
Head:	Thread

Step 1: Place the hook in the vise and wrap a thread base that starts about one eye width back on the hook and covers the front one-fourth of the shank. Tie on a section of Z-lon to form the spinner wings. Adjust the length of each wing so they are as long as the hook shank. Tie on four Micro Fibbets as you wrap to the end of the shank. Criss-cross between them to divide the tail. Leave the thread near the back of the hook.

Step 2: Select a large brown hackle feather and strip all the fibers from the stem. Tie it on the hook by the tip at the end of the shank. Wrap the thread forward to the wings then follow with the stripped stem forming the abdomen. Tie it off behind the wings and trim the waste end.

Step 3: Tie on the biot butt end first with the pointed end facing back. Be certain the shiny side is facing down. Apply a small amount of dubbing to the thread and apply it to the hook to form a thorax. We find crisscross wraps help provide the correct profile. Leave the thread hanging just behind the eye.

Step 4: Fold over the biot and anchor it with the tying thread. Trim the excess material, apply a whip finish, and cut off the thread. Apply a coating of head cement or Aqua Head.

Crown Royal Streamer

When Bud set out to improve on a Royal Coachman streamer he wasn't sure just how he would do so; it was already a darned good fly. We were so impressed with his modification we just had to try it, and the Crown Royal proved as attractive to the fish as it did to us.

The two applications of golden pheasant tippets, first in the tail and then in the beard provide two bright spots that act as strike zones for the fish. We have never experienced short strikes with this fly that we sometimes do with other Matuka streamers. It's our premise that the bright spots serve the same function that eyes do on LaFontaine patterns. Bud's concept has found its way into several of our streamer patterns, including the one featured here. If you look in our streamer boxes you'll find a strong influence from both Gary LaFontaine and Bud Heintz.

Crown Royal Streamer

Hook:	Mustad 79580, size 2-10
Thread:	Black
Tail:	Golden pheasant tippets
Rib:	Fine wire
Body:	Peacock herl and red floss
Wings:	Silver or golden badger feathers
Beard:	Golden pheasant tippets
Hackle:	Badger, tied as a collar
Head:	Black ostrich, thread

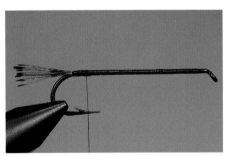

Step 1: Place the hook in the vise and apply a thread base that covers almost all of the hook shank. Leave a small section of bare hook directly behind the eye to allow room for the head in a future step. Tie on a tail of golden pheasant tippets that is equal in length to one-fourth the hook shank. Leave the thread hanging near the back of the hook.

Step 2: Tie on a four-inch section of fine, gold wire for use later as a rib. Tie two or three peacock herls on the hook by the tips and wrap them to form the butt section of the body. Advance the thread forward to the one-fourth position and tie on a section of red floss.

Step 3: Wrap the floss to the back peacock herl butt and then forward to the starting point. Tie on two or three peacock herls by the tips and wrap a segment similar in size to the rear application. Trim any waste ends and leave the thread just in front of it.

Step 4: Match four silver badger feathers into a wing unit that is twice as long as the hook shank. Make sure the dull sides of the feathers face each other. Tie it on the hook to the front of the body. Wrap the rib forward binding the wing to the body Matuka style. Tie off and trim the excess wire.

Step 5: Select a clump of golden pheasant tippets of similar proportions as the tail. Tie them on the hook as a beard. Adjust their length so they equal the tail.

Step 6: Strip the waste fibers from the stem of a silver badger feather and tie it on the hook directly in front of the beard. Wrap six turns, tie it off, and trim away the excess. Tie on a black ostrich herl and wrap four turns tight against the hackle. Tie it off and trim off the waste end. Form a thread head, whip finish, and remove the thread. Apply a coating of head cement or Aqua Head.

HENRY HOFFMAN

Retired hackle producer, Henry Hoffman grew up near Santa Rosa, California. While in high school he started fishing near Bodega Bay for saltwater rockfish. In 1953 Henry almost drowned after being swept off a reef at Stewart's Point. After that experience he decided to fish in the safer, nearby, Russian River. Henry often hitch-hiked there to fish, sometimes catching a ride with fly-anglers like Bill Schaadt and Grant King. From them he developed an interest in fly-fishing.

Before he ever saw anyone tie a fly he learned about their construction by taking apart samples he found along the river. Without the aid of tools, Henry would then reassemble the flies using his mother's sewing thread. He also tied a few other patterns with feathers from his parents' chickens and other materials from around the house.

The next time Henry hitched a ride with a fly-fisherman he proudly shared his "trashy looking flies." The man explained he could do much better if he got tools and an instruction book through Herter's catalog. With a new set of tools and the book he quickly became a good fly-tier and also started raising chickens for hackle. The birds were purchased from the Murray McMurray Hatchery in Webster City, Iowa. By 1955 he was selling many of the flies he produced, but always keeping a few for his own use.

Henry spent the years of 1957 to 1959 in the US Army. While stationed in Germany he did his duty and tied flies or fished in his spare time. Henry recalls a day while on KP duty, an officer and a couple of sergeants bought a person to relieve me and told him to get his fishing gear from the barracks. They took him in their jeep several miles to a creek and asked him to catch them some trout. Henry caught a dozen for them before an indignant landowner told them to get off his property! In Europe there is very little public fishing water.

In 1961 Henry moved to Astoria, Oregon where he became a logger,

Henry Hoffman

longshoreman, and commercial fly-tier. He again pursued his hackle production hobby after purchasing two barred rock bantam chickens at a fair and matched them up with a half dozen more from the McMurray Hatchery. None of these birds had been bred for fly tying so Henry had his work cut out for him. He sold the hackle he didn't use himself for $3.00 per neck and $.75 per bag of saddle hackle.

By the early 1970s he had married his wife, Joyce and was well along in developing the world's best hackle. The two worked hard through the lean years and eventually made Hoffman's Hackle Farm a success. In 1989 they sold their genetic strain of birds to Tom Whiting with the agreement they could maintain a flock of their own for the next six years.

During the last eleven years Henry's main interest has been developing new fly patterns from chicken body feathers—rooster soft hackle, chicken marabou, and knee hackle. He tested his new patterns in a clear-water tank and what looked good there went to the field for testing. In 1998 Henry caught 909 fish and over 800 of them were caught on flies he developed from rooster body feathers. He has shared these flies with fellow anglers in the Federation of Fly Fishers since 1974. They are works of art, as you will see here.

Author's Note: We've known Henry for a number of years and consider him to be one of the most innovative fly-tiers we know. He is the person who took fly-tying hackle from the dark ages to the awesome feathers available today. We are especially pleased with his participation in this book.

Beaver & Knee

In the recent past, Henry was on an extended fishing trip to Lenore Lake in Washington. The fishing was so good he was losing flies on a regular basis and resorted to tying replacements in his motel room at night. Eventually Henry's supply of materials for a soft-hackle Pheasant Tail ran out and he had to resort to substitution. He used brown beaver dubbing because it was similar in color to the pheasant-tail fibers and rooster knee hackle because that was all he had.

In the following days, the substitute pattern quickly proved itself as a top producer, far surpassing the original pheasant tail. Henry likes to keep the body quite slender to more effectively represent a mayfly nymph. It went on to save the day at the Douglas

Lake Ranch in British Columbia when the finicky Kamloops would touch no other fly.

We feel it's important to talk a bit about "knee hackle" because many of you have probably not been exposed to it. The feathers are similar in appearance to a small hen cape feather and are found on a rooster's lower leg where the kneecap would be if chickens had such a thing. We love these little feathers for soft hackles and also for streamer wings on some of the miniature streamers we often tie and fish. Henry has only a few of these feathers left in his supply, so we suggest you have your local fly shop request this product from Whiting Farms in Delta, Colorado.

Beaver & Knee

Hook:	Mustad 9671, size 10-16
Thread:	Brown & yellow
Bead:	Spirit River gold glass bead
Tail:	Brown Chickabou
Body:	Brown beaver dubbing
Rib:	Fine gold wire
Hackle:	Grizzly dyed brown knee hackle

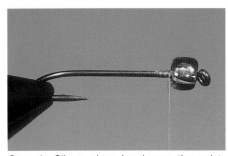

Step 1: Slip a glass bead over the point, around the bend, and onto the shank. Place the hook in the vise and apply a yellow thread base directly behind the eye. Leave the thread hanging tight against the back of the eye. Slide the bead forward so it's touching the thread, bring the thread over the bead and anchor it behind. Twist the bead on the hook so that the thread strand anchoring it in place is positioned on the underside. Apply a drop of super glue and allow it to run onto the thread wraps inside the bead. Allow the glue to set-up before going to the next step.

Step 2: Whip finish, remove the yellow thread, and attach the brown directly behind the bead. Wrap it to the end of the shank and tie on a sparse tail of brown Chickabou that is as long as the shank. Trim off the waste end.

Step 3: Tie on a section of fine gold wire for later use as a rib. Apply brown beaver dubbing to the thread. Be sure to remove any offending guard hairs. Start wrapping forward, shaping a tapered body in the process.

Step 4: Finish wrapping the body. Follow with the wire rib, tie it off, and trim away the waste end.

Step 5: Select a grizzly dyed brown knee hackle, remove the fluff from the base end, and bind it to the hook at the bead. Trim the excess stem.

Step 6: Wrap two or three turns of hackle, tie it off, and trim the waste end. Whip finish and remove the thread. Apply a coating of head cement or Aqua Head.

Bright Eyes

Henry has been tying his damselfly nymphs with Chickabou for several years and finds the pattern to be very effective. One day on his way home from a fishing trip he stopped at a craft store and ended up buying a string of bright, metallic plastic beads. When Henry added the bright eyes to the nymph the fish went crazy.

It is especially productive in off-colored water or when there is an algae bloom. Henry tells us, "A good retrieve is to draw the line in with the stripping hand while jiggling the rod tip with the other hand." Also he likes to fish a dropper fly ahead of the damsel so it looks like the damsel is chasing the other nymph.

Bright Eyes

Hook:	Mustad 9672, size 8-14
Thread:	Olive
Tail:	Olive Chickabou
Wing case:	Grizzly dyed olive knee hackle
Eyes:	Metallic green bead chain
Head:	Olive beaver dubbing

Step 1: Apply a thread base to the hook that starts at the eye and stops at the end of the shank. Select an olive Chickabou feather and tie it on the hook at a tail equal in length to the shank. Trim away the waste end.

Step 2: At the end of the hook attach an olive Chickabou feather by its tip. Select a segment of fine gold wire and tie it on for later use as a rib. Trim any excess material.

Step 3: Wrap the feather about three-fourths of the way forward on the hook shank and tie it off. Counter wind the wire as a rib and tie it off as well. Trim the waste ends from both materials.

Step 4: Take a soft-hackle feather and strip a clump of fibers from the stem. Bind them to the off side of the hook and trim away any waste ends. Repeat the process on the near side of the hook.

Step 5: Select a knee hackle or hackle tip, coat it with head cement, stroke it one time to pull the fibers together, and allow it to dry. Tie the prepared feather on the hook as a wing case and trim away any excess material.

Step 6: Cut two beads from a length of metallic green, bead chain. Tie them on the hook slightly forward of the wing case as a pair of eyes. Anchor the eyes with several figure-eight wraps then apply a drop of Super Glue to cement them in place.

Step 7: Apply olive dubbing to the thread. Wrap around and in front of the eyes to form a head.

Step 8: Whip finish, trim off the thread, and apply head cement or Aqua Head.

Chickabou Crab

Henry got the idea for this pattern after fishing with Dave Whitlock's crab pattern. It is constructed from clipped deer hair that looks very realistic but has a slow sink rate in the water column. He decided to substitute Chickabou for the deer hair so he could speed up the crab's descent to the depths.

The resulting fly looked great and Henry chose the bonefish at Christmas Islands as testing subjects. First he cast a Crazy Charlie to cruising fish. Often they would retreat back into the blue water. Then he tried his crab near a drop-off and had immediate success. Ever since, this fly has served him (and your authors) very well.

It is tied on a saltwater jig hook allowing the point to ride up in the water. This feature is especially helpful when working the pattern on or near the bottom. It certainly helps avoid hanging up. It is very simple to adjust the colors based on the natural crabs in your area.

Chickabou Crab

Hook:	Size 4-8, saltwater jig
Thread:	Gray
Claws:	Grizzly dyed gray, trimmed
Body:	Gray and blue dun Chickabou, trimmed
Eyes:	Artificial flower stamens, black
Legs:	Grizzly dyed gray soft hackle

Step 1: Apply a thread base to the complete hook starting behind the eye and stopping at the end of the shank. Select a gray chicken breast feather and trim the fluff one-fourth-inch wide on both sides of the stem. Tie it on the hook at the end of the shank.

Step 2: Wrap the thread forward several turns so it is even with the hook point. Wind the feather three or four turns, tie it off, and trim the waste end. Criss-cross wrap the thread through the feather application to strengthen it. Use a curved pair of scissors to trim it into a ball shape.

Step 3: Select a grizzly soft-hackle feather and trim the barbs off the right side of the stem. Identify the right side when holding the feather with the natural curve away from you. Tie it on the hook at the front edge of the Chickabou ball.

Step 4: Turn the hook over in the vise. Place a coating of head cement over two grizzly soft-hackle feathers. When they are dry, trim the barbs on the base end of each feather to form stubble on the sides of the stems. Then clip off the tips of each feather to shape the claws. Set one aside for future reference and tie the other on the hook just forward of the Chickabou ball. Notice the natural curve of the feather is pointing down. Henry tells us the stubble on the feather base makes it much easier to position the claws.

Step 5: Pre-trim a light-and-dark Chickabou feather so the fibers are three-eighths inch on each side of the stem. Tie on the dark and wrap it several turns. Secure it with a couple of thread wraps then trim the waste end. Tie on the light-colored feather in front of the dark and repeat the previous process. Tie on the flower stamen eyes as illustrated.

Step 6: Trim away the waste ends of the eyes. Apply several more light and dark feather bands until you reach the point on the shank where it angles to meet the eye. Stop at that position and leave the thread there for the next step.

Step 7: Pick up the pre-formed claw from Step 4, tie it on the hook at the front of the shank, and trim away the waste end. Pull the one-sided, grizzly feather placed in Step 3 forward and anchor it at the front of the shank to form the legs.

Step 8: Trim away the waste end of the grizzly feather. Use your scissors to clip spaces in these fibers to better define the legs. Whip finish, trim off the thread, and apply a coating of head cement or Aqua Head.

Chickabugger

For several years Henry fished this fly in a color range more consistent with standard Woolly Buggers—black, brown, or olive. He has found that sometimes the color red is best. He tells us the best times to use the red version is after sunset or during the day when the wind is stirring up mud and debris along the shore line. During these conditions fish will move into the dirty water to feed on what is churned up. The red fly is easier to see under low visibility situations.

Does the fly catch fish? We'll let Henry tell you in his own words,

"On May 17, 2001 I was fishing a lake when several spin fishers started snagging fish as they cruised the shore line. I called the game department and an officer put an end to the snagging. The official advised me to leave the area to prevent any possible reprisals. Reluctantly I drove seven miles to another area and quickly caught two large trout on a number-eight red Chickabugger—one fish was 27 inches and the other was 30." We needed no more convincing; you'll find several red Chickabuggers in our fly boxes.

Chickabugger

Hook:	Mustad 9671, size 6-10
Thread:	Red
Tail:	Red Chickabou
Body:	Red Chickabou
Rib:	Red copper wire
Hackle:	Red soft-hackle feather
Eyes:	Silver Spirit River Real Eyes
Head:	Red Chickabou or extra-fine chenille

Step 1: Wrap almost all of the hook shank with red polyester sewing thread to form a base that stops directly above the hook point. Bind a strip of 30-pound monofilament to each side of the shank to help shape the body. Cover the side shims with the sewing thread, whip finish, and trim it from the hook. Coat the thread with Super Glue and allow it to dry before continuing to the next step.

Step 2: Tie on the red tying thread directly above the hook point and trim away the waste end. Select a red Chickabou feather and tie it on the end of the shank to form a tail that is about as long as the complete hook. Trim off the excess feather.

Step 3: Prepare a red soft-hackle feather by trimming the fibers from one side of the front part of the feather. Do not trim away the real fuzzy fibers near the end of the stem. Tie the feather to the hook by the tip and trim the waste end.

Step 4: Tie on a section of red copper wire to later use as the rib; then attach a red Chickabou feather by the tip. Trim off the excess materials and advance the thread forward to a position about one-fourth back from hook eye.

Step 5: Tie the eyes on top of the shank with several criss-cross thread wraps. The positioning of the eyes causes the hook point to ride up while in the water.

Step 6: Wind the Chickabou feather forward to form the body and tie it off behind the eyes. Trim off the unused portion of the feather.

Step 7: Palmer the hackle forward to the eyes. Be certain to wrap at least one turn of the fuzzy fibers to form a collar directly behind the eyes and tie the hackle off there. Counter wrap the rib and tie it off as well. Trim off all excess materials.

Step 8: Tie on a long-fibered red Chickabou feather by the tip. Figure-eight wrap around the eyes to form the head. Tie off the feather at the hook eye, whip finish, and trim off the excess materials. Apply a coating of cement or Aqua Head.

Hank's Foam Damsel

One day while fishing Georgetown Lake in Montana Henry encountered trout being particularly selective. He observed the fish taking the adult damsels as they skimmed above the surface or when they briefly touched the water. Their bodies were prominent, but the moving translucent wings were barely visible. Henry designed this pattern with white hackle and post so the fish looking up at it would see body and little else. The white foam post helps the fly float and makes it easier to see on the water, especially when a breeze makes the water choppy.

Henry likes to fish the fly early in the season when the nymphs are migrating to the shore. He casts it close to the bank where the fish will be preying on the newly-hatched adults. He tells us, "Later when the hatch is about done, the adults will spend the nights and early mornings along the shoreline hiding in the grass, weeds, brush, etc. At about 10:00 a.m., warming temperatures will bring the damsels back over the water." From that point, the trout will illustrate where to fish, often jumping clear out of the water to capture a hovering insect.

Hank's Foam Damsel

Hook:	Mustad 94840 or 80000, size 12
Thread:	Blue polyester & Gudebrod BCS 136
Body:	Blue closed-cell, black marker
Thorax:	Spirit River peacock blue dubbing
Wing post:	White closed-cell foam
Hackle:	White or silver badger
Eyes:	Spirit River monofilament

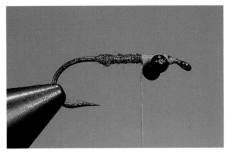

Step 1: Apply a thread base that covers the front three-fourths of the hook shank using polyester sewing thread. Whip finish the thread and trim it from the hook. Coat it with Super Glue and set the incomplete fly aside to dry. When the Super Glue is no longer tacky, attach the tying thread to the shank just behind the hook eye. Bind the Spirit River monofilament eyes on the shank with several criss-cross wraps. Henry suggests tying the eyes to the underside of the shank to allow more room for the hackle in a last step.

Step 2: Apply the dubbing to the thread and wrap a body that covers the complete hook shank both in front of and behind the eyes. Leave the thread hanging at the back of the shank.

Step 3: Cut a strip of 1/16-inch blue foam so it's the same width as it is tall. Use a fine-point felt-tip marker to color black bands on the strip. Bind the foam to the back of the hook with several tight wraps. Pull the excess foam up and advance the thread forward about half way to the eyes. Bring the foam strip back to the hook shank and again bind it with several thread wraps. Advance the thread to the eyes using the same process just outlined. Bind the foam to the shank one last time and trim away any excess.

Step 4: Prepare a white or silver badger hackle feather by removing the fuzzy fibers near the base of the stem. Tie this feather to the hook directly behind the eyes and trim away any excess stem.

Step 5: Cut a strip of one-sixteenth-inch white foam so it's about one-fourth inch wide. Trim one end so it comes to a point. Tie this end to the hook directly behind the eyes and stand it up to form the parachute post.

Step 6: Wrap the hackle around the post several turns, tie it off, and trim away the excess. Whip finish the thread, cut it off the hook, and trim the post short to finish the fly. Apply a coating of cement or Aqua Head.

Hank's Braided Snail

Frustration is often the impetus behind development, whether we speak of fly-tying or going to the moon. In Henry's case it all started one day when he was fishing Clear Lakes Country Club near Twin Falls, Idaho where the rainbows seemed to be rising to an unseen hatch. He soon found to his amazement the trout were taking snails floating in the surface film. Shortly after that day he again witnessed this phenomenon on Yellow Lake in British Columbia.

Henry later learned this happens when the water is warm with lower oxygen content. He also learned trout feed on those same snails whether they are on the surface or on the bottom, so he has developed patterns to fit both situations. We present both versions and three colors here. It's a simple pattern anyone can tie, but oh so effective!

Hank's Braided Snail

Hook:	Size 10-14, dry or wet fly
Thread:	Black or brown
Eyes:	Melted monofilament
Shell:	Black or brown rope, shoelace, or foam
Body:	Thread

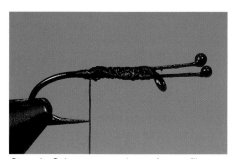

Step 1: Select two sections of monofilament and melt one end of each with a cigarette lighter. Mark them with a brown or black felt-tip marker to finish the eyes. Place the hook in the vise and apply a thread base that covers the front half of the hook. Bind the eyes in place starting at the eye and ending near the center of the hook. Trim away the excess monofilament.

Step 2: Dye sections of braided nylon rope, parachute cord, or shoelaces to brown, gray, or black. Cut a short section of black-dyed cord and tie an overhand knot in it. Trim away one waste end and tie the other to the hook. Trim it at a severe angle and cover the trimmed end with thread. The knot forms the shell.

Step 3: Whip finish the thread and trim it from the hook. Coat the body area with epoxy or Aqua Tuff. You just completed a sinking version of Henry's fly.

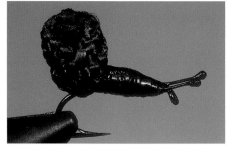

Step 4: Here is a brown version of the same style.

Step 5: The gray foam strip produces a floating snail.

Step 6: A felt-tip marker changes the pattern to black and is our favorite.

Jig Head Chickabou

Henry's fishing log shows he caught his first bass on June 24, 1953 on the Russian River in California. He didn't fly-fish at that time, but by the early 1960s he regularly caught largemouth bass in his parents' farm pond.

In 1994 Henry started developing patterns for the Umpqua River's smallmouth bass. He found 1998 to be a very good year when he tested seven different patterns in a variety of colors and sizes. In an eight-day period, he fished six miles of the river on the Big K Ranch near Elkton, Oregon and caught 464 smallmouth bass. The best pattern was the Jig Headed Chickabou and the best colors were orange and black; the pattern you see here!

Jig Head Chickabou

Hook:	Mustad 9672, size 6-10
Thread:	Black
Tail:	Black Chickabou
Rib:	Fine gold wire
Body:	Black & orange Chickabou
Hackle:	Black soft hackle
Eyes:	Spirit River Real Eyes
Head:	Fine black chenille

Step 1: Use an un-waxed sewing thread for this step because it will better absorb the glue. Select two segments of 25-pound monofilament that are a bit shorter than the hook shank. Attach the tying thread behind the eye with a couple of turns then bind the two segments of monofilament to the sides of the shank stopping even with the hook point. Coat this application with super glue and allow it to dry before continuing. The flattened base helps keep the eyes from moving around on the hook.

Step 2: Whip finish and trim off the sewing thread. Tie on the standard tying thread near the end of the shank. Select a black Chickabou feather and bind it to the hook as a tail that is as long as the shank. Trim the excess material.

Step 3: At the end of the shank, tie on a black Chickabou feather by its tip. Also tie on a section of fine gold wire to later serve as the rib.

Step 4: Wrap the thread forward and leave it hanging just in front of the hook point. Wrap the Chickabou forward to meet the thread and tie it off.

Step 5: Tie on an orange Chickabou feather by the tip and wrap several turns to form a band in the center of the body. Tie if off and trim away the excess. Repeat the process with a black feather. Be sure to leave enough room for the eyes, hackle, and head. Counter wrap the wire for the rib, tie if off, and cut away the waste end.

Step 6: Tie on the Spirit River eyes on top of the shank. Place a drop of Super Glue to anchor them in place.

Step 7: Behind the eyes, tie on a black soft-hackle feather by the tip. Wrap two or three turns, tie it off, and trim the waste end.

Step 8: Tie on a segment of fine black chenille. Wrap between and in front of the eyes to form the head. Tie it off and trim the excess. Whip finish the thread, trim it from the hook and apply a coating of head cement or Aqua Head.

DAVID HUNTER

David currently works for Regence Blue Cross Blue Shield of Oregon and has done so for the past twelve years. He lives in Salem with his lovely wife Carolyn who is very supportive of his fly-fishing and fly-tying interests. His other hobbies include upland bird hunting (grouse and chukars), as well as deer or elk hunting in the nearby Cascade Mountains.

In his letter to us David tells us, "When I first moved to Oregon in the late 1980s, I was excited to start fishing in such a beautiful state with so many rivers and lakes. I started spin fishing rivers and ponds with great success. One day I wandered into McNeese's Fly Shop. I had some very interesting conversations with Forrest Maxwell over the next few weeks and before I knew it I had purchased my first fly rod, a Cortland 5/6 with matching reel and line."

From that moment, he haunted the local library for books on casting, flies, entomology, etc. While devouring those books he practiced casting on his lawn in the evenings, all the while ignoring comments from his neighbors. He soon learned that the different current speeds treated his line differently than did the grass on the lawn. David remembers, "I recall how excited I was the first time a trout devoured the dry fly on the end of my line, and all the information I had read came to make sense on the river."

He believes it makes him a much better fisherman to spend more time observing what was going on rather than jumping into the water and starting to throw a line. David likes to observe all aspects of the

David Hunter

fish's environment—insect size and shape, life-cycle phase, weather, etc. He always covers the water in a slow, quiet, methodical manner.

David recalls the impetus behind his fly-tying, "After my first few fly-fishing experiences, I ended up with more flies in the bushes and trees than I had left in my fly box at the end of the day. Waiting for pay day to purchase more flies made it seem like it took forever to build up a good selection." Carolyn came to his rescue when she presented him with his first fly-tying vise as a birthday present.

With the help of Forrest Maxwell and library books, he was soon catching fish on flies created by his own hand. Over the years, David has strived to learn all aspects of fly-tying, from small trout patterns to full-dressed Atlantic salmon flies. He credits Rich Youngers, David Barlow, and Harry Gross with much of his growth as a fly-tier. Today he teaches beginning fly-tying classes for the Creekside Flyfishing Shop. David closes, "I enjoy getting people excited about fly-tying and fishing, because I want them to have the same satisfaction and adventure that I have been fortunate enough to experience." David is obviously a person who wants to give back as much as he has received. What a great outlook on life.

Hunter's Stonefly

This pattern is the result of David's observation on the Santiam River where he saw large stoneflies clinging to the brush and grass along the bank. Often the clumsy insects would fall into the river and only float for a short distance before disappearing in the swirl of a feeding trout.

He struggled with several design ideas, finally determining an extended body would serve very well. After questioning friends about extended-body construction he learned about using a needle in the vise to shape a section of foam. This was the answer to his problem.

He would glue two different colors of foam together then cut the assembly to shape. When Foust's Chernobyl Fly Bodies became available, David no longer needed to make his own.

David tells us, "I enjoy fishing this pattern during the spring and summer months when the adult stoneflies are fluttering about. I use a loop knot, so the fly has a free action." It works well either as a skater or dead drifted for steelhead or trout. The foam body provides excellent floatation and durability.

Hunter's Stonefly

Hook:	Size 4-8, salmon-fly style
Thread:	Orange
Body:	Chernobyl Fly Bodies, orange/black
Tail:	Brown biots
Dubbing:	Orange Seal-Ex and brown muskrat mix
Wing:	Cream Antron under fox squirrel tail
Antenna:	Brown biots
Head:	Thread and black stripe

Step 1: You have the option of either constructing the body or using a pre-made one. The body illustrated on the top is available commercially; the one on the bottom was made by welding two colors of foam together with epoxy then using a pair of scissors to shape it.

Step 2: Place a needle in the vise jaws and wrap a couple of turns of thread near the end. Bind the foam tightly to the needle with three or four tight wraps then apply a whip finish. Do not cut off the thread. Pull the foam up and wrap the thread toward the vise jaws a couple of turns. Push the foam back down to the needle and wrap several tight wraps followed by a whip finish. Again pull up the foam and wrap a couple more turns toward the jaws. Push the foam back down and tie a third segment with several tight wraps. Tie on the biots for the tail, one per side. Trim the waste ends, whip finish the thread, and cut it from the assembly. Slip the prepared body off the needle and turn the unit over in your hands. You will note a short piece of thread between each whip-finished segment. Trim them off the body and apply head cement to each thread application.

Step 3: Place the hook in the vise and attach the thread to the shank slightly forward of the point. Bind the body unit to the hook over the first segment tied in the previous step. Mix a small amount of orange seal fur (or Seal-Ex) with brown muskrat dubbing. Dub this on the hook until you reach the center of the shank. Leave the thread hanging there in preparation for the next step.

Step 4: Pull the loose end of the foam over, tie it to the shank, and trim off the waste end. Dub over the trimmed foam and forward on the shank to a position 1/4 back from the hook eye.

Step 5: Tie on the Antron under wing and trim it to length. Clean the short fibers and under fur out of a clump of squirrel-tail hair. Do not stack it but do remove any extra-long fibers. Tie the clump on the hook tips forward. Make certain it is long enough to reach to the end of the tail when it is folded over in the next step.

Step 6: Fold over the squirrel-tail wing and bind it in place forming a fairly large head. Tie a biot on each side to simulate the antenna. Trim any waste ends, wrap a thread head, whip finish, and trim away the orange thread. Use black tying thread to construct a band in the center of the head. Whip finish and remove it as well. Coat the head with epoxy or Aqua Tuff.

GERALD JAMES

Gerald James

Gerald lives in Grants Pass, Oregon with his lovely wife Arlene. He is retired from the country road survey crew and she is the Deli Manager at the local Safeway. They raised two children who have given them four grandchildren. Son Stephen (an orthopedic spine surgeon) lives with his wife Janice in Atlanta, Georgia with two sons—Collin and Nicholas. Daughter Christina (Manager of Cendant Travel) lives with her husband Rob in Oklahoma City with their two children—Stephen and Katie. Both Stephen and Christina tied commercially through their high school years buying their clothes, bikes, cars, etc. with money they earned tying flies.

At the young age of three Jerry received a blow to the head and has suffered migraine-type headaches continually since. In spite of the continual pain we have never seen him when he didn't display a smile and cheerful attitude. He says, "I humbly thank the Lord for allowing me to have the talent to tie flies in spite of my condition. I hope I am an encouragement to others who have disabilities."

Jerry first remembers fly-fishing at the tender age of five. It was May 1946 when he first went fly-fishing with Mr. Rightmeir, an elderly neighbor who lived across the street from his parents' home. That home was only one block from the Rogue River. Mr. Rightmeir coached Gerald like a grandfather. He always fished two wet flies: the main fly was the Royal Coachman and the dropper was a Gray Hackle Yellow. Jerry remembers, "He would almost always have a trout on, sometimes two, one on each fly. When I saw this I was *hooked* on fly-fishing."

Gerald's fly-tying mentor was Frank Jones, a wheelchair-bound commercial tier who operated Jones's Bait and Tackle. Frank's business was only four blocks from Jerry's home. It was only a matter of time before his tenacity convinced Frank to teach him how to tie. Gerald apprenticed under Frank for the next five years until Frank's death in May 1959. After that Jerry was on his own, but always remembers Frank's stern advice, "It takes a lifetime to get a good reputation, tie your best at all times. It only takes one fly, poorly tied, to get a bad reputation. Don't ever tie that first poor one."

In January 1978 he began tying flies for the famed fly tier, and author of *Tying and Fishing the Fuzzy Nymphs*, Polly Rosborough (1975 Buz Buszek Memorial Award Recipient). From 1978 to 1992 Jerry was Polly's only fly tier. Polly tied left-handed so Gerald learned to tie his flies backward so they would look exactly like Rosborough's.

In 1994 Gerald opened Ye Olde Fly Fishing Museum. He advises, "I have beautiful exotic bird mounts, 450-gallon jars of assorted materials, and exotic feathers for tying flies. There are fish carvings, displays of vintage fishing tackle, color plates tied by many fine fly tiers, bamboo rods, reels, books, a Polly Rosborough display, a Ginger Rogers display, and many antiquities showing fly-fishing over the centuries. I buy and trade for old fishing tackle to add to my museum." We think it is quite a place and suggest you place it on your siteseeing list the next time you are in Grants Pass. You won't be disappointed.

Hole-In-One Stonefly

Gerald developed this fly quite by accident. He was talking on the telephone while rolling an orange golf tee in his fingers. All of a sudden the lights flashed and he realized the golf tee would make a great stonefly body with only a minimum of modification. First he removed the large end of the tee then cut a slot length-wise to accommodate the hook shank. An application of Shoe Goo cemented the body to the hook. The wing is constructed from a rip-stop automotive material Jerry painted gray then stamped with the vein markings. He finishes by spraying the wing with a clear acrylic to waterproof it.

Is the fly effective? You bet it is and easy to cast as well! Jerry calls it "ultra-dry" because it is almost impossible to sink. The fly hits the water with a telltale splash that alerts the fish to its exact location. From there it's a matter of setting the hook because the fish is going to strike. Jerry designed it to be a trout fly, but has caught bass and steelhead on it as well.

Hole-In-One Stonefly

Hook:	TMC 200R, size 4
Thread:	Orange & fluorescent orange
Tail:	Black biots
Body:	Hot orange golf tee
Over back:	Black latex
Rib:	Black Larva Lace
Wing:	Automotive upholstery fabric
Head:	Deer hair, bullet style
Eyes:	Melted monofilament
Legs:	Rubber leg material
Antenna:	Black wild boar hair

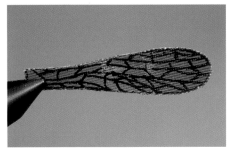

Step 1: Prepare the wing by coating the rip-stop upholstery fabric with a thin coat of gray water-based paint. Allow it to dry, then cut the wing to shape as illustrated. Apply the vein markings with a felt-tip marker or stamp. Spray the wing with clear acrylic to waterproof it. Set it aside to dry. Also cut a half-inch section of monofilament and melt the ends to form a set of eyes. Color them with a black marker and set them aside as well.

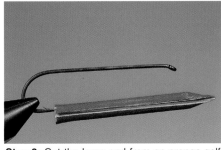

Step 2: Cut the large end from an orange golf tee and discard it unless you plan to use it as a pan-fish popper head. Saw a slot length-wise in the remaining slender portion that is deep enough to cut about half way through the piece. We've stuck the prepared golf tee on the point of the hook for illustration purposes only. It is mounted on the hook in the next step.

Step 3: Mount the body on the hook using Shoe Goo or epoxy and allow it to dry. Be sure the front 1/4 of the hook shank remains bare. The body should extend beyond the end of the shank no more than 3/8 inch. After the glue is dry, color the top of the body with a black felt-tip marker.

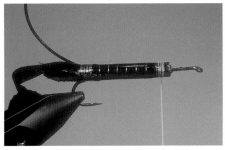

Step 4: Attach the orange thread at the very end of the hook shank and trim the waste end. Tie a black biot on both sides of the body as a tail and cut off the excess material. While at the end of the shank, tie on a 1/4-inch-wide strip of black latex directly on top of the body. Next attach a section of black Larva Lace on the off side of the body. Wrap the thread forward to the front of the body forming evenly spaced turns later to be covered by the rib.

Step 5: Fold the latex over, tie it down at the front of the body, and trim the excess. Wrap the black Larva Lace forward to form a rib, spacing the turns so it covers the thread placed in the last step.

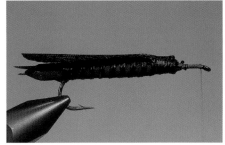

Step 6: Position the wing on top of the body, bind it in place, and trim away the waste end. Apply a coating of head cement to the wing/body juncture. Whip finish the orange thread and trim it from the hook. Tie on the fluorescent orange thread and advance it to the hook eye.

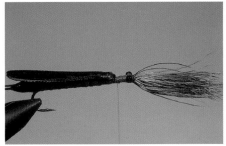

Step 7: Select, clean, and stack a clump of deer hair. Adjust it so the fibers are equal in length to the hook shank then spin it around the front of the hook with the tips pointing forward. Trim off the waste end then cover them with a thread base. Tie on the eyes shaped in Step 1 then tie on two wild-boar fibers to form the antennae; they should extend forward one-half inch.

Step 8: Pull deer hair over to form the bullet head. As you bring the hair back take care to allow the antennae to remain pointing forward. Form the head and bind it in place. Cut two sections of rubber leg material and tie one of them to the off side of the hook so one end sticks out next to the eye and the other next to the body. Repeat the process on the near side of the hook. Whip finish the thread and trim it from the fly. Trim the legs to length and spot them with several drops of black head cement to provide texture. Apply a coating of cement or Aqua Tuff to the bullet head and orange thread wraps.

KIM JENSEN

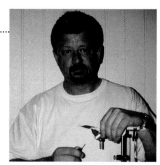

Kim Jensen

South Weber, Utah fly tier Kim Jensen is a project manager for a national marble and granite installation company. It is a constant struggle for him to find time for work and other activities like tying flies, fly-fishing, camping, and hunting. Kim also enjoys practicing martial arts, having achieved the rank of fifth-degree black belt in Karate. All that said, his most valued moments are spent with his friends, wife Tammy, five sons (Brandon, Steven, Travis, Chris, and Val ages seventeen to twenty-five), and two granddaughters.

Kim started his life-long love of fly-fishing and tying at twelve years of age. As a paperboy he worked to save the money to purchase his first fly rod, a six-weight fiberglass purchased for the enormous sum of $25.00. One of his fondest memories of those early years learning to fly-fish was in Utah's Uinta Mountains when he caught his first fish. Equipped with his new fly rod and an old automatic reel given him by his father he fished hard all day but with no luck. Finally, as the family was getting ready to go home, a small trout inhaled his fly. Kim was so surprised he launched it right over his shoulder and into the stream behind him where thankfully it came off the hook and disappeared. He has been a hooked fly-fisher ever since.

With a simple set of tools and a Herter's vise Kim learned fly-tying basics from his father while home convalescing from an illness. He tied very little after his introduction, but retained an interest that would be rekindled some twenty years later. In the spring of 1993 Kim was schedule for hip replacement surgery. His wife Tammy thought fly-tying would be a good activity to keep him preoccupied while recovering. She scheduled him for fly-tying classes with Dave Scadden at the Anglers Inn fly shop. For Kim this experience was like coming home to an old friend.

This reintroduction kindled an insatiable thirst for fly-tying knowledge only partially satisfied by books and videos. Kim took lessons from anyone willing to teach him. His skills rapidly developed until he was asked to share them via public tying demonstrations. He entered and won fly-tying contests, local to international in scope. His patterns have been featured in several books and magazines. Kim considers demonstrating at Federation of Fly Fisher's conclaves a highlight in his fly-tying career; a pleasure he's experienced four times to date. We are confident he will enjoy demonstrating at many future national and international shows.

Many people have helped Kim enjoy his current success. They include his mother and father (Roy and Leola), Tammy, the kids and a list of helpful friends too long to present here. Suffice it to say that many featured within the pages of this book are on it. Most of all, Kim thanks God for the ability to express through his eyes and hands what has been placed in his heart and mind.

Kim's Cased Caddis

Inspiration for this pattern came from two different directions. After purchasing a package of Caddis Tube Bodies from Umpqua, Kim was browsing through Gary LaFontaine's marvelous book *Caddisflies* looking for ideas on how to effectively use the new material. Gary is well known for his woven-body flies, so it was only natural to put the two together.

When Kim first started tying this fly it was intended to be an artistic rather than fishing fly. To his surprise it proved effective on the water, especially after replacing the pheasant-tail legs with those constructed from rubber.

Kim fishes it without weight, casting up stream and allowing it to dead-drift back downstream. The Cased Caddis is most productive in clear, moderately fast-moving water like sections of the Provo or Weber rivers near his home in Utah.

Kim's Cased Caddis

Hook:	Mustad 80150 BR (Swimming Nymph), size 14-16
Case:	Umpqua Caddis Tube Body coated with gravel
Body:	Wapsi Round Rib, yellow and olive, woven
Legs:	Black pheasant-tail fibers or fine rubber legs
Thread:	Black, chartreuse
Coating:	Five-minute epoxy

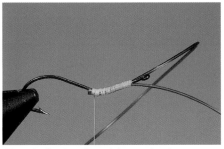

Step 1: Start a thread base about one eye-width back on the shank. Wrap back to the first bend near the middle of the hook. Cut a four-inch segment of yellow and olive tubing. Lay the olive aside for a moment and bind the yellow to the off side of the hook shank ending near the eye. Tie on the olive to the near side ending in the middle of the hook. Be sure the tubing is on the sides of the shank.

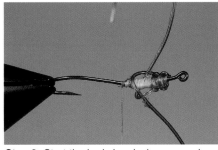

Step 2: Start the body by placing an overhand knot in the tubing, slipping it on the hook, and then tightening it. Be certain to keep the olive on the top and yellow on the bottom. Place a series of these knots on the shank, each one getting closer to the center of the hook. Some tiers find this operation easier if they turn the vise so the hook points either toward or away from them.

Step 3: Once you reach the center of the hook, tighten the last knot then bind the two tag ends of the tubing to the shank. Trim away the excess then apply a thread base to the rest of the shank ending up back in the middle. Whip finish the thread and trim it off.

Step 4: Apply black thread to the hook directly behind the hook eye. Select six black pheasant-tail fibers and bind them to the underside of the hook as legs. Trim away any excess fibers. Dub a black head, whip finish, and cut off the thread.

Step 5: Trim the body so it is as long as the hook shank. Remove the hook from the vise and slide the point inside the body. Half way into the tube pierce it with the point and slide it part way onto the shank.

Step 6: Apply a coating of super glue to the thread wraps and finish sliding the body tube on the hook shank until it reaches the woven body completed in Step 3. Hold the tube in place until the super glue works its magic.

Step 7: Remove the hook from the vise and secure it in a pair of hemostats. Mix five-minute epoxy and coat the body tube with it. While it is still wet, dip it into a container of fine gravel making certain it is evenly coated on all sides. Kim uses parakeet gravel available at pet supply stores or fine gravel from the body of water he plans on fishing.

Step 8: Here is Kim's rubber leg version. This has become our go-to searching pattern for streams we fish in Idaho. If caddis are an important insect in your part of the world you owe it to yourself to try this pattern. It is awesome!

BOB LAY

As a youth growing up on the shores of Lake Erie, Bob was not exposed to fly-fishing nor did he have an occasion to think about it. It wasn't until he moved to Boulder, Colorado in the late 1960's that he found the avenue to pursue his interest in the sport.

When he lived in New York City he tried to get information on "how to get started." When he made inquiries at a sporting goods store well known for its fishing department he became disillusioned with their attitude. They convinced him he must have blue blood and have been born with a silver spoon to fly-fish. Tying flies also seemed out of the question. These were the day when patterns called for "urine-stained fox fur" which was a prized possession of the same nobility who discouraged him from fly-fishing. This experience and the attitude of others caused Bob to become determined to tie flies and become the accomplished instructor he is today.

Finding a Herter's catalog was the springboard for a life-long passion and made him realize he could afford what he needed to get started. Not long after that, a neighbor suggested they attend a fly-fishing club in Fort Collins, Colorado together. It was there that Bob joined the Federation of Flyfishers and met Eric Pettine who was conducting a fly-tying class. This class gave him the start, and later the purchase of two fly-tying books written by Jack Dennis helped round out his skills.

In 1978 Bob, his wife Pat, and two children moved to Kalispell, Montana where they lived for many years. Bob started attending the

Bob Lay

FFF National Conclaves.

Through his work in the telephone industry Bob became friends and started fishing with a fellow fly-fisher and tier from northern Idaho, Al Beatty. A skilled fly tier in his own right, it was Al who asked Bob to assist him in a fly-tying class he was teaching at the National Conclave. Through Al's encouragement, Bob started teaching and demonstrating fly tying. As you recall, Bob experienced some difficulty in getting started. It was this bad experience that made him determined to become proficient in instructing others. He often says, "I wasn't born with this knowledge, I have no business keeping it to myself." Bob gladly imparts his knowledge to anyone interested and willing to work at learning.

Bob has demonstrated and taught fly tying throughout the United States at different fly-fishing shows and for various clubs. In addition he has demonstrated and taught in the United Kingdom and Europe.

In 1988 Bob retired from a management position with an insignificant telephone company based in Louisiana. Today he and his wife travel the United States managing various telephone construction projects. He looks forward to the day he can retire to join his children (Susan and Jim) in Bozeman, Montana. There he hopes to fly-fish, tie flies, and write.

Missouri River Caddis

Bob tells us, "This pattern, like many, evolved from another similar fly. Several years ago I had a commercial order of LaFontaine Sparkle Caddis Emerger flies. I had a really difficult time forming the gas bubble on the top and bottom of the hook. After that experience I set out to make the fly easier to tie and what you see here is the result." Bob changed the hook style, wing material, and the method of form-

ing the bubble he found so difficult on the LaFontaine pattern.

Bob and your authors have tested this fly extensively and found it produces in a multitude of situations. We cast it either to individual fish or quartering down stream and across. When the fish seem to stop feeding on dry flies, even though the caddis as still on the surface, we often change back to this pattern and resume catching fish.

Missouri River Caddis

Hook:	TMC 2487 scud, size 10-18
Body:	Wool dubbing or yarn, color to match the natural
Bubble:	White Z-lon or Antron
Antennas:	Six strands of woodduck flank fibers
Head:	Peacock herl

Step 1: Place the hook in the vise and apply a thread base that covers the back 2/3 of the hook shank. Bind the Antron or Z-lon fibers over the thread base, wrapping to the back of the hook. Apply wool dubbing to the thread and construct a body while advancing the thread back to the 1/3 point on the shank.

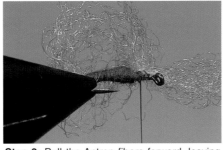

Step 2: Pull the Antron fibers forward, leaving them fairly slack and secure them with two loose turns of thread just to the front of the body. Those fibers should form a one-inch loop over the body. Separate the loop into two parts and pull them to the sides of the fly.

Step 3: Slip a bodkin through the near-side loop, under the hook shank, and through the far-side loop. Rest the bodkin on the bottom of the hook bend near the barb and pull the Antron fibers tight.

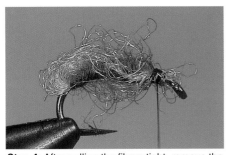

Step 4: After pulling the fibers tight, remove the bodkin, apply several thread turns to anchor the bubble, and trim away the excess material. Use your fingers or a bodkin to tease the bubble fibers in place around the body.

Step 5: Tie on several woodduck fibers to form antennae that extend beyond the end of the hook. Tie on a peacock herl by its tip, trim off any excess material, and advance the thread forward to the hook eye.

Step 6: Wrap the peacock herl forward to form the head, tie it off, and trim the waste end. Whip finish and remove the thread. Apply a coating of cement or Aqua Head.

Parachute Hopper

ob discovered this pattern in the early 1990s and immediately added it to his box of favorite patterns. Al has fished with him for a number of years and can truthfully say that he has never seen a parachute Bob didn't like. He acknowledges, "I have to say, without bias, I feel the Parachute Hopper works far better than the standard patterns."

Bob likes to fish this hopper tight to the bank where the natural insects often end up in the water. Its size causes it to create a disturbance as it lands on the water; the "ker-plunk" often attracts fish. Bob doesn't just fish this fly dry. He often sinks it under an indicator and fishes it as a drowned insect. This method is particularly effective when presented to highly selective fish.

Parachute Hopper

Hook:	TMC 200R, size 6-12
Thread:	Tan
Parachute post:	White poly yarn
Body:	Tan dubbing
Rib:	Gold wire
Wing:	Turkey quill
Legs:	Knotted pheasant fibers
Hackle:	Grizzly

Step 1: Place the hook in the vise and apply a thread base that starts at the eye and stops at the end of the shank. For the purposes of this discussion we identify the end of the shank as a position directly above the throat of the barb. Tie on the gold wire as you wrap forward to the 1/3 point. Cut a two-inch section of poly yarn and tie it to the hook in the middle of the material with several very tight thread turns. Pull both ends of the yarn up straight and wrap the thread around them multiple times to form a parachute hackle platform. Leave the thread hanging in front of the post. Take a mottled turkey feather and coat the fibers with Tuff Film or Aqua Flex. Set it aside to dry.

Step 2: Select a grizzly hackle feather and strip the waste fibers from the stem. Tie the feather to the hook directly in front of the post then bind it to the post as well. Make certain you are binding bare stem to the post.

Step 3: Apply tan dubbing to the thread and construct the body that covers the complete hook shank. Wrap the gold wire forward as a rib. Tie it off at the hook eye and trim off the waste end. Wrap the thread back so it is hanging behind the post.

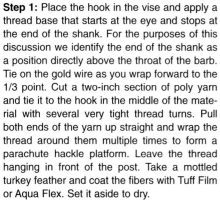

Step 4: Select several pheasant-tail fibers and place an over-hand knot in them to form a leg. Repeat the process and set the legs aside for a moment. Cut a strip of turkey feather, as treated in Step 1, that is as wide as the hook gape. Round one end with your scissors to form the end of the wing. Tie this strip on the hook with the rounded end extended slightly beyond the end of the hook. Attach the legs one per side with several tight thread wraps. Trim off all waste ends.

Step 5: Apply tan dubbing to the thread and wrap a thorax behind and in front of the post. Leave the thread hanging at the hook eye.

Step 6: Wrap the hackle around the post starting at the top and placing each subsequent turn closer to the body. When you reach the body pull the hackle forward and tie it off at the hook eye. Trim off the excess feather, whip finish the thread, and remove it from the hook. Apply a coating of cement to the head and the top of the parachute post.

Texas Shrimp

Bob found the pattern several years ago while working in Houston, Texas. Prior to his move south he had lived and fished his whole life in western waters. The Clark Fork and Missouri river's are two that come to mind. He experienced a learning curve associated with the unfamiliar coastal waters, but the Texas Shrimp made the process much easier.

Bob included this pattern here because it definitely produces fish, is easy to tie, and he thinks it should be shared with others. He has fished it from Texas to the southern tip of Florida and has observed redfish leave grass cover and move across the flats to sample this delightful morsel.

Texas Shrimp

Hook:	Mustad 34007, size 2-6
Body:	Tan craft fur and dubbing
Body hackle:	Brown, palmered
Eyes:	Medium black bead chain
Hook guard:	Craft Fur, pearl & gold Krystal Flash

Step 1: Place the hook in the vise and wrap a thread base from the hook eye, to the end of the shank, and down slightly into the bend. Advance the thread forward a short distance back to the end of the shank. Select a two-inch section of tan craft fur and trim it from the backing. Comb out the under-fur and set it aside to use as dubbing in a future step. Tie this on the hook starting at the end of the shank and binding it into the bend. Wrap back to the end of the shank and tie on the bead-chain eyes. Leave the thread hanging behind them.

Step 2: Select and prepare a brown hackle feather by removing the fuzzy material at the base of the stem. Tie it to the hook behind the eyes.

Step 3: Retrieve the under-fur remaining from Step 1 and apply it to the thread. A dubbing wax like BT's Tacky Wax helps with this process. Construct a dubbed body behind and in front of the eyes wrapping almost all the way back to the hook eye. Leave a 1/8-inch space between the front of the body and the back of the hook eye.

Step 4: Wind the hackle forward over the dubbed body. Tie it off just short of the hook eye.

Step 5: Trim away the excess hackle feather and cut the palmered hackle from the top of the shank. Turn the hook over in the vise or rotate the vise a half turn if you are tying on a true rotary vise like our DanVise.

Step 6: Tie a section of pearl/gold mixed Krystal Flash on the under side of the hook shank and trim it so it is even with the first application of Craft Fur. Top this with another section of tan Craft Fur and trim off any excess material. Wrap a head, whip finish and remove the thread from the hook. Use a brown felt-tip marker to place mottling bands on the body sections. Note: We've also illustrated this step with the vise rotated a half turn.

NED LONG

Master fly-tier John "Ned" Long passed away quietly at his home in Tahoe City, California on June 23, 2002 while under hospice care for recurring cancer. We will long remember his crooked smile, his wonderful outlook on life, and his many contributions to our sport.

He was born on December 8, 1922 in Delaware, Ohio and at the age of four moved to Glendale, California. His mother gave him the nickname "Ned" almost at birth and it stuck for the rest of his life. He met his wife Betty on a blind date while attending the University of Southern California. At the time of his passing they had been married 54 years and had three children (James, Katie, and Patti). For thirty years Ned had a successful insurance business in Pasadena. He eventually moved to Tahoe City where he started another insurance venture until he decided it was time to retire, tie flies, and go fishing.

Ned learned how to fly-fish at the early age of ten from his older brother Jim. The two brothers loved fishing area waters around Mammot. Don Martinez lived in Hollywood and owned the fly shop that later became Bud Lilly's in West Yellowstone, Montana. In 1949, Don helped Ned start tying flies and it became a life-long addiction. By the mid 1950's Ned was teaching fly-tying to patients at the Vista del Arroyo Veterans Hospital. Betty tells us Ned probably owned every book ever written about fly-tying and fly-fishing.

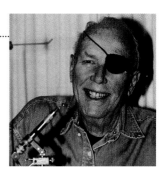

Ned Long

He joined the Federation of Fly Fishers in the late 1960s and was one of the founding fathers of the Tahoe Truckee Fly Fishers. Over the years he served the club in every possible officer position including president. Ned was also a long-time Director for the Northern California Council of the FFF and was the chairman of their first Conclave. That show continues today every fall at the Kings Beach Community Center.

It wasn't long before his fly-tying skills were in demand at all levels within the FFF including the international Conclave. He demonstrated his unique style of flies at all Conclaves since 1988 and in 1996 he was the recipient of the prestigious FFF Buz Buszek Memorial Fly Tying Award, the highest honor a tier can receive.

We are very sad to bid farewell to our friend Ned Long. He was an innovative fly-tier and a true gentleman in every sense of the word. He will be missed, but not forgotten. Ned lives on through the many people he touched by personal example or through shared fly-tying skills.

Ned's Fold Over

When we sent the requests to the fly tiers for this book Ned wanted to participate, however, his failing health robbed him of the energy he needed to assemble the items we requested. Two months before he passed we saw him at the East Idaho Fly Tying Exposition and promised that Al would tie his fly for him so he could participate. Here it is.

Fold-over hackling is not a tying style he developed to be sure, but

Ned certainly refined the technique. He was the first tier we know who used Super Floss, to apply the hackle to the hook. The material would stretch making it much easier to perfectly fill a section of fly with hackle. Prior to the use of Super Floss getting the right amount of hackle on the hook was difficult. Now all you have to do is stretch the floss to fit the designated area and the hackle moves along with it.

Ned's Fold Over

Hook:	Size 12-18, scud style
Thread:	Brown
Tail:	Pearl Krystal Flash
Body:	Pale orange Super Floss
Thorax:	Peacock herl
Wings:	Any color hackle, fold-over style

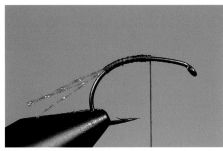

Step 1: Place the hook in the vise and apply a thread base that starts in the center and goes well into bend of the hook. Attach a sparse tail of pearl Krystal Flash that is as long as the hook. Wrap back to the center of the hook and trim any excess material.

Step 2: Select a section of Super Floss and tie it to the underside of the hook shank, wrapping the thread to the back of the hook then forward again to the center. Wind the Super Floss forward, forming the body, and tie it off the floss with thread wraps advancing part of the way into the front section of the hook. Wrap the thread back to the center of the hook. Do not cut off the excess floss.

Step 3: Pull the loose floss straight back and anchor it in the center of the hook. Now pull it straight up and secure it in a gallows tool. Select a hackle feather, strip the web from the butt end, and tie it to the hook directly in front of the floss.

Step 4: Wrap the hackle up the floss about 1/4 inch then back down to the hook. Tie the hackle off in the center of the hook. Trim away the waste end.

Step 5: Release the floss from the gallows tool and pull it back into the material keeper. Attach a couple of peacock herls and wrap the thorax. Tie them off at the hook eye and trim off the waste ends.

Step 6: Pull the hackle-covered floss over the thorax and tie it off at the hook eye. Trim off the excess, whip finish the thread, and remove it from the hook. Apply a coating of head cement.

RONN LUCAS, SR.
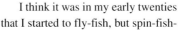

Ronn is a dental technician by trade and has operated his own dental lab since about 1969. Close-up, precise work is not unfamiliar to him since he creates gold and porcelain teeth during the day and flies for fishes' teeth at night. Ronn has lived all his life in Portland, Oregon.

Ronn tells us, "I have been creating things with my hands all of my life. I was a pre teen in the mid fifties when I met a lady by the name of Audrey Joy. Mom would drop me off in the sporting goods section of a large Portland department store when she was shopping. Audrey tied flies at a card table in the middle of the department. My folks weren't outdoors people so I had never even fished in those days, but I was fascinated by the "bugs" Audrey created out of bits of fur, feathers and hooks. I sat and watched her for hours on end. Finally one day, Audrey gave me some feathers, hair, and a few hooks to take home and try tying something.

I was excited by the prospect that I might create some of the flies like Audrey tied so off I went. When I got home, mom gave me some black sewing thread and a bit of candle wax. I had no vise, no bobbin, none of the tools we Tiers are so fortunate to have these days. In the days that followed, I tied a couple dozen of the world's best and most beautiful flies. Mankind had never seen such beautiful creations.

The next time mom and I went to the store I took the flies I had tied. My chest swelled with pride when I dumped the collection of flies out on the now-familiar card table in front of Audrey. Time has dulled my memories of those days, but I can't recall her frowning or finding much fault with those humble creations. Somehow, a few more than a dozen of those flies have survived the years and now rest in a frame. Every time I pass by and look at them I am struck by how crude and homely they are.

Ronn Lucas, Sr.

I think it was in my early twenties that I started to fly-fish, but spin-fishing was more likely than not my usual method. Later, fly-fishing became more and more the method of choice and now I fish almost exclusively with the fly.

When I started to tie again, I did so pretty much alone and, for the most part, I am self-taught. Later I read books and magazines on the topic until it became something of an obsession. I collected feathers and fur with reckless abandon. The most recent focus of my tying attention is tying the fully dressed flies.

Over the years I have had a few of my patterns published in magazines and books, won a few contests and have recently begun to do some writing. My current project is building an Atlantic Salmon & Steelhead tying section for FlyAnglersOnLine.com, the Internet's best on-line magazine.

In addition to working in the lab, my wife Chris and I make and sell a line of tying materials both for general tying and tying Atlantic salmon flies." (We highly recommend their materials. You can get them via www.flyanglersonline.com.)

Iridescent Gold Stone

Ronn developed this pattern several years ago after a fishing trip to the Metolius River in central Oregon. The golden stones had hatched and were everywhere, but nothing in his well-stocked fly box interested the selective fish. Ronn tells us, "I prefer to think the fish were selective rather than consider the problem could have been my poor fishing skills." He snapped a couple of photographs of the bugs and later used them to design the pattern you see here. Ronn calls this a "damp" rather than a dry fly because it is fished in, rather than on, the surface.

His tying style tends more toward realistic thus added features like eyes and antennae are part of the dressing. Ronn is not concerned with the time required to tie the fly because that process is also part of his fly-fishing experience.

Iridescent Gold Stone

Hook:	Daiichi 2220, size 4-12
Thread:	Orange
Body:	Gold Stone Iridescent Dubbing
Wing:	Elk hair
Thorax:	Gold Flashback
Hackle:	Brown
Eyes:	Glass beads on melted monofilament
Antenna:	Stripped hackle stems

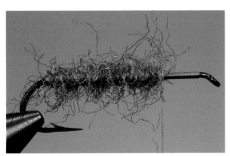

Step 1: Apply a thread base to the back 2/3 of the hook shank. Dub over this thread base with Gold Stone Iridescent Dubbing. Advance the thread in close wraps to the eye and back to the front of the dubbed body.

Step 2: Select, clean, and stack a clump of elk hair. Tie it on as wings that are slightly longer than the body.

Step 3: Trim the waste hair ends. Strip the fibers from the stems of two grizzly feathers and tie them on the sides of the shank to form antennae. Slip two black beads on a short section of monofilament, then melt each end of it with a cigarette lighter. Tie this unit on the front of the hook shank to form the eyes. Anchor them in place with tight figure-eight wraps.

Step 4: Tie in a 1/4-inch strip of Gold Flashback with the iridescent side facing down. As you wrap back, take a couple of looser wraps at the start of the body to bring the flared hair under control.

Step 5: Prepare and tie on a brown hackle feather. Apply dubbing to the thorax and around the eyes. Leave the thread hanging behind the eyes.

Step 6: Wrap the hackle forward through the thorax and tie it off. Trim off the waste end.

Step 7: Advance the thread in front of the eyes. Pull the Flashback forward and tie it to the hook with a couple of thread turns. Wrap back one turn leaving the thread hanging behind the eyes.

Step 8: Fold the Flashback back and anchor it. Trim off the excess, wrap a whip finish, and cut off the thread. Apply a coating of head cement or Aqua Head.

CHRIS MIHULKA

Chris Mihulka

A native Oregonian, Chris is the third generation of his family to have the opportunity to travel to the great fishing spots of the Northwest. His grandfather and uncle started Adam's Taxidermy in the late 40's and explored many of the area waters where Chris got his first fishing experiences with his father at the age of two. Crappie and bluegill filled these waterways, and were the perfect introduction to a lifelong passion.

Summer trips to the home of John and Lola Crabtree on the McKenzie River with his parents were an enlightening experience. John was an avid fly-fisher, and one of a group of brothers that helped settle a section of Oregon north of Springfield. On these trips, the Mihulka family would use spinning gear to fish a deep, turquoise-colored pool at the base of Eagle Rock, near the town of Nimrod. When the large pool finally tailed out, it formed a long, smooth, crystal-clear run. During one trip, when Chris was five years old, John Crabtree brought his fly rod and joined the family at the river. The large gravel bank along the riffle made an excellent teaching area, and gave Chris his first chance to try a fly rod. It was a life-changing experience.

A few years later, a bunch of fur and feathers from his relatives' taxidermy shop got Chris into the next step: fly tying.

Growing up in Springfield, which sits directly between the McKenzie and Willamette rivers, gave Chris many chances to hone his tying and fishing skills over the decades. One day, while sitting on the bank of the McKenzie, taking a break from a March brown hatch, a drift boat being rowed by Kim Short came by. Kim was the President of Skykomish Flies, a company that packaged and sold fly-fishing items through department stores. Kim offered Chris a job starting a new division of the company to be called McKenzie Flies. Chris was Production Manager for McKenzie Flies, which included traveling the world training factory fly tiers, showing products at trade shows, and giving demonstrations at consumer shows. The original McKenzie Flies has been sold several times, and is now owned by Scientific Anglers, where Chris is a member of the Product Design Pro Staff.

Chris also owns a fly-fishing-related business called Northwest Fishing Stuff, which sells flies, fluorocarbon fly leaders, tying materials, and custom-built rods. He has hosted segments of a Saturday morning fishing show called "On The Fly" on ESPN, and currently shoots and produces fishing, tying, and outdoor videos through his own production studio.

Chris' most recent adventure has been teaching his six-year-old twins, Ben and Sarah, to fly cast and tie. They recently joined him at The 2002 Northwest Fly Tyers Exposition in Eugene, Oregon. Chris believes that the future of the sport lies in starting kids early and teaching them to love the experience and the environment. Kids fishing with dad are not joining gangs or taking drugs.

Mr. Right

An avid smallmouth bass angler, Chris started fishing the Umpqua River for them in the late eighties. He found they could be quite selective and searched for a productive pattern. Although the simple Woolly Bugger would attract fish, the bass would often just play with the fly rather aggressively take it.

Chris set out to develop a pattern that would fit his fishing needs. He tells us, "When I developed the current pattern, I found a combination of balance and attraction that take fish on a regular basis. The heavy eyes point the hook eye down for a controlled dive, the tail creates a slowing drag effect, the rubber legs give life, and the hook shape makes the fly always land on the bottom with the point up, hence the name Mr. Right."

When presenting the fly, allow it to sink on a slack line. If a fish does not pick it up on the dive, let it land on the bottom, and watch it. Chris advises, "I have had several very large bass swim to the fly, turn away, and come back several times before deciding to taste it to see what it is. If there are more than one fish, they will usually race for it." Whatever its attraction, we've found it to be a very effective fly and believe you will as well.

Mr. Right

Hook:	Mustad 37160 or TMC 205BL, size 2-6
Thread:	Black
Eyes:	Dumbbell, chartreuse and black
Tail:	Black marabou blood quill
Body:	Black chenille
Legs:	Black rubber leg material
Hackle:	Black saddle

Step 1: Place the hook in the vise and apply a short thread base directly behind the hook eye. Securely tie in the eyes on top of the shank with several figure-eight wraps then coat them with head cement.

Step 2: Tilt the hook down in the vise and wrap the thread to the end of the shank. Tie on a tail that is as long as the complete hook. Trim away any excess material.

Step 3: Advance the thread forward to the dumbbell eyes then tilt the hook back up in the vise for the rest of the steps. Tie on a section of black chenille starting directly behind the eyes and wrap the thread toward the end of the shank.

Step 4: Continue binding the chenille to the top of the shank until you reach the tail material. Place the chenille in the material keeper, select a black saddle hackle feather, stroke back the fibers, and tie it to the hook by its tip. Wrap the thread forward to the center of the hook and leave it there for the next step.

Step 5: Select two sections of round rubber leg material. Tie one to the off side of the hook and the other to the near side.

Step 6: Advance the thread forward to the eyes. Retrieve the chenille stored in the material keeper and wind it forward to the eyes.

Step 7: Tie off the chenille and trim away the waste end. Wind the hackle forward over the body. Take care when placing it around the rubber legs.

Step 8: Continue wrapping the hackle to the dumbbell eyes, tie the feather off, and trim away the waste end. Whip finish the thread and remove it from the hook. Trim the hackle off the top of the fly over the area between the eyes and the legs. Here Chris has illustrated the fly as it would appear in the water column or resting on the bottom.

BILL MURDICH

Bill grew up in the suburbs of New York City. Although he came from a non-angling family he was intrigued by a fishing show on television. He was particularly taken with the possibility of catching a fish on an artificial lure. One June morning in 1964 Bill's mother gave him a copy of *Outdoor Life* magazine. He recalls, "Reading the articles, and looking at the pictures mesmerized me. I would never have imagined that anything like this even existed. I think this is when I became a fisherman."

After a couple of years reading magazine articles about catching fish on self-constructed lures young Bill decided fly-fishing was for him. He started tying with materials borrowed from his mother and a fly-tying kit from a local hobby shop. The vise in the kit soon gave out and Bill substituted it for one from Herter's. Now he started producing bass bugs in earnest!

With his newly tied flies in hand, he set out to catch fish. Bill soon discovered he had much to learn like how to cast or what a leader was. He loved to tie flies and in time the fish started coming to hand as well. He started with bass and sunfish, graduated to trout, and then advanced to striped bass and bluefish.

During the college and graduate school years Bill lost his fly-fishing and tying direction focusing instead on education and grades. His first job out of college was a research position with the National Marine Fisheries Service in Galveston, Texas. Much of his work was offshore with time available for fishing. Bill was soon again involved with fly tying and then presenting his creations to both inshore and offshore fish.

Bill Murdich

After relocating to Gainesville, Florida he saw a fly-tying course offered in a continuing education brochure. The instructor was Dana Griffin, a superb fly tier and teacher. As a self-taught fly tier Bill was pleased to learn easier methods Dana shared with his students. He had been doing many things the hard way and Dana's encouragement and guidance opened a whole new world to him.

In 1988 Bill moved to Tampa, Florida and shortly thereafter became one of the founding members of the Tampa Bay Fly Fishing Club. There he met Tom Theus who was impressed with Bill's tying skills. Tom arranged an invitation for Bill to demonstrate fly tying at the Federation of Fly Fishers 1996 Conclave in Livingston, Montana. Your authors are pleased to know the invitation they sent him is framed and hanging in his office. He comments, "My annual trip to Montana is always one of the highlights of my year."

Not long after demonstrating at his first Conclave Bill met Jeff Fryhover from Umpqua Feather Merchants at an outdoor show at Cypress Gardens, Florida. Bill gave Jeff one of his flies to test on local waters. The fly's action impressed him and he suggested Bill submit it to Umpqua for their marketing program. The company accepted the fly and Bill became one of their Designer Tyers. We believe Bill has many more accomplishments destined for him in the future.

Sugar Shrimp

Bill tells us, "The pattern came about because I felt I could improve on the currently most popular shrimp flies. I had done some research on penaid shrimp and handled perhaps a couple hundred thousand of the animals during the course of the study. I knew what a shrimp looked like. I also had preserved specimens that I could constantly check against my developing pattern."

Bill's test patterns were more slender than the natural creature until he added the rattle. It not only solved the fly's profile problem but also added the snapping sound of a fleeing shrimp flicking its tail. He has tied the pattern in a range of colors including pink, white, tan, chartreuse, and root beer. Adding the "weight post" finalized the Sugar Shrimp allowing the angler to fish the same fly with a varied sink rate.

Sugar Shrimp

Hook:	Mustad 34011, size 1
Thread:	Beige
Antennae:	Root beer Krystal Flash
Mouth parts:	Root beer Krystal Flash
Rattle:	Viper Mini Rattle
Body & legs:	Large pearl Cactus Chenille, tan maker
Back & rostrum (horn):	Tan Ultra Hair
Weight post:	Melted monofilament
Tail:	Tan marabou feather tip
Head:	Thread, Aqua Flex

Step 1: Glue two black beads to a short section of heavy monofilament and set them aside to dry. Place the hook in the vise and apply a thread base that starts behind the eye and stops at the end of the shank. Select six root beer colored strands of Krystal Flash that are twice as long as the shank and bind them to the hook with several firm thread wraps. Add a short, dense clump of the same Krystal Flash to represent the mouthparts. They should be as long as the gape is wide. Trim away any excess material.

Step 2: Retrieve the black beads/monofilament assembly and bind it to the shank directly above the hook point to represent the eyes. Tie the Viper Mini Rattle to the under side of the shank with several tight thread wraps. Leave the bobbin hanging directly in front of the rattle and apply a coating of head cement to all of the thread wraps.

Step 3: Wrap the thread back between eyes and the hook bend. Bind the Cactus Chenille to the shank, trim off the waste end, and advance the thread forward in front of the rattle. Wrap the chenille one turn around the hook, figure-eight around the eyes, and advance forward covering the rattle. Tie off the Cactus Chenille and trim away the waste end. Color the chenille with a tan felt-tip maker then trim it flat on top of the shank.

Step 4: Select a short section of six-pound monofilament and melt a small ball on one end. Tie it to the hook in front of the rattle pointing down so it is slightly shorter than the gape is wide. We found bending the monofilament at a 90-degree angle really helped to accomplish this step. Trim away the waste end.

Step 5: Attach a clump of tan Ultra Hair with several tight thread wraps. Trim off the waste ends then cover them with the tying thread. Apply a coating of Aqua Flex or Dave's Flexament to the Ultra Hair and work it into the material with a toothpick by stroking the hair toward the hook bend. As the Flexament begins to set, and becomes less tacky, squeeze the hair from both sides between your fingers immediately above the mouthparts. This will form the "horn" at the end of the shrimp's carapace. Let the cement dry completely then trim the hair into an upward-sweeping point.

Step 6: Tie the marabou feather tip on the underside of the shank with its end extending forward of the hook eye. Trim away the waste end, shape the thread head behind and in front of the marabou, whip finish and remove the thread. Apply a coating of Aqua Flex or Dave's Flexament. It's up to the fly-fisher whether additional weight is needed on the fly. Here we've illustrated it with a removable split shot attached to the weight post.

JOHN NEWBURY

John Newbury

John Newbury lives in Chewelah, Washington where some forty years ago he caught his first fish in Paye Creek, a spring creek meandering through his grandfather's pasture. John's father and father's Dad (Grandpa) were die-hard stream fishermen, with John and his brother Tom always hoping to tag along on their outings. Tackle consisted of a metal telescopic rod, monofilament line on a Perrine automatic fly reel, and a wicker creel slung over a shoulder. He recalls, "Later I learned the technique we used was referred to as dapping."

His other Grandpa introduced John to lake fishing. He liked to troll lead-core line, using flies, small spoons, rooster tails, or a flatfish. When you went trolling with Pa, it was an all-day event. Mom was always afraid he'd lose one of the kids over the side of the boat, but somehow he always got them home with a few fish and a smile.

In 1978 he met Tim Peterson who convinced John to join him in fly-fishing from a float tube. At about the same time he met the daughter of a lady in his apartment building, Judy Bartness. John recalls, "Boy-oh-boy, could she cast!" Judy taught him how to cast and along with Tim the three experienced some great fishing trips together.

It wasn't long before John started tying his own flies. In 1980 he started teaching sixth grade in Colville, Washington where he met fly-fisher and tier extraordinaire, Jake Guhlke. Over the next couple years John honed his skills under Jake's watchful eye.

In 1983 John was diagnosed with cervical, oromandibular, and spasmodic dystonia, a neurological movement disorder resulting in sustained muscle contractions. No longer able to teach, John retired. He spent the next couple years regaining his health to a point where he could at least drive, tie flies, and fish. Now living in Spokane, John had the good fortune to meet former casting champion, Everett Caryl. Under his guidance, John's skills rapidly advanced. Everett died in 1989 and is now a member of the West Coast Fly Fishing Hall of Fame.

During his time in Spokane, John also met Joe Roope (junior and senior) who introduced him to Al Beatty (one of your authors) and Jimmy Nix. Through this contact with Jimmy he was invited to demonstrate his fly-tying skills at the 1988 Federation of Fly Fisher's Conclave. Since then he has demonstrated at twelve of the last fourteen Conclaves, taught classes on entomology and realistic flies, and assisted Al Beatty with his hair-wing class.

For a number of years John operated an exotic game-bird farm supplying his fellow FFF fly tiers with the feathers needed to dress Atlantic salmon flies. Today you'll find John in a float tube on a favorite lake in eastern Washington or British Columbia. He is also one of the few experts on the Upper Columbia River.

Big Daddy

When John shared this fly with us at the East Idaho Fly Tying Expo we were stunned. It looked so real! We were on the way to work and didn't have time to check it further until preparing John's materials for this book. It is really the unique blend of a spin-fishing lure and fly-tying materials as only the creative mind of John Newbury could produce. We are not suggesting everyone construct flies in this manner, but present it for what it is, a blend of two worlds.

In his own words Johns tells why he created the Big Daddy, "This fly was created to use on the Colville River where monster browns are known to dine on crawdads. My biggest brown to date is a 27-inch buck that weighted 6 3/4 pounds." That is quite a fish, what else can we say?

Big Daddy

Hook:	Size 3/0, salmon
Thread:	Olive
Eyes:	Black pushpins
Claws:	Replacement Claws
Carapace (front):	Olive Fury Foam
Legs:	Olive brown ram's wool
Carapace (rear body):	G4 rubber band
Tail:	Olive Swiss straw

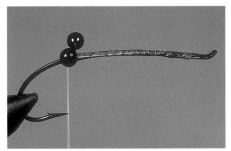

Step 1: Take two black pushpins, dip the ends in epoxy, and place them on a rotating wheel to dry. Place a hook in the vise and apply a thread base from the eye to a position directly above the point. Remove the now-dry pushpins from the rotating wheel and place a 90-degree bend in each about one-eighth inch from the black bead. Bind them to the sides of the hook forming the pattern's eyes. Leave the thread hanging behind the eyes.

Step 2: Secure a set of replacement Claws to the shank behind the eyes with the claws pointing past the end of the hook. Work through the legs, binding them to the shank while traveling first toward the front of the hook and then back to the point where the claws were tied on. Cut a section of olive Furry Foam that is about 1/2-inch wide and tie it to the hook just to the rear of the eyes.

Step 3: Tie on three clumps of ram's wool starting to the rear of the eyes, but forward of the Furry Foam. The first clump is shorter and sparser than the other two, the second positioned in the middle of the leg area is the largest of the three, and the third is at the end of the legs. All clumps are tied with the wool tips pointing to the rear of the hook, *or* the front of the crawdad. Trim any waste ends and leave the thread in the center of the hook.

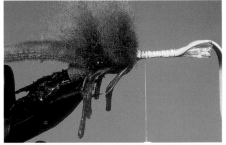

Step 4: Select a section of olive Swiss straw and fan it out. Bind it to the hook shank starting in the center and wrapping to the hook eye. Trim the crawdad tail to length. Cut a rubber band in half to make a single strand and tie it to the hook while wrapping the thread back to the hook center. Trim off any waste end.

Step 5: Wrap the rubber band to the center of the hook adjusting the tension on it to shape the profile of the body. Tie it off in the center of the hook.

Step 6: Color the rubber band part of the body with an olive felt-tip marker then coat it with nail polish or Aqua Flex. Divide the ram's wool legs in half and pull the Furry Foam over and tie it to the center of the hook. Trim off the waste end, whip finish (in the center of the hook) and remove the thread. Apply a coating of Aqua Head or cement to the whip finish.

Fry-N-Egg

We certainly got a chuckle out of the name John gave this fly. It is a very simple, but effective pattern as all the flies he shares with us seem to be. Maybe he only shares the ones that work. Whatever the reason, this fry pattern looks to be a very attractive fly with all the triggering mechanisms we have come to expect. We've not had the oppor-

tunity to test it but have confidence in John; if he says it's good, we believe him.

John tells us, "I fish this fly on a full-sink line in early spring and late fall using a variety of retrieves representing the erratic movement of a minnow. Big fish really wallop this pattern so hang on!"

Fry-N-Egg

Hook:	Mustad 34011, size 6, 3XL streamer
Thread:	Gray
Tail:	Light gray marabou
Body:	Pearl Flex-Cord
Eyes:	Stick-on, silver with black pupils
Egg:	Hot glue

Step 1: Place the hook in the vise and apply a short thread base at the end of the hook shank. Select a light gray marabou feather and discard the real fuzzy fibers at the base and along the sides for the stem. Use the tip of the feather only to construct a tail that is 1/3 the hook shank in length. Trim off the waste ends and leave the thread at the back of the hook for the next step.

Step 2: Take a section of Flex Cord and tie it to the hook at the end of the shank. Build a whip finish and trim the thread temporarily from the hook. Place a drop of head cement on the whip finish.

Step 3: Trim the section of Flex Cord that sticks out beyond the front of the hook so it is equal to the width of the hook gape. Take two loose turns around the Flex Cord that is sticking out in front of the hook but do not tighten up on those wraps. Pull back on the Flex Cord (with the thread around it) causing the tubing to flare and bringing the loose end just behind the hook eye. Now tighten up on the thread turns to anchor the tubing to the hook. Place several more thread wraps, whip finish, and trim it from the hook. Apply a coating of head cement to the whip finish.

Step 4: Stick a silver/black eye on the offside of the hook just behind the thread head. Repeat the process on the nearside of the hook. Use a hot-glue gun to apply a small egg ball from a transparent orange glue stick. Allow the egg ball to cool then coat it and the eyes with a layer of epoxy. Place the fly on a rotating wheel to allow the epoxy to set up evenly.

Peacock Dragon

John is one of the best stillwater fishers we know. He can dredge up fish after fish when others on the same water (including us) are scratching their head wondering what to try next. He studies what's happening around him and uses that observation along with knowledge of the bottom structure to put together an effective plan. John's not always the first fly-fisher in the water but when he does slide into his float tube you can bet the action will soon start.

He fishes this pattern on a fast sinking line so the fly will quickly be close to the weed beds where the fish and bugs live. John normally uses a hand-twist retrieve with an occasional three or four inch erratic strip. He finds this fly particularly productive on the lakes near his home in April and May but we've found it works quite well on any body of water that has a population of dragonflies.

Peacock Dragon

Hook:	Partridge H3ST, size 6
Thread:	Black
Eyes:	Melted monofilament
Body:	Peacock herl
Legs:	Golden pheasant tail
Head:	Peacock herl
Wing case:	Peacock herl

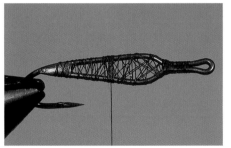

Step 1: Place the hook in the vise and start a thread base behind the hook eye. Wrap it to the end of the shank and back about one half way. Note how we use cross wraps to stop the thread from slipping on the many up- and down-hill slopes a tier encounters on this Draper-type hook.

Step 2: Attach several strands of peacock herl to the back part of the hook and leave them pointing to the rear. Trim off any waste ends then advance the thread forward almost to the hook eye. Attach a pair of monofilament eyes with several crisscross wraps to anchor them.

Step 3: Wrap the peacock herl forward forming the body. Often a second bundle of herl is required to complete the body. John recommends wrapping the tying thread to the back through the body to the end of the hook and then forward to the eye to strengthen the herl application. Leave the thread hanging behind the monofilament eyes.

Step 4: Select four or five fibers from a golden pheasant tail, tie them to the hook directly behind the eyes on the offside of the shank, and trim away any waste ends. Repeat the process on the nearside of the hook.

Step 5: Attach two or three peacock herls behind the eyes and construct a head around the eyes using figure-eight wraps. Tie the herl off behind the eyes and trim away the waste ends. Strip the fuzzy material from the base of the stem of a peacock back feather and tie it to the hook with two or three loose thread wraps.

Step 6: Pull forward on the feather until it has slipped into the proper position to shape the wing case then pull the loose thread-wrap tight. Pull the feather up straight temporarily and advance the thread forward to the hook eye. Pull the feather back down and anchor it at the hook eye. Trim away the waste end, whip finish, and remove the thread from the hook. Complete the fly with a coating of Aqua Head over the whip finish.

Peacock Spider

John is a highly-skilled steelhead fly-fisher and this fly has contributed much to his success. He tells us in his own words, "This is my most productive steelhead fly and thus my favorite. I have great confidence in this fly and it seems to produce under a variety of water conditions.

"The Peacock Spider has been responsible for hooking and landing steelhead on the Snake, Grand Ronde, Methow, Deschutes, Clearwater, Babine, Bulkley, Kispiox, and Morice rivers. It has blessed me with seven fish over the years that have weighted 20 pounds or better. The largest, caught on the Babine in 1998, was a monster measuring 42 1/2 inches long and it had a 24-inch girth!" Now we know the reason for John's steelhead success. We were also surprised how this fly was tied; the hackle went on differently than we had assumed.

Peacock Spider

Hook:	Size 2/0-2, salmon
Thread:	Red or reddish brown
Body:	Peacock blue Diamond Braid
Hackle:	Peacock breasts feathers
Head:	Thread

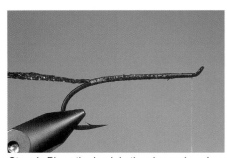

Step 1: Place the hook in the vise and apply a thread base that starts at the eye and stops at the end of the shank. On this hook we identify "the end of the shank" as the position directly above the throat of the barb. Select a 10-inch section of peacock blue Diamond Braid and tie it to the top of the hook while advancing the thread back to the hook eye.

Step 2: Wrap the thread back from the eye to the start of the looped platform and leave it there. Wrap the Diamond Braid forward forming the body. Notice the material has a tendency to twist, but it is quite easy to place a counter twist as each turn of the diamond Braid is applied to the hook thus producing a nice, smooth body.

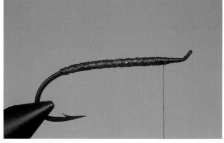

Step 3: Continue wrapping the body material forward to meet the thread. Tie it off and trim away the waste end.

Step 4: Prepare two (size 2 hook) or three (size 2/0 hook) peacock breast feathers by stripping away the fuzzy material at the base of the stems. Tie the feathers to the shank, staggering their position; in this case we are using a 2/0 hook so they are placed on the near side, top, and far side of the hook. This positioning is what surprised us. John's flies always looked so neat we just assumed the hackle was constructed from one feather only!

Step 5: Start with the offside feather and wrap it one turn around the hook. We suggest working that feather behind and in front of the other two while making the wrap. Tie it off and remove any waste end.

Step 6: Now select the top feather and wrap it the same as described in Step 5. Tie it off and trim the waste end. Wrap the last hackle in front of the other two, tie it off, and remove the excess. Build the thread head tight against the hackle to force all three feathers together. Whip finish and remove the thread. Apply a coating of Aqua Head or cement to the whip finish.

Wiggle Damsel

John developed the Wiggle Damsel in 1985 during a discussion at Joe Roope's fly shop. The goal was to tie a damsel nymph that combined realism with movement for a more precise imitation. John wanted the hook at the rear of the fly to limit short strikes, which meant he had to add an appendage that hinged. Single-strand stainless-steel wire leader (38-pound test) was his choice, it hinged in the eye well, was easy to work with, and wouldn't rust. To this articulating hook John added some marabou, Swiss straw, eyes, and a thorax of seal or goat dubbing. With the fly complete it had to be field tested.

The first test was Chopaka Lake—one of north-central Washington's quality waters. That day was and still is memorable for John—72 fish landed and released ranging in size from 14 to 20 inches. John was pleased to say the least. What would happen on the next outing? It was at Dry Falls Lake where he caught and released 35 fish ranging in size from 16 to 23 inches. From those days to today it remains John's favorite stillwater fly. We suggest you give this superb pattern a test drive. We are confident it will serve you as well as it has us, and John.

Wiggle Damsel

Hook:	Mustad 9672, size 14
Thread:	Olive
Tail/abdomen:	Golden olive marabou
Hinge:	Stainless-steel leader
Eyes:	Spirit River Inc. Mono Eyes
Wing case:	Golden olive Swiss straw
Thorax:	Olive brown seal or Angora goat dubbing

Step 1: Select a good-quality marabou feather and prepare it for application by stripping away the fibers at the base end of the stem. Place the hook in the vise and apply a thread base that covers the complete hook shank. Tie the prepared marabou feather on the hook at the end of the shank to form a tail that is as long as the gape is wide. Advance the thread forward to the hook eye and leave it there for the next step.

Step 2: Wrap the marabou feather forward to meet the thread, tie it off, and trim away the waste end. Whip finish the thread and remove it from the hook. An alternate method would be to leave the thread at the back of the hook and advance the feather/thread together.

Step 3: Cut a one and 1/4-inch section of 38-pound stainless-steel leader material. Use small needlenose pliers to bend it into thirds forming an articulated hinge. Slip it into the eye of the hook remaining from Step 2.

Step 4: Remove the hook from the vise and place the hinge in the jaws. Apply a thread base over most of the hinge snug enough to tighten the two ends. Twist the hinge 1/2 turn to form a ring eye. Bind a pair of Spirit River Mono Eyes to the center of the hinge. If you wish, substitute melted monofilament eyes. Notice the hook point slipped in the slot between the jaws; it's much safer there for the fly tier.

Step 5: Tie on a section of golden olive Swiss straw behind the eyes and leave it extending back for the moment. Apply dubbing with most of it behind the eyes. We'll finish dubbing in front of them in the next step. The bobbin should be left hanging behind the eyes.

Step 6: Fold the wing case (Swiss straw) over and bind it to the hook behind the eyes then fold it back out of the way again. Apply a small amount of dubbing to the thread and finish constructing the thorax ending in front of the eyes. Fold the wing case over again, tie it off, and trim the waste end. Whip finish and trim the thread. Use a bodkin to pluck out the dubbing creating the image of legs extending from the thorax.

MARVIN NOLTE

Marvin Nolte

Bar Nunn, Wyoming resident, Marvin Nolte retired in 1993 so he could tie flies full-time. This decision had two unintended but fortunate consequences. The first is that he has more time to practice tying than most folks (he says that he can surely use it); the second is that he is able to do what he likes best: travel for fishing and teaching. His love of giving classes and workshops, and availability, has led to tying and fishing adventures in seven foreign countries.

Contrary to most people's experiences, Marvin began tying flies before he started fishing with them. Beginning in 1974 with a fly-tying kit, a gift from his wife Victoria, he began a progression from trout flies through fully dressed salmon flies. Although best known for his salmon flies and the Grainger Collection, Marvin assures us that he can tie trout flies—and that they work. While giving a fly-tying demonstration at a Fly Fair in Sweden he was approached by a member of the delegation from Scotland. This gentleman said he and some friends were going to practice some Spey casting in the local river, and they needed something to put on the end of the line. Marvin tied them an Andelle Dragon. The next morning at breakfast the Scottish gentleman told him, with a broad grin, that he had caught a nice rainbow on the fly, and asked for a few more.

His first fly-fishing experience was with friends from the Nuclear Weapons School in Albuquerque, New Mexico. Fishing in the San Juan River, he caught his first trout on an old fly pattern, the Cow Dung. That experience led to lifelong passions, both for fly-fishing and tying old style flies. (*Author's note: In another life Marvin was a bomb disposal officer for the United States military but we'll let him tell you about that at another time*).

Henry's Lake Pupa

This fly started out as the Andelle Dragon, which was an inspiration by the French dry-fly pattern called the Andelle. It is identical to the Henry's Lake Pupa except the body is green seal's fur. In mid-summer on Henry's Lake, a very large caddisfly emerges at twilight. During a day's fishing, the empty husks from these caddis can be seen all over the water. This pattern was designed to imitate the emerging caddis.

Marvin likes to fish the Henry's Lake Pupa on a full-sink line, counted down so it is almost on the bottom, and retrieved with slow, short strips. He keeps the leader short and stout; about three feet of 2X tippet. We've had the opportunity to fish with Marvin on several occasions and yes this interesting fly really does produce fish.

Henry's Lake Pupa

Hook:	Mustad R74, size 8
Thread:	Brown
Body:	Tan Antron dubbing
Body/bubble/tail:	Lemon woodduck flank
Hackle:	Partridge, tied as a collar
Head:	Brown dubbing

Step 1: Place the hook in the vise and apply a thread base that covers most of the hook shank. Be sure to leave a long tag of tying thread at the back of the shank for use in a future step; store it in the material keeper for now. Also leave enough room at the front of the fly to later form a head.

Step 2: Apply tan Antron dubbing to the thread and wrap a body that covers the back 2/3 of the hook shank. Leave the tying thread hanging at the 1/3 point on the shank at the front of the body.

Step 3: Select a Woodduck feather with fibers long enough to form the bubble and the tail in the next step. Tie it on the hook by its tip at the front of the body and wrap a wet-style collar. Tie off the feather and trim away the waste end.

Step 4: Retrieve the tag of thread remaining from Step 1. Pull the woodduck fibers back over the body forming a bubble and anchor them with the thread at the end of the shank. The remaining ends form the fly's tail. Whip finish the thread and trim it from the hook. Place a drop of head cement on the whip finish.

Step 5: Select a partridge feather and sweep the fibers back along the stem. Tie it on the hook by its tip and wrap a two-turn wet-style collar. Trim off the waste end.

Step 6: Form a head of brown dubbing. Whip finish the thread, cut it from the hook, and apply a coating of head cement.

TED PATLIN

Ted Patlin

Ted Patlin from Lodi, New Jersey tells us, "I started fly-fishing, well, really roll casting, with a worm and dropper; just about the same time that I started fishing with my dad…45 years ago! Trout were the preferred quarry, but carp and sunfish also taught me at a young age to observe and learn different rules of the game. I started wrapping feathers around a hook about the same time and found out that was called fly tying."

Tastes change, but never the thrill of the game. Most of us commenced with one species of fish and the techniques to entice them, then logically branched out into different arenas. Ted feels very lucky to have been brought up in New Jersey. This little, highly populated state holds an incredible diversity of game fish, including trout, most of the warmwater species, and of course the fish of the Atlantic Ocean. Ted calls New Jersey fly-fishing opportunities "10X to 10 weight."

The same factors that affected his growth as a fly-fisherman are the reasons he loves to tie all types of flies. He thinks it odd that he is recognized as a classic Atlantic salmon fly tier while like his fishing venues he has no favored style.

Ted shares some of his accomplishments, "I have been fortunate to be chosen as the Northeast Council's Fly Tyer of the Year (1989) and to win seven international fly tying tournaments; Federation of Quebec Salmon Association (5) and the Mustad Scandinavian Open (2). I've been invited to many places, from Gatlinburg up to Calgary, over to England and south into Holland to demonstrate my craftsmanship. Many of my flies have been exhibited in various publications including: *Rare and Unusual Fly Tying Materials,* Vol. 1 & 2, and *Forgotten Flies,* by Paul Schmookler & Ingrid Sils; *FFF Fly Pattern Encyclopedia,* by Al & Gretchen Beatty and few other FFF volumes."

Over the years he has developed a unique style of framing angling art, for which he received the Northeast Council's Extraordinary Craftsman Award in 1993. Regularly his work is commissioned by some of the most prestigious museums dedicated to the art of fly-fishing. These include: The American Museum of Fly Fishing in Manchester, Vermont; The Catskill Fly Fishing Center and Museum in Livingston Manor, New York; and The International Museum of the Federation of Fly Fishers in Livingston, Montana.

Ted closes, "Frequent contributions by groups such as the FFF, TU, Christie's Auction to save the Atlantic Salmon (North Atlantic Salmon Fund), and Tie-a-Fly for Freedom remind me that we cannot become nonchalant about issues pertaining to our environment, we must always look ahead. Education is my profession—*education through fly-fishing* is an obsession."

Fiery Brown Calamari

This pattern (like many) is a variation of Lefty Kreh's Cactus Striper and Bob Popovic's Shady Lady squid. Ted thinks the name Calamari sounds romantic while squid echoes of bait fish. No matter which name is used, it's just a meal to the predators in the ocean, in fact one of their primary food groups. He uses the K.I.S.S. (keep it sparse stupid) principle in many of his fishing flies. Ted advises, "A sparsely tied fly, fished in a manner that the fish are accustomed to, a baitfish type action, will be much more productive when the times are slower."

A sparser pattern is better suited when you must get a fly down 15 or 20 feet into a strong ocean current. Ted uses a sink-tip or full-sink line to adjust his fishing depth. If he needs to go deeper than either of these will produce, he ties his patterns with a cone head or weighted eyes. Once he gets to the depth of the fish, he adjusts his retrieve until he starts scoring.

Fiery Brown Calamari

Hook:	Size 5/0-2, salt water
Thread:	Brown
Mouth parts:	Fluorescent red Estaz
Legs:	Fiery brown saddle hackles
Eyes:	Taxidermists
Body:	Fluorescent red Estaz
Swimming flukes:	Rusty-brown craft fur

Step 1: Place the hook in the vise and apply a thread base that starts behind the hook eye and stops at the end of the shank. Tie on a section of red Estaz and wrap a small ball. Tie it off and trim away the waste end. Tie on a single feather slightly forward of this ball and trim off the unused part of the stem.

Step 2: Tie five more feathers on the hook again slightly forward of the chenille ball making certain they are evenly spaced around the hook. Trim the waste ends. The closer the thread is wrapped to the chenille ball, the more the feathers will flare out; wind the thread toward the ball until they stick out at a 45-degree angle. Bend a 90-degree angle in the stem of each eye and tie them on the sides of the hook. Apply a coating of Aqua Flex to the hook shank.

Step 3: Tie on a section of red Estaz in front of the eyes and figure-eight around them a couple of times. Advance the chenille forward to the hook eye, tie it off, and trim away the waste end.

Step 4: Tie on two sparse bundles of craft fur to each side of the shank directly behind the hook eye. Trim off any excess, apply a whip finish, and remove the thread from the hook. Coat the windings with Aqua Head to finish the fly.

TIM PAXTON

Robert Paxton, who goes by the moniker "Tim," was born in Orange, California 60 years ago, and remembers when you could ride your bike from Anaheim to the pier at Newport Beach in an hour, and only have one stop sign along the way. He got hooked on fishing in his teens casting from the piers on Southern California coastal waters. Tim carried his interest for fishing into the six years he spent with the United States Army testing various waters within country and as well as in Germany.

In 1964 he relocated to Eureka in Northern California and immediately became interested in fly-fishing and fly-tying. There were not very many fly-tying books available at that time so Tim taught himself how to tie. He remembers ordering most of his supplies from a Herter's catalog. There were two fishing shops in Humboldt County at the time. Art Dedini ran one of the shops and Lloyd Silvius (originator of the Silver Hilton and Brindle Bug) operated the other. Lloyd retired soon after Tim arrived and Art had very few fly-tying supplies in his store, so Tim was pretty much on his own.

Not long after settling in Eureka, Tim married Roxie and started his apprenticeship as an electrical lineman for Pacific Gas & Electric. Years later he transferred to the gas department as a field meter man eventually retiring from the company after 30 years of service. They have one son, Steven, an avid fly-fisher who makes his home in Corvallis, Oregon.

Tim Paxton

In the early eighties, Tim started a business call Buggy Nymph selling a fine translucent dubbing. This business began his adventures traveling to many sports shows, conclaves, and exotic fishing locations to show/field-test his products. Tim tells us he has met many wonderful, knowledgeable fly-tiers and fly-fishers through that business. Through their association he has developed into a highly skilled fly-fisher and fly-tier.

Tim has developed many flies that have been featured in magazines, books, and videos. They include Tim's Twit, Humboldt Honey, Buggy Nymph Hare's Ear, Roxie's Rainbow (named for his wife), Herniator, and Soft Pop. His most recent creation, the Herniator, was originally called the Terminator but when using it on the Klamath River one fine October day, his fishing companion developed a hernia while stripping in so many fish and was hospitalized the next day, thus the name change.

Many young people in the Eureka area have knowledge of fly-tying thanks to Tim. He has taught courses for 4-H, fly shops, and local schools during the years, giving a little of what he's learned back to the community.

Tim's Twit

Tim developed this fly in preparation for a baby tarpon fishing trip to Venezuela. He knew he would need poppers and really hated the idea of taking the time to tie them out of spun hair. Jerry Silvers, a fellow fly tier and Federation of Fly Fishers member, told him about using foam-caulking rods to make his popper heads. He located the material in the glass department in a home improvement center. By using it, the poppers fairly flew out of his vise; they were that easy to tie.

Since discovering this material he's made a few modifications until the pattern evolved into what you see here today. He likes it colored yellow or green for bass and white with red hackle for baby tarpon. The foam construction makes it light and easy to cast on a rod, as light as a five-weight.

Tim's Twit

Hook:	Mustad 3407 (salt) or 2-10, TMC 8089 (bass), size 1/0-2
Thread:	White
Tail:	Grizzly dyed yellow saddle hackle
Body:	Foam cylinder (3/8, 1/2, 5/8 inches)
Body color:	Felt-tip markers, colors of choice
Legs:	Foam strip, loop style
Hackle:	Grizzly dyed yellow
Head:	Thread

Step 1: Cut a caulking rod "plug" 7/8 inches long and sand the surface to remove the glaze. Starting 5/16 inch from one end, slice a 45-degree angle. The longest dimension will be the belly of the fly. Starting at the blunt end of the plug, insert the hook point just above the belly and "thread" it through the body lengthwise and parallel to the belly until the hook eye is flush with the popper face; point down. Place the hook in the vise.

Step 2: Start the tying thread at the back of the hook and capture the tapered end of the foam. Wrap forward, slightly compressing the foam at the back of the body. Apply a coating of head cement to the thread.

Step 3: Select a sheet of 1/8-inch foam and cut a 1/8-inch strip five inches long from it. Identify the center of the strip, slip it under the hook near the bend, and tie it to the underside of the hook with several tight figure-eight wraps. Loop the free end of the nearside segment over, bind it to the hook directly behind the body to form a looped leg, and trim off the waste end. Repeat the process with the farside segment.

Step 4: Use felt-tip markers to color the body a design of choice. We have found the color is much more durable if we coat the body and legs with Aqua Flex before continuing to the next part of this step. Select a fairly long saddle hackle feather and tie it to the hook as the center of the feather allowing the tip to extend to the back of the shank as a tail.

Step 5: Grab the large end of the saddle feather and wrap a wet-style collar. Tie it off and trim away the waste end. Whip finish and trim off the thread. Apply a coating of cement or Aqua Head.

Step 6: Here is a Tim's Twit designed for baby tarpon. The tail is shaped from two splayed neck-feather tips and the collar is constructed from the remaining portion of each. *Note: There is a kit available from Umpqua Feather Merchants packaged under the name Paxton's Easy Popper. It includes hooks, loop legs, and body material.*

ERIC PETTINE

Eric grew up in northern New Mexico in an extended family whose idea of recreation was to head up into the mountains to hunt, fish, and tent-camp. Until he was 16, Eric believed that all fishing flies were classic wet flies in one of three patterns: a Royal Coachman, a Gray Hackle Peacock, or a Rio Grande King. These were the only patterns he and his father fished. The flies came in boxes of a dozen, snelled on heavy monofilament. He still remembers catching his first rainbow by lying on his stomach on a log over the Gallinas River and dragging a Coachman repeatedly across the surface of the water. Eric claims that his fishing technique fifty-five years later is somewhat more sophisticated (he usually stands up for instance) but he's as hooked on fly-fishing today as on the day he caught that first fish at age five.

He also remembers the kindness and generosity of the man who gave him his start in fly tying. Eric was an undergraduate student at the University of Colorado with a new wife, a baby on the way, en route to a career in dentistry, and chronically empty pockets. Each day on his way home from school he would detour a couple of blocks to stop at Hank Robert's Fly Shop. Hank was always dressed in his signature white shirt and tie.

Although Eric spent a good deal of time studying the shop's variety of fishing gear and bins of flies, the only fly-tying gear he owned was a book his wife Ann had bought him (*Family Circle's Guide to Trout Flies*). He had repeatedly read the instructions for tying a Fan-Winged Coachman, the only "how to" section of the book. He also

Eric Pettine

spent time watching Roberts' tiers, especially Gracie a talented Native American fly dresser. He was ready to tie his first fly, but didn't have the money to purchase the tools and materials.

One day while browsing wistfully through the tying materials, Roberts asked if he was a shoplifter because he never bought anything. Eric explained he really wanted to learn to tie but could not afford the materials at the moment. Embarrassed by his impoverished state Eric hurriedly left the shop. Fortunately he didn't stay away long because at his next visit Roberts gave him a basic tying kit and gruffly ordered him to go upstairs and take a lesson from Gracie. He's been tying just about every day since that memorable day 42 years ago. Eric has tied professionally, but now ties for himself, friends or clients on those days he guides for Saint Peter's Fly Shop in Fort Collins where he has lived and practiced dentistry since 1969.

He finds the Federation of Fly Fishers annual Conclave to be the single most important educational resource for him as a fly-tier and fly-fisher. It was at one such Conclave that Eric watched his friend Bill Heckle from Illinois demonstrate the use of biots to tie a dry fly. Bill's pattern, with slight modifications, became Eric's standard imitation of a mayfly dun.

Baetis Dun

Eric tells us about this fly, "I first saw this pattern at a Federation of Fly Fishers Conclave in Livingston, Montana when Illinois fly tier Bill Heckle demonstrated this style of fly. Like all fly tiers I've modified it somewhat from the sample Bill gave me in that I changed the wing and tail material to better suit the water I fish and guide on. It has become my standard mayfly imitation, all I do is change the size and color to suit the situation."

Eric favors this fly for spring-creek type conditions where the trout get ample time to scrutinize the imitation. He believes if you pick the right size and shade and make a good presentation, even the most discriminating trout will eat it. Eric doesn't believe in "magic" patterns that work all the time, but this fly works often enough to let the angler know it will fool fish.

Baetis Dun

Hook:	Size 12-24, dry fly
Thread:	Gray
Tail:	Gray Micro Fibetts
Body:	Olive/gray biot
Wing:	Stalcup's Medallion Sheeting
Thorax:	Olive/gray biot
Hackle:	Dun
Head:	Thread

Step 1: Place the hook in the vise and apply a thread base that covers the back 2/3 of the hook shank. Tie in the Micro Fibett tail then use a soft figure-eight with the tying thread to separate the fibers. Trim off any waste ends. For a size sixteen or smaller we suggest two Micro Fibetts and for larger flies we recommend four. Put a half twist in the Medallion Sheeting and tie it on the hook at the point of the twist. Cut the wing to shape.

Step 2: Wrap the thread back to the end of the shank and tie on a biot by its tip. Wrap it forward forming a body that stops just behind the wings. When tying on the biot we placed the dark edge up to get the look you see in the illustration. The appearance is much different if the dark edge is placed down. We suggest you select the "look" you want.

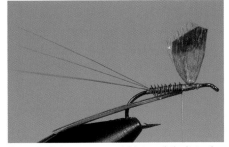

Step 3: Select a second biot and tie it to the hook by its tip positioned behind the wings. Trim away the waste end and leave the thread behind the wings.

Step 4: Select and size a blue dun hackle feather. Prepare it by removing the web near the base of the stem and tie it to the hook behind the wings. Wrap the hackle, placing a couple turns behind the wings and several more in front. Tie off the feather and trim away the waste end.

Step 5: Evenly separate the hackle on the underside of the hook then pull the biot forward and anchor it in front of the hackle. The hackle on the far side of the hook tends to point at an angle; pull up on those fibers so the hackle on both side point straight out from the hook.

Step 6: Trim off the waste end of the biot then wrap a thread head. Apply a whip finish and trim off the thread. Coat the thread wraps with Aqua Head to finish the fly.

BRITT PHILLIPS

Britt Phillips

We consider this Arroyo Grande fly tier one of the more creative individuals we've had the good fortune to call a friend. Although his start in fly tying was a little shaky, his skills have literally exploded as his thirst for knowledge grew. It all started, though, with an accident. Shortly after Britt started fly-fishing in the late 70s, he was on the banks of the San Joaquin River when he dropped his only box of flies into the river and watched as it floated downstream, merrily on its way to the Pacific Ocean. The flies were all store bought and replacing them presented a problem; buy more or learn to tie. Britt figured if he was going to continue fly-fishing he did not want to be tethered to a fly shop for his patterns. Britt began the learning process the very next week after losing that box. He took one lesson in which he learned the hand half hitch and from there has never looked back.

Books, magazines, and videos gave him a strong foundation. Britt's biggest advancement though was attending Federation of Fly Fisher's Conclaves and tying events. There he asked questions, watched, took notes, and drew pictures. Fly tiers like Dave Hughes, the late Gary LaFontaine, Charles Jardine, Andy Burke, John McKim, Eddie Chiles, and the late Ned Long all greatly influenced him with their skills and ability to convey their knowledge to him, especially on a one-to-one basis. He was really hooked on his new hobby. Little did he know in those formative years he would end up a skilled instructor and a fly shop owner as well.

After years of the learning process, Britt began to innovate techniques for simplifying the steps or processes, with a main underriding thought of re-using materials as much as he could in his flies. He also began scrounging for all sorts of materials to put into his flies. Wire from auto relays, craft yarns, synthetic wig hair, and fabric store finds all took on new meaning as they worked their way into his patterns. On long fishing trips to the "trout heavens" from his home in "trout hell" he would conjure up steps and possible ways of using different materials. His mind's eye "fly stormed" things like reversing the tie in, a different material, and substitutes. The more Britt got into fly design the more he became aware there were no rules, no bounds, no reason to stick blindly to tradition, and no failure, only opportunities to play.

By the 80s Britt's skills had grown to the point he was less a student and more the teacher. He started teaching fly tying to Santa Lucia Fly Fishers club, the local 4H youths, and demonstrating at some the same shows that a few years earlier were his classrooms.

Today his patterns have appeared in several publications like *Patterns from the Masters* and articles by John McKim in *Western Outdoors* magazine. Britt is a regular demonstrator at the ISE Shows in Sacramento and San Mateo, California. He is owner and operator of a great fly shop in Grover Beach called the Hole in the Wall. He chuckles and says, "Maybe its successful because there are no other fly shops within 150 miles!" We think it's because he is knowledgeable, pleasant, and willing to share.

BH Squirrel Nymph

We first saw Britt demonstrate his technique for constructing a dubbing hackle collar at a recent fly-tying exposition. We were so impressed we wanted the technique illustrated in this book. Britt explains how it all happened, "One night at a fly-tying roundtable at my shop, I was asked to demo a Dave Whitlock pattern, the Red Fox Squirrel Nymph. I tried to duplicate the picture that was supplied to me from a magazine and got frustrated with my initial attempts as I followed the directions. I decided to swap materials using partridge for the tail and squirrel guard hairs for the hackle.

"I used part of a technique demonstrated by the late Gary LaFontaine which he called touch and spin. The technique I stumbled on I call STP (Spin the thread, Touch the dubbing, and Push the dubbing up to the hook). The resulting fly sure looked good and subsequently caught fish as well." We loved the technique and have incorporated it into many of our flies. We've been wondering how we could use this idea to produce a parachute hackle on a dry fly, but have not done so yet! Who among you will take the challenge and come up with that technique?

BH Squirrel Nymph

Hook:	Size 10-16, nymph
Thread:	Orange
Tail:	Partridge fibers
Rib:	Mylar tinsel
Body:	Squirrel belly dubbing
Hackle:	Squirrel dubbing
Head:	Bead, color of choice

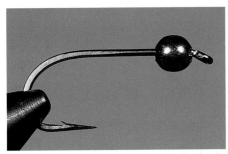

Step 1: Take a bead and slip it on the hook. Place the hook in the vise and slide the bead forward to the hook eye.

Step 2: Attach the tying thread behind the bead, place several wraps, and trim the waste end. Select a clump of partridge feather fibers and bind them to the hook as a tail while wrapping the thread to the end of the shank. The tail should be no longer than the distance of the hook gape. Trim a short section of Mylar tinsel from its spool and tie it to the hook while wrapping the thread most of the way back to the bead. Place it in a material keeper for future reference.

Step 3: Put wax on the thread then apply squirrel belly dubbing to it. Wrap a body starting at the back that reaches almost all the way to the bead. Be sure to leave room for the hackle. Wind the tinsel forward forming the rib. Tie it off and trim the waste end.

Step 4: Place wax on the thread then spin the bobbin. While the bobbin is spinning, touch the squirrel back dubbing to the thread. The spinning thread distributes the dubbing/guard hairs around the thread forming a dubbing brush.

Step 5: Stop the spinning bobbin with the right hand. Using the left hand push the dubbing brush up the thread to the hook, compressing it into a clump.

Step 6: Wrap the bundle/thread around the hook, sweeping the fibers back in the process. Wrap the thread tight against the fibers to force them back into a wet-style collar. Apply a whip finish and trim the thread from the hook. Coat the windings with Aqua Head to finish the fly.

Greby

This is another fly that employs the STP soft-hackle technique. Britt developed this pattern after observing how emerging insects drift helplessly in the surface film. The fact he loves fishing for trout in the "near-surface" was another good reason. Britt tells us, "I believe that most flies are extremely over-dressed and complicated. I do my best to distill my flies to their simplest form once they prove their worth."

Britt likes to fish this fly quartering upstream on a dead drift. As it draws across from him he throws a mend upstream then allows the fly to drag across the current as it travels downstream. He tells us, "Be sure to let the fly hang straight downstream for a few seconds before retrieving it slowly using the hand-twist method."

Greby

Hook:	Size 12-20, wet fly
Thread:	Orange
Abdomen:	Mylar tinsel
Wing:	Mylar tinsel
Thorax:	Ice Dubbing, color of choice
Hackle:	Squirrel dubbing
Head:	Thread

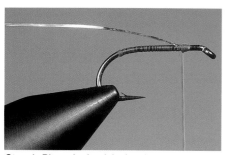

Step 1: Place the hook in the vise and lay down a thread base that covers all of the shank except a short section near the eye. Tie a strand of Mylar tinsel at the front end of the thread base. Trim off the waste end and leave the thread at the front of the hook.

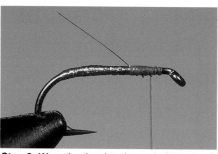

Step 2: Wrap the tinsel to the end of the shank then back to the starting point near the hook eye. Tie off the tinsel on top of the shank, pull straight back on it, and bind it to the hook to form a miniature wing. Stop the thread wraps at the 1/3 point on the shank. Trim the tinsel so it is even with the end of the hook.

Step 3: Select Ice Dubbing in a color of your choice and apply it to the tying thread. Construct a thorax ending with the thread near the hook eye. Be certain to leave enough room for the hackle in the next steps.

Step 4: Apply dubbing wax to the tying thread, spin the bobbin, and while the bobbin is spinning, touch a clump of squirrel back dubbing to the thread. The spinning, waxed thread grabs the dubbing on all sides evenly, creating a dubbing brush.

Step 5: Stop the spinning bobbin with the right hand, place the left thumb and forefinger around the thread next to the bobbin barrel then push the dubbing up the thread to the hook. This pushing motion takes the elongated dubbing brush and compresses it into a bundle tight again the hook. Wrap the thread around the hook, distributing the bundle evenly around the shank. At this point the fibers are sticking out in all directions.

Step 6: Sweep back the helter-skelter fibers and build a thread head that forces them to stay back wet, collar style. Whip finish and trim the thread from the hook. Apply a coating of Aqua Head to the whip finish to complete the fly.

PT Brassie

Britt advises, "Give a job to a lazy person, me, and I will come up with an easier, less work method of doing anything. I don't like to pick up things more than once, cut and re-tie materials, and get all complicated in steps." Britt sure minimized motion with this fly and it's a really effective pattern as well. It falls into a category we call "guide flies," patterns that are easy to tie and produce fish.

It is an assembly of several flies but what we like about it is Britt's use of the materials. The dubbing is the only material used for just one function. He tells us with a grin, "Unfortunately the dubbing had only one use. Dang! I'll figure another use for it yet." Knowing Britt, we have no doubt he will.

PT Brassie

Hook:	Size 10-16, wet fly
Thread:	Orange
Tail:	Pheasant-tail fibers
Abdomen:	Copper wire
Thorax:	Hare's ear dubbing
Wing case:	Pheasant fibers

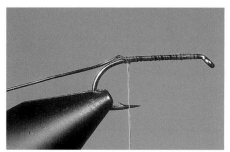

Step 1: Place the hook in the vise and attach the tying thread just behind the eye with a couple of wraps. Select a length of copper wire and bind it to the top of the shank while winding the thread to the back of the hook. Leave the thread at the end of the shank.

Step 2: Select five or six pheasant-tail fibers and tie them to the hook as a tail that is as long as the hook gape is wide. Advance the thread to the hook eye, binding the tail fibers to the top of the shank in the process. At the eye form a loop from the excess tail fibers. Do not trim any of the fibers.

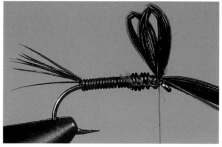

Step 3: Bring the wire under the tail to tilt it up then wind it forward using tight wraps forming the body. At the eye, reverse the direction and wind several turns of wire back to about the 1/3 position on the shank. Cut the waste end with a pair of pliers then press the tag end tight to the hook. Leave the thread hanging at the hook eye in preparation for the next step.

Step 4: Place dubbing on the thread and wrap a thorax from the eye back to the one-third position on the hook shank. Leave the thread there for tying the wing case in the last step.

Step 5: Pull the pheasant fibers remaining from Step 2 over and bind them to the hook to form a wing case. Trim the waste ends, apply a whip finish, and cut the thread from the hook. Coat the wing case with Aqua Flex to finish the fly then pick out the guard hairs to represent legs.

TED ROGOWSKI

Ted Rogowski

Ted fondly recalls his "early years" fly-fishing for bass and bream. At that time his flies were carved from balsa wood in the shape of a grasshopper with feathers glued into place taken straight from the chicken yard. The wood was leftover scraps from a model airplane project. Ted remembers with a grin those first assembled rather than tied flies often only lasted for one or two fish. He graduated to trout fishing at Amherst College where a stream flowed through the campus. The call of the stream often interfered with springtime studies. At Amherst he sponsored an Intercollegiate Trout Tournament among New England colleges. Ted tells us, "Fly-fishing has been a lifetime pursuit and joy."

His first job out of college was production manager for the Phillips Fly and Tackle Company in Pennsylvania with 20 fly tiers. There he had the good fortune to fish with George Harvey, the well-known fishing instructor/professor at Penn State College. That fun was to be short lived as Ted was drafted into the Korean war.

Upon his return from military service in 1953, the G. I. Bill brought him to Columbia Law School and a Wall Street law practice, to his wonderful wife Margie (who passed on May 20, 2000), and to the Angler's Club of New York. All three were instrumental components in shaping his future. While in New York he traveled with Lee Wulff to Newfoundland, Labrador, Scotland and Norway in pursuit of Atlantic salmon. Ted filmed Lee Wulff's pioneering salmon and trout fishing movies for CBS-TV and ABC-TV, then chronicled those adventures in Esquire magazine. Also while in New York he became a founding direc-

tor and charter member of the Federation of Fly Fishers and the Theodore Gordon Fly Fishers. He was the FFF Legal Counsel during the West Yellowstone years, watching the Federation grow from a few clubs to over 250.

In 1966 he joined the federal government serving under Stuart Udall and then William Ruckelshaus in the newly established U. S. Environmental Protection Agency. Ted served as Senior Water Counsel to establish the Clean Water Act for water-quality standards in all states. In 1970 Ted and Margie moved out West where he continued as counsel for Region 10 (Alaska, Idaho, Oregon, and Washington) until 1993, responsible for implementing all U. S. Environmental Protection Agency laws. Today Ted continues to practice environmental, corporate, and business law in Washington and New York.

During his federal tenure, Ted retired from FFF and private legal duties on an ethical conflict basis, but today he is again active in the Federation of Fly Fishers and Trout Unlimited conservation of water resources legal matters. Ted is one of those little known champions of the fly fisher and the environment who deserves recognition for his contribution. Maybe this short profile will correct that deficiency in a small way. We are proud to name Ted and his lovely new wife, Joan Wulff, (married in August 2002) among our federation friends.

Emerger #1, #2, & #3

Ted's contribution to our sport does not focus on water quality and the environment alone. He is also considered by many to be the father of the emerger style of imitation. This fly series had its beginning on Minipi Lake in Labrador where Ted and Lee Wulff experienced a frustrating day filming the trout gorging themselves on hatching drakes. They spent hours capturing a film sequence of the trout swirling at the surface often refusing dry flies.

Ted tells us, "When I returned to the City, what I was seeing through the movie camera lens staged a repeat performance in my mind's eye. The New York subway train rattled my brain in creative problem solving. The trout were gulping emerging mayflies at the water's surface, often refusing dry flies. A new kind of fly was conceived to deceive such trout—I had the 'magic moment' to dare to reproduce a series of nymphs in their various stages of hatching, like those I saw at Minipi."

In the fall of 1957 Ted introduced the Emerging "Silk Stocking" Nymphs to Ernie Schwiebert and Dick Clark at a New York Anglers Club Crackerbarrel Fly-Tying session. Ernie saw the creations as a significant new form of "matching the hatch" that imitated significant life forms of mayflies. The fly series included the mayfly as it struggled through the water column to the surface, with a wing-case bursting; their partially unfolded wings with the fly still attached to the nymphal shuck; their riding the shuck as a new fly, curved body and tails pointing to the sky.

Ernie captured the moment of discovery in his book *Nymphs*:

"However, there is also a transistory stage of hatching between the first appearance of the wings and their full-blown

development just before the winged state. Several years ago Ted Rogowski and I began experimenting with a new emerging nymph material.

It was Rogowski who hit on the technique, and I merely suggested the insects with hatching behavior best suited to the imitation of emerging wings, along with some thoughts on proportions. Rogowski outlined the theories in his *Crackerbarrel Discourses,* which appeared in an anthology, The Gordon Garland, compiled by the Theodore Gordon Flyfishers in 1965. His theories involved a piece of fine-denier nylon stocking.

What are these wings? I asked at their debut. *Nylon?*

Right! Rogowski laughed and handed me several more hatching nymphs.

They come in great colors these days!"

(*Nymphs*, p. 279, 1973 Winchester Press)

Ted did have to endure a certain amount of good-humored razing as the result of his nylon-stocking fetish! He tells us about it, "Sparse Grey Hackle, ever alert to history in the making, gave the world a more beguiling report in Red Smith's *New York Herald Tribune* angling column. His account was headlined with a warning to the females of the City: "Fly-tyers on Prowl for Silk Stockings – Ladies Beware." According to Sparse, fly-tying had proceeded from clipping scarce plumage from ladies' bonnets to a now more subtle search for dun-colored silk, and stocking silk most closely matching the semi-opaque emerging wings of the subimago drake."

We were very pleased to present Ted's revolutionary fly designs in our last book, the *Federation of Fly Fishers' Fly Pattern Encyclopedia.*

Stage #1, #2 & #3: *Represented here are all three stages of the emerging insect as observed by Ted Rogowski and Lee Wulff.*

Emerger #1, #2, & #3

Hook:	Size #10 - #20, 2XL
Thread:	Match the insect
Tail:	Wood duck fibers
Abdomen:	Dubbing to match the insect
Stage 1 *Wing:*	Nylon stocking
Stage 2 & 3 *Wing:*	Nylon stocking
Stage 2 & 3 *Filling:*	Plastic bubble
Stage 1 *Hackle:*	Grouse or hen, beard style
Stage 2 *Hackle:*	Color to match the insect
Thorax:	Dubbing to match the insect

Step 1, Stage 1: Place the hook in the vise and apply a thread base that covers the back 2/3 of the hook. Tie on a wood-duck fiber tail that is as long as the hook shank and trim away any waste ends. Apply dubbing to the thread using any good dubbing wax like BT's. Make the first turn with the dubbed thread under the tail to elevate it then wrap forward to the 1/3 point, constructing the abdomen.

Step 2, Stage 1: Nylon stocking mesh readily takes dye or felt-tip markers. Color a block of mesh tan (or color to match the insect). Cut the colored mesh into two-inch squares, roll one of them to form a bubble, and tie it to the hook at the 1/3 point. Keep the length of the bubble fairly short to represent the emerging wing.

Step 3, Stage 1: Trim off the excess wing material. Select a clump of grouse, partridge, or hen hackle fibers and tie them to the under side of the hook beard style. Trim off any excess fibers. Apply dubbing to the thread and construct the thorax on the front part of the hook. Whip finish and remove the thread. Apply a coating of Aqua Head to finish the fly. Note: Ted changed the materials in the tail in the photograph to illustrate the flexibility one has in creating a range of patterns to represent just about any mayfly.

Step 1, Stage 2: Here Ted added several brown hackle fibers to provide support to the woodduck tail. To aid floatation he places a plastic ball inside a single square of tan nylon mesh when constructing the wing. A dry-fly hackle is substituted for the beard to further aid floatation.

Step 1, Stage 3: Here we create a freshly emerged insect still riding on its nymphal shuck. The shuck is created just like we did the back part of the fly in the previous step. Before adding the hackle or thorax, tie on a tail and body of the hatched-out insect constructed from a woodduck feather tied Harry Darby "one fly" style. Trim away any waste ends. Complete the fly as done for Stage 2.

Author's note: Ted tied Stages 2 & 3 with Whiting champagne hackle. We think the superbly speckled colors are prefect for emerging insects.

JOHN RYZANYCH

An avid fly-fishing enthusiast for over twenty years, this Castro Valley, California fly tier recently transferred his experience in the field to the creative efforts of developing specialty products and innovative patterns for the fly-fishing market. Thinking outside the box is the practice that supports John's novel and practical approach to design, earning him and his products the reputation of being on the leading edge of innovation.

John is the owner of ICON Products that produces SOFTEX and FLY STAGES. He also sits on the pro staff of several other tackle companies. John is credited with stylizing the popular Airhead topwater fly, the Soft Head large-profile pattern, and the Hackle Back technique for realism in wet-fly patterns he often demonstrates at tying exhibitions throughout the U.S. and abroad.

Another recent innovation is the Line Label technique of marking a fly line with easy-to-read identification typed on one's home computer.

During his childhood, John was introduced to fly-fishing by his father during a family vacation in Oregon, and after a stint with bait- and lure-fishing returned to the greater satisfaction of fishing with flies and the pursuit of what eats them. The progression through the

John Ryzanych

freshwater species fostered his first exposure to the blue waters of the Sea of Cortez. Since then, the attraction of *fast predators* has taken him through the waters of the South Pacific, Atlantic Ocean, Australia, and much of Mexico, where he continues adding to his seemingly endless list of fly-caught species, and contributions of style and technique to the art of fly tying.

Airhead

In 1995 John was introduced to braided tubing, a product of the high-pressure hose and wiring harness industries. Like many fly tiers, he experimented with the newly discovered material and magic happened when he married the tubing with SOFTEX produced by his company ICON Products. The body produced by the two materials is light, easy to cast, and flexible allowing for a more natural feel with better hook ups.

John suggests using a single- or two-handed retrieve pulling the fly across the water producing a "V" wake. He tells us the best method is the two-handed constant-motion retrieve. The Airhead is remarkably durable. The coating allows tooth damage to be easily repaired with the addition of more SOFTEX over the problem area followed by a ten-minute dry time.

Airhead

Hook:	Size 2/0-6, TMC 511S
Thread:	White
Body:	Pearl EZ Body tubing sized to the hook
Back:	Two grizzly, dyed olive hackle feathers
Coating:	SOFTEX
Tail:	Hackle, green and white Krystal Flash, silver tinsel
Eyes:	Stick-on, silver with black pupils

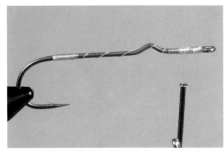

Step 1: Place the hook in the vise and start a thread base at the end of the shank. After several close wraps at the end of the shank spiral forward and construct a similar base just behind the hook eye. The result is a dense front and rear thread base with the bobbin hanging just behind the hook eye.

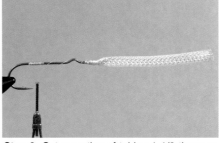

Step 2: Cut a section of tubing 1 1/2 times as long as the hook shank. Slip it over the hook eye and anchor it there with several tight thread wraps. Trim any unused tubing then wind the thread to the back of the hook.

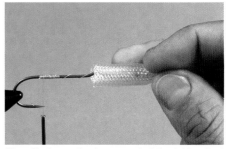

Step 3: Grasp the loose end of the tubing that is sticking out in front of the hook. Push back on it forcing the tubing to turn inside out.

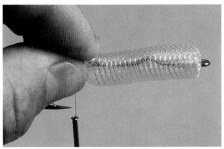

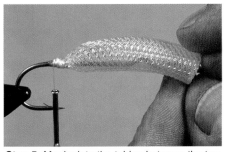

Step 4: Push the tubing all the way back then reverse the direction and press forward on it. This motion allows it to expand and shape the body's profile. Anchor the tubing at the back of the hook and trim any waste ends.

Step 5: Manipulate the tubing between the two tie-in points with the thumb and index fingers. Pinch while stroking the tubing from the rear of the hook to taper the body and form the concave face.

Step 6: Tie on the tail materials starting with the white Krystal Flash, then put on the silver tinsel, and lastly apply the green Krystal Flash. Tie off the thread and trim away the bobbin leaving a twelve-inch tag. Apply SOFTEX to the whip finish and the entire body bridging the tube strands but not filling the cavity.

Step 7: While this coating is still wet, place the first hackle feather across the back anchoring it in place. Place a second coat of SOFTEX over this feather and apply the second hackle over the first. Secure both hackles at the back of the hook with the thread tag left in the last step. Whip finish and remove the thread tag. Allow this to dry for a few minutes.

Step 8: Trim the feathers at the front of the body, use a felt-tip marker to color the face, and add the eyes. Coat the entire body by immersing it into the container of SOFTEX then rotate it for thirty seconds to prevent sagging. Use a wood toothpick to clean the hook eye and the excess SOFTEX from the face. Place it on a rotating wheel to finish drying.

BOB SCHEIDT

Bob Scheidt

Bob was born and raised in Fresno, California where he lives today with his wife Colleen. His home waters are the lakes and streams of the Sierra Nevada Mountains and the San Joaquin Valley offering a diversity of fish species and water types. Bob says the Sierra creeks are his passion because they offer lots of small fish and some serious exercise getting to the best of them.

In 1973 he took a fly-tying and casting class with the oldest fly club in California, The Fresno Fly Fishers For Conservation. "I really respected those veteran anglers who showed great patience teaching a teenager tying and casting," Bob recalls. "Those conservation pioneers knew then that the environment had to have someone looking out for it."

After that class, Bob continued tying and fishing on his own. The fishing was a lot easier for him but the tying was a real struggle. Then there were few books on the subject and no Internet or videotapes; things are much different today. Through the mentoring efforts of Clarence Butzbach, Bob was able to learn the finer points of fly-tying. He recalls Clarence telling him, "This Western Coachman could use about ten percent more hair on the wing." Under his direction, Bob learned the difference between a mediocre and well-tied fly.

He continued tying and fishing, and was rewarded with a few nice trout and a four-pound bass all caught on his own creations. One day he wandered into a fly shop in Dunsmuir and soon discovered he had just met the legendary Ted Fay. After listening to him talk about tying and fishing Ted really got Bob fired up about the sport. On another trip to Northern California he met master steelhead tier Ed Haas. He spent a memorable afternoon in Ed's cabin on the Forks of the Salmon River talking and learning about tying. Bob tells us, "Mr. Haas was a unique, extremely intelligent man and a brilliant fly tier."

Fly tying helps Bob with his vocation as an electronics technician. The manual dexterity and eye-to-hand coordination that fly-tying brings to him make it easier for Bob to deal with very small parts and assemblies.

Today he has been tying and fly-fishing for thirty years. He enjoys angling with traditional patterns that give him a sense of the history of fly-fishing. His attention to detail led him to dying his own materials and over the years has become quite proficient at it. Bob now teaches tying at all levels from beginner through advanced. He really enjoys the tying shows where ideas are exchanged and friendships are made. We met Bob at one of these shows and yes, we consider him a good friend.

Adams Tommy Twist Parachute

Bob learned this parachute technique from Tom Leggler in Fresno, California. This pattern demonstrates splitting the tail with the thread tag and blending two hackles to produce a more attractive fly. The disadvantage is some hackle fibers will splay upwards, but can be easily cut off. On the other hand, the advantage is both hackles are twisted together and wrapped as one producing an evenly mixed hackle.

Bob fishes this fly like any angler would, quartering upstream on a dead drift. He also finds it is very productive when presented with a check cast on a downstream dead drift. This method is particularly effective when used over very selective fish.

Adams Tommy Twist Parachute

Hook:	Size 8-20, dry fly
Thread:	Gray or black
Tail:	Moose hair
Post:	White poly yarn
Body:	Gray dubbing
Hackle:	Brown and grizzly mix

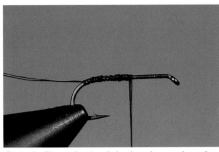

Step 1: Place the hook in the vise and apply a thread base that covers the back half of the hook. Do not cut off the waste end of thread, instead loop it and tie the loose end to the hook while wrapping the thread back to the center of the shank. Place the "waste thread loop" in the material keeper for use in the next step.

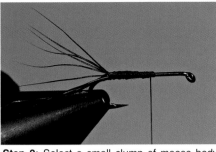

Step 2: Select a small clump of moose body hair, clean out the under fur, and even the tips in a stacker. Tie them to the hook as a tail that is as long as the hook shank. Trim off the waste ends. Retrieve the thread loop from the material keeper, bring it through the tail fibers splitting them in two bundles, and anchor the loop to the hook shank. The amount of tension on this loop will determine how wide the two tail bundles are split.

Step 3: Advance the thread to a position 1/4 of the shank length back from the hook eye. Tie on a section of white poly yarn, and trim off the waste end. Stand up the yarn to form the wing using several thread wraps tight against the front. Wrap several turns around the yarn to construct a parachute platform. Select a brown and a grizzly hackle feather and prepare them by stripping the fuzzy material from the base of the stems. Tie them to the hook and the platform part of the parachute post.

Step 4: Wax the tying thread then place dubbing on it. Wrap the dubbed thread to construct a body ending with the thread hanging at the hook eye.

Step 5: Secure the two feathers in a pair of hackle pliers. Twist them about six or eight turns in preparation for the next step.

Step 6: Wrap the twisted feathers as if they were one, forming a parachute hackle. Tie the feather off at the hook eye and trim any waste ends. Whip finish and remove the thread from the hook. Cut the wing to shape, then trim any unwanted hackle fibers. Apply a coating of Aqua Head to the thread windings to finish the fly.

Bob's Flying Ant

This pattern is Bob's choice for the flying ants that usually appear in early summer in the Sierras. They can ruin a picnic or make a day of fishing because the fish really go for them. He is convinced the mallard wings are key to the pattern. They are light in color and just look alive. It is also a unique use for duck flank feathers.

The flying ants don't land lightly, so it is okay to splat the fly hard on the water. After applying fly floatant, Bob makes sure to turn the fly over hard so it lands firmly on the water, but the fly line lands softly. The strike can be explosive!

Bob's Flying Ant

Hook:	Size 12, dry fly
Thread:	Black
Abdomen:	Black rabbit dubbing
Post:	White poly yarn
Wings:	Mallard flank
Hackle:	Black
Thorax:	Black rabbit dubbing

Step 1: Place the hook in the vise and attach the thread about four eye-widths back on the shank. Tie on the yarn, trim the waste end, and construct a parachute post. Select a black hackle feather, strip the fuzzy material from the end of the stem, and bind it to the hook/post. Trim the waste end of the feather and leave the thread hanging behind the post.

Step 2: Place wax on the thread then apply the rabbit dubbing to it. Wrap a large dubbed ball to form the abdomen.

Step 3: Tie a clump of mallard flank fiber to the off side of the hook by the tips. Bob advises tying them on by the tips is important. Repeat the process on the near side of the hook. Trim off any waste ends and leave the thread in front of the post.

Step 4: Wrap the parachute hackle down the post then tie it off in front but not all the way forward to the hook eye. Trim the excess feather.

Step 5: Place wax on the thread and apply a small amount of dubbing to it. Gently pull the hackle out of the way and dub the thorax in front of the post. Whip finish and remove the thread from the hook.

Step 6: Trim the mallard wings to length so they are slightly longer than the hook. Last cut the parachute post to length then finish the fly with a coat of Aqua Head on the thread windings.

Ladybug

Bob is not sure if the fish take this fly for a beetle or a ladybug because they can't see the spots on the back. It is a good, year-around terrestrial pattern. They are important insects on lakes of the western side of the Sierras because hatches can be few and far between.

Ladybugs fly and can be quite thick on the water when you do find them.

Bob fishes it with short twitches, casting it toward the shore early and late in the day. He applies fly floatant to the legs only so it will sit low in the water like the natural insect.

Ladybug

Hook:	Size 14-16, dry fly
Thread:	Black
Back:	Orange foam
Body:	Black rabbit dubbing
Legs:	Black hackle, trimmed
Antenna:	Two moose fibers
Dots:	Black paint

Step 1: Place the hook in the vise and apply a thread base that covers the back 7/8 of the shank ending near the hook eye. Cut a section of foam that is as wide as the distance of the hook gape. Tie it to the top of the hook wrapping first to the end of the shank then back forward almost to the eye.

Step 2: Wax the thread then apply the dubbing. Wrap a medium-thick body ending just short of the hook eye. Be sure to leave a bit of bare hook at the front. Wrap the thread back over the front part of the dubbed body and leave it there for the next step.

Step 3: Select a black hackle and prepare it by stripping the fuzzy material from the base end of the stem. Tie it to the hook and trim the excess stem. Wrap the thread forward to the front of the dubbed body then follow with the hackle. Tie off the feather and trim away the excess material.

Step 4: Pull the foam over the back, anchor it behind the hook eye, and trim off the unused portion. Select two moose hairs and tie them to the hook just behind the eye. Trim them short to represent the antenna. Whip finish and remove the thread from the hook.

Step 5: Trim the bottom of the hackle even with the underside of the body. Cut the legs to length so they are even on both sides. Coat the head with cement.

Step 6: Paint black dots on the foam back with a round toothpick. Place the fly in a rotating wheel to dry.

JIM SCHOLLMEYER

Jim has fished most of his life, starting with his early years in North Dakota spent catching bullhead, walleye, and northern pike employing any means possible. His favorite fishing was with a spinning rod, casting a spoon to pike holding along the edges of lakes.

After moving to Oregon in the early 70's, Jim spent most of his time fly-fishing for steelhead and an occasional trout. A few years after his relocation he took a basic entomology class from Rick Hafele and Dave Hughes. From them Jim learned the importance of aquatic insects as a food source for trout, and that by studying their life cycles he would have a better understanding of when and how to fish for them. With this knowledge and great excitement, Jim started chasing hatches and tying flies to match the insects he collected. Later he started photographing aquatic insects to document the hatches and to have images of their different life cycles. These photographs made it easier to tie flies that matched the shape, size, and color of the naturals. He learned his lessons well because today he is one of the best macro photographers involved in the fly-fishing publishing industry.

Jim advises, "I think catching trout on a fly is a great sport, but it is just a small part of the whole experience of being outdoors. The more you know about a subject, the more you will enjoy it. Once you start studying trout and their ecology, you will begin an incredible journey, and those travels will be some of the best times of your life.

Jim Schollmeyer

A good way to start this journey is by joining a local fly-fishing club and or one of the national fly-fishing organizations like the Federation of Fly Fishers or TU. By becoming an active member of one of these groups you will meet people with similar interests, increase your fishing knowledge and skills, help protect trout, trout fishing, and their environment."

Jim manages "Patent Patterns", a fly-tying contest featured in each issue of *Flyfishing & Tying Journal* published by Frank Amato Publications. His recent book *Patent Patterns* is a review of 1500 unique flies submitted to the contest over the past several years. He is half of the team (Leeson & Schollmeyer) who produced the incredible book, *The Fly Tier's Benchside Reference.*

Today Jim makes his home in Salem, Oregon with his wife Debbie where he makes his living as a writer and professional photographer. His work has appeared in numerous fly-fishing books, periodicals, and general outdoor magazines. Jim's books include *Tying Emergers, Hatch Guide for Western Streams, Hatch Guide for Lakes, Hatch Guide for the Lower Deschutes River,* and *Fly Casting* (with Frank Amato).

Krystal Flash Nymph

This pattern came about because Jim needed a small blue-winged olive nymph imitation that would break through the water's surface tension, but not sink very fast. Its design allows it to be fished close to the surface by itself or trailing as a dropper behind a dry fly or strike indicator.

The Krystal Flash body and wing case provides the density to break through the surface tension without adding additional weight to the fly. The tail and picked-out dubbing in the thorax slow the sink rate of the fly, making it an excellent pattern to use when trout are feeding on emerging nymphs close to the surface. Black Krystal Flash imitates the color of mature *Baetis* nymphs, but peacock or root beer Krystal Flash can be used for the abdomen for more color variations.

Krystal Flash Nymph

Hook:	Size 16-20, wet fly
Thread:	Black
Tail:	Dark-dun hen fibers
Abdomen:	Black Krystal Flash
Wing case:	Black Krystal Flash
Thorax:	Brown or olive-brown Hare-Tron dubbing

Step 1: Place the hook in the vise and apply a thread base from the front of the hook to the end of the shank. Select a small clump of dark-dun hen fibers and tie them to the hook as a tail that is slightly shorter than the hook gape is wide.

Step 2: Tie on two to four strands of Krystal Flash while advancing the thread forward to the middle of the hook. Twist the Krystal Flash into a rope and wrap them forward forming the abdomen. Tie them off, but do not trim off the excess.

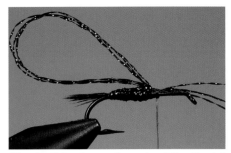

Step 3: Take the waste ends of the Krystal Flash and fold them forming a short loop twice as long as the complete hook. Tie it to the hook in front of the abdomen with a couple of thread wraps. Do not trim off the waste ends.

Step 4: Again, take the waste ends and form two more loops just like those constructed in the last step. Now trim away the waste ends. Wrap the thread back over the loops keeping them on top of the abdomen until reaching the middle of the hook.

Step 5: Apply dubbing to the thread and wrap forward forming a thorax. Be sure to leave room for the head. Pull the Krystal Flash loops over the thorax, forming the wing case, and secure them with several tight thread wraps.

Step 6: Trim off the waste ends of Krystal Flash. Cover the trimmed ends with a thread head, whip finish, and cut the thread from the hook. Apply a coating of Aqua Head to finish the fly. While the head cement is drying, pick out the dubbing in the thorax to form legs.

CLINT SMITH

Clint Smith

It's our pleasure to introduce this great young fly tier from Nampa, Idaho. His skills far surpass his seventeen years of age, but he got a good start. Clint spent his pre-teen years exposed to a wealth of knowledge while hanging out in Boise's busiest fly shop. Employees and patrons alike were always willing to share their experience with an attentive young person. With knowledge so available, Clint soon grew into an avid fly-fisher and tier. With this great foundation he continues to blossom in both areas.

Growing up in southwest Idaho, the birthplace of the float tube, Clint had the opportunity to fish many magnificent lakes and blue-ribbon trout streams from a very young age. He enjoys tying bluegill and steelhead flies (you should see his awesome Spey flies). Clint is rapidly becoming an excellent Atlantic salmon fly tier. He credits Mick Miller, Ken Magee, Dave Tucker, and his dad Jeff Smith with much of his growth. On a more recent basis he credits your authors with his development in trout-fly techniques. He offers a special thank you to those who helped him get to where he is today.

Clint will be in his senior year of high school next year and hopes to work in the fly-fishing field while completing his studies and continuing on to college. He is leaning towards a major in natural resources, which would complement his love of fishing and the outdoors. He feels privileged to have the support of a family that also enjoys spending time in the open air. There is never a lack of people to fish with in his home. Clint considers it an honor and privilege to participate in this book and share what he has learned in his short seventeen years.

Clint is a modest person and neglected to share some of his accomplishments, so we'll do it for him. He is the youngest member ever of the Boise Valley Fly Fishermen's Board of Directors, has chaired several committees for club functions, and is a great demonstration fly tier. We predict you haven't seen the last of Clint Smith and expect to see his name in print before many years go by.

Bead Head Stepchild

Clint's dad Jeff wanted to incorporate several elements of existing proven patterns into one fly. It has become one of the "go to" patterns for those anglers lucky enough to make its acquaintance, including your authors. It has taken many trout and is Clint's favorite bluegill fly. The pattern represents just about everything a fish wants to see, from a leech to a baby crayfish.

The weighted shank gives the fly a distinct football shape and the bead provides a jigging action. Here we've illustrated the fly tied with Canadian brown SLF, but other colors are equally effective. We believe this color is best to represent the baby crayfish in our area, but purple is great for attracting bass. Don't let its simplicity fool you! It's a very productive pattern.

Bead Head Stepchild

Hook:	Size 6-14, 2XL nymph
Thread:	Tan
Weight:	Non-lead wire
Tail:	Grizzly dyed brown marabou
Body:	Canadian SLF dubbing
Horns:	White biots
Collar:	Peacock herl
Head:	Bead

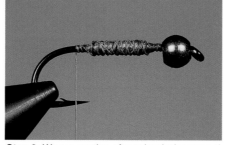

Step 1: Slip a bead on the hook, slide it forward to the eye, and mount the hook in the vise. Apply a thread base that starts behind the bead and ends at the back of the hook.

Step 2: Wrap a section of non-lead wire around the hook shank covering much of the thread base. Crisscross wrap the thread over the wire to further anchor it, ending up at the back of the hook.

Step 3: Select a grizzly marabou feather over-dyed brown and tie it to the hook as a tail equal in length to the shank. Trim off the excess material.

Step 4: Form a loop of thread at the back of the hook, place Canadian color SLF in it, and twist it into a dubbing brush. Wind the thread forward to the bead and leave it there for a moment. Wrap the twisted brush forward, tie it off at the bead, and trim away the excess material.

Step 5: Select two white biots and tie them on the hook behind the bead as horns. Trim away the waste ends.

Step 6: Tie on a strand of peacock herl between the horns and the bead. Wrap it to form a collar, tie it off, and remove the waste piece. Whip finish and remove the thread from the hook. Apply a drop of Aqua Head to the whip finish to complete the pattern.

Clint's Dragon

Hours of seining and observing at local, stillwater fisheries inspired Clint to develop this fly. A dragonfly is high-calorie food causing a motivated fish to strike aggressively. His pattern is very effective on all species that live in the waters frequented by dragonflies.

Double lead wire provides the large profile of the natural insect and also sinks the fly like it was a rock. The copper wire rib provides segmentation and durability to the plastic shellback. The CDC tail gives the illusion of the anal gills of a natural insect.

Clint's Dragon

Hook:	Size 2-10, curved nymph
Thread:	Tan
Eyes:	Colored bead chain
Weight:	Non-lead wire
Rib:	Copper wire
Tail:	Tuft of CDC
Body:	Peacock green dubbing
Shellback:	Clear plastic bag
Legs:	Hungarian partridge, collar style
Head:	Peacock green dubbing

Step 1: Place the hook in the vise and apply a short thread base behind the eye. Cut a two-bead section from a length of colored chain and mount it on the hook as eyes using several crisscross wraps. Wind the thread back on the shank stopping even with the point. Double wrap a strand of non-lead wire to heavily weight the hook. Anchor the application in place with several back and forth wraps.

Step 2: Select a short tuft of natural CDC and tie it to the hook behind the non-lead wire turns. Trim the waste end. Notice the tail material fills in the area behind the lead.

Step 3: Tie on a section of copper wire to the under side of the hook to use as a rib in a future step. Cut a strip of clear sandwich bag that is not quite as wide as the hook gape and tie it to the top of the shank so it is sticking out the back of the hook. Apply wax and dubbing to the thread and construct a body that covers the back 2/3 of the hook shank.

Step 4: Pull the plastic strip over the top of the body, bind it to the hook, and trim off the excess. Advance the copper wire forward as a rib to segment the body and provide a bit of flash.

Step 5: Prepare a Hungarian partridge feather by stripping off the fuzzy material near the base of the stem. Tie the prepared stem to the hook and wrap a one-turn collar. Wrap the tying thread tight against it to force the collar back wet style.

Step 6: Apply dubbing to the thread and construct a head around the eyes. Whip finish and remove the thread, then apply a coating of Aqua Head to complete the fly.

Red Ass Willy

In the early 90's, at Sheep Creek Reservoir near Owyhee, Nevada, Ken Magee was enjoying great fishing using a little red midge pattern. Unfortunately he lost them all on big fish and had to find a substitute fly. He resorted to using materials available in his tying kit and also the pattern had to be simple because spending time tying flies when the fish were going crazy wasn't in his game plan. The RAW was the result and it proved to be a fly that outfished the one he was trying to substitute.

Its greatest attribute (beside catching fish) is its ease of tying and use of common materials. The floss tail provides illumination and action while the peacock rib defines segmentation. Besides, who ever saw a bad fly with peacock herl in it? Clint acknowledges Ken Magee as the originator of this super simple but effective pattern. We found the RAW one of our best patterns for stillwater and often coat the body with Aqua Flex before wrapping the rib to improve its durability.

Red Ass Willy

Hook:	Size 8-20, wet fly
Thread:	Red
Weight:	Non-lead wire
Tail:	Red floss
Body:	Red floss
Rib:	Peacock herl
Counter Rib:	Copper wire, optional
Eyes:	Stick on, optional

Step 1: Place the hook in the vise and apply a thread base over the complete hook shank. Wrap several turns of non-lead wire over the thread base then crisscross wrap the thread over it to further anchor it. The thread should be hanging at the back of the hook.

Step 2: Select two strands of red floss and tie them to the top of the shank while advancing the thread forward to the hook eye. Trim off the waste end then cut the floss tail to length; we like it almost as long as the hook shank. Leave the thread at the back of the hook.

Step 3: Tie on a single peacock herl while advancing the thread to the front of the hook. Trim off the waste piece. Tie on a strand of red floss at the front of the hook, wrap it to the end of the shank, and back forward to the eye. Tie it off and remove the waste end.

Step 4: Wrap the peacock herl forward to form the rib, tie it off, and trim the remainder. Wrap a fairly large thread head, whip finish, and remove it from the hook. Apply a coating of Aqua Head to the whip finish to complete the fly. An option copper wire rib (counter wrapped) can also be added or stick-on eyes coated with Aqua Flex, it's the tier's choice.

JEFF SMITH

The painted fly plates of Preston Jennings, Ray Bergman, and Joe Brooks inspired Jeff's youthful attempts at tying flies. Shortly after the discovery of his deceased grandfather's cane rod in a basement corner he needed a steady supply of them to use on the local drainage ditches. Few pursuits have drawn Jeff away from the tying bench in the more than thirty years that followed his infection.

He could not have been born in a better place than the southwest corner of Idaho, the birthplace of float-tube fly-fishing. Thanks to a patient Dad and Mom (she drove him to fly-tying classes in the evenings), Jeff mastered trout and panfish flies under the influence of Ken Magee, Ruel Stayner, Marv Taylor, and many more of the float-tube crowd.

In the mid 80's he met David Tucker, who at that time was the Boise area's only practicing tier of the full-dress Atlantic salmon fly. Dave has been a true friend and mentor in all of the years since, sharing many great hunting and fishing adventures. Jeff believes Dave has influenced his ability and style more than any other person he has met. He continues to learn the art and science of fly dressing, very few days go by that he doesn't spend at least a few hours at the vise.

Jeff's wife Debbie and sons Clint and Steve (both accomplished fly tiers) have been his biggest supporters over the last twenty years.

Jeff Smith

Debbie lives among an endless supply of furs, feathers, rods, reels, lines, and, don't forget, the dyes in her kitchen with very little complaint. Clint and Steve are always ready to go fishing or hunting, he never has to look far to find good companions.

Jeff maintains a very strong belief that our young people will be the means to conserve the resource that we all love. He is therefore a strong supporter of the Federation of Fly Fishers and the local affiliate club, the Boise Valley Fly Fishermen. Jeff is twice past and also current president of the BVFF, Debbie is the Treasurer/Banquet Chair, and Clint is the youngest member of the board of directors. Jeff has also been the fly-tying chair for the rapidly growing Treasure Valley Fly Fishing Seminar.

Jeff lives with Debbie and the boys in Nampa, Idaho. This location allows them many diverse outdoor opportunities. Self-employment offers Jeff the freedom to spend time enjoying his passion (Debbie says obsession) with fishing and hunting pursuits. The fly-tying bench is a focal point in the Smith home. Seldom do visitors leave without a few flies or a great exchange of ideas.

Barney

The fly was developed during the time Jeff's children were watching the popular purple dinosaur on television. At the time very few anglers were fishing Spey-style flies on Idaho's steelhead waters. Inspired by the elegant flies in the patterns books he studied, Jeff designed a fly using the colors most successful for him at that time.

He suggests using one piece of tinsel to make the tip and then as an under wrap for the tag. When constructed in this manner, the floss tag's color is much more brilliant when wet. Mounting the bronze mallard wings takes a bit of practice, but having good-quality materials is most important of all. Jeff cautions, "Pick good quality matching duck plumage and don't try to use too much of each feather as there is a limited number of good usable wing sections in the center of each."

Barney

Hook:	Size 2/0-4, salmon
Thread:	White
Tag:	Gold tinsel, fluorescent green floss
Tag Rib:	Fine gold wire
Tail:	Dyed red pheasant crest feather
Body:	Purple floss, purple Seal-EX
Rib:	Silver oval tinsel
Body Hackle:	Blue ear pheasant feather
Hackle Collar:	Teal, one side stripped
Wing:	Bronze mallard, tent style
Cheeks:	Jungle cock
Head:	Black thread

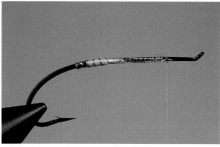

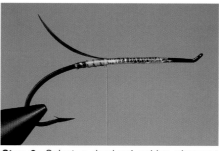

Step 1: Mount the hook in the vise and apply a white thread base from the eye platform back to a position directly above the point. Tie a section of fine gold wire to the under side of the shank and store it in a material keeper. Also on the under side of the hook, tie on a piece of flat gold tinsel. Wrap several turns of tinsel to form the "tip" part of a tag then wind it forward forming an under wrap for the floss part of the tag. Tie it off, but do not trim the waste end. Tie on a strand of fluorescent green floss, wrap it back to meet the tinsel tip, and then forward to its starting place. Tie it off on the under side of the hook and again do not trim away the excess floss. Take the gold wire out of the material keeper and wrap it over the tip/tag assembly forming a five-turn rib. Tie it off, then advance the thread forward to the looped-eye platform binding the wire, tinsel, and floss to the bottom of the hook. Now cut off the waste ends.

Step 2: Select a dyed-red golden pheasant crest feather and strip off the fuzzy material at the base of the stem. Tie it on the top of the shank to form a tail that is as long as the width of the gape of the hook. Notice it is tied along the complete length of the shank to also provide a smooth under body. Leave the thread at the back of the hook.

Step 3: Attach a section of silver oval tinsel to the bottom of the hook while advancing the thread forward to the eye platform and then back to the center of the hook. Mentally divide the remaining part of the hook into thirds and construct a floss body-part on the rear 1/3. Select a blue-eared pheasant feather, fold the fibers, and tie it on the hook by its tip. Form a thread loop, place purple Seal-Ex in it, and twist it into a dubbing brush. Wrap the thread forward and follow it with the dubbing brush forming the front 2/3 of the body. Fuzz up the fibers with a bodkin or dubbing picking tool. Tie off the white thread and attach the black.

Step 4: Wrap the silver tinsel forward forming a five-turn rib. Tie it off and trim away the waste end.

Step 5: Wrap the blue-eared pheasant feather forward tight against the three forward turns of rib. Tie it off and trim the waste end.

Step 6: Strip the fibers from one side of a teal feather, tie it to the hook by its tip at the eye platform, and wrap a single-turn hackle collar. Tie it off and trim away the excess feather.

Step 7: Select two slips of bronze mallard from matching feathers and tie them to the hook as tent wings long enough to reach the end of the tail. Trim the waste ends. We often use a cauterizing tool to burn away any errant fibers, but must also exercise caution to avoid burning the thread.

Step 8: Match a pair of jungle cock nails and strip off the fuzzy material below the white part of the stem. Tie them to the sides of the fly to form cheeks, then trim the waste ends. Wrap a thread head, whip finish, and remove it from the hook. Apply a coating of Aqua Flex to the head and place the hook on a rotating wheel so the glue will dry to a smooth, even finish.

Lava Point Crawdad

This pattern was developed over the course of several summers of experimentation while pursuing Snake River smallmouth bass and channel catfish. Since the early 90's it has produced most of the large bass and catfish Jeff and his companions have caught. It has also fooled brown and rainbow trout on a variety of waters throughout the West.

The months of June and July have proven to be, by far, the most productive time frame to fish this fly. In larger boulder-strewn water, try fishing it dead drift under a large strike indicator. On waters with a sandy or gravel base, use a sinking line just dense enough to reach bottom then retrieve it in short hops and jerks.

Lava Point Crawdad

Hook:	Size 2/0-2, offset worm
Thread:	Tan
Mouthparts:	Krystal Flash, dyed deer hair
Weight:	Dumbbell eyes, non-lead wire
Claws:	Grizzly dyed brown marabou
Body:	Canadian SLF, dubbing brush
Rib:	Copper wire
Legs:	Grizzly dyed brown hackle
Carapace/Wing:	Grizzly dyed brown marabou

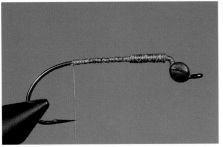

Step 1: Place an offset-worm hook in the vise and apply a thread base that covers the short section behind the eye. Tie on a set of dumbbell eyes in the corner of the offset using several crisscross wraps. We suggest further anchoring them with a drop of Krazy Glue. Wrap the thread around the corner and half way down the shank. Place several turns of non-lead wire on the front part of the shank then crisscross wrap the thread to further anchor them. Wrap the thread to the end of the shank and leave it there for the next step.

Step 2: Select, clean, and stack a clump of dyed reddish-brown deer hair. Trim the butt ends after stacking the clump and flare it in place near the end of the hook shank. We like to position this clump of hair slightly past the end of the shank into the start of the hook bend.

Step 3: Prepare two brown marabou feathers by stripping off the fuzzy material at the base of the stems. Tie the first one on the off side of the hook against the flared deer hair. Repeat the process on the near side of the hook to complete a set of claws. Tie on several strands of pearl Krystal Flash to complete the mouthparts. Notice the flared deer hair keeps the marabou claws spread apart.

Step 4: Tie on a section of copper wire and temporarily store it in the material keeper. Prepare a grizzly dyed brown hackle feather by stripping away the fuzzy material at the base of the stem. Tie it to the hook at the end of the shank. Form a loop of thread and place Canadian color SLF dubbing it. Wrap the thread forward to the eyes. Twist the loop to form a dubbing brush then wrap it forward to the front of the hook where it meets the eyes, forming the body. Tie it off and trim away the extra material.

Step 5: Place the tip of the feather in a pair of hackle pliers and palmer it over the back half of the body. Allow the weight of the hackle pliers to temporarily hold the wrapped feather in place. Counter wrap the copper rib through the hackle and forward to the front of the hook. Tie it off and trim away the waste end. The counter-wrapped rib also anchored the palmered hackle into position, so trim off the excess feather hanging near the center of the hook.

Step 6: Turn the hook over in the jaws or rotate the head depending on the type of vise used. Tie on a grizzly/brown marabou feather as a wing/carapace. Whip finish and remove the thread from the hook. Apply a coating of Aqua Head to the whip finish to complete the fly. Notice we photographed the fly with the jaws rotated a half turn.

Max Canyon Spey

This pattern evolved from Jeff's affection for orange and black steelhead flies. Being somewhat overdressed, it deviates from classic Spey-fly style, however, fished greased line it has a great deal of motion under very little tension. When fished deep on the swing it has a very definite profile.

Jeff suggests picking your Spey hackle with care looking for fine stems and fibers to aid in tying and fishing. Wrapping the hackle from the butt or root of the feather will cause it to stand out from the body. He prefers to use natural black feathers for the collar due to their iridescent color.

Note: In the Fly Pattern Encyclopedia *on page 140, the center fly should have been identified as the Max Canyon (a Doug Stewart fly). Our thanks to Jeff for helping set the record straight and sharing one of his favorite flies in the process.*

Max Canyon Spey

Hook:	Size #2/0 - #4, salmon
Thread:	White
Rib:	Gold oval tinsel
Body Hackle:	Orange saddle
Body:	Orange floss, black Seal-EX
Hackle Collar:	Black saddle or schlappen
Wings:	Four white saddle feathers
Head:	Black thread

Step 1: Place the hook in the vise and apply a white thread base from the looped-eye platform to a position directly above the throat of the barb. Select a section of gold oval tinsel and tie it to the bottom of the hook using two thread wraps. Do not trim the waste end yet. Prepare an orange saddle hackle feather by stripping off the fuzzy fibers at the base of the stem. Tie the stripped stem on the bottom of the hook adjacent to the tinsel. Wrap the thread forward anchoring the stem and the tinsel to the bottom of the shank. Stop at the looped-eye platform and trim off any waste of the two materials. Tie off the white thread and attach black for the rest of the steps.

Step 2: Wrap the thread to the center of the hook and tie on a length of orange single-strand floss. Wrap the floss from the center of the hook to the end of the shank and back to its starting point. Tie it off and trim away the waste end. Form a dubbing loop of thread, place black Seal-EX into it, and twist the unit to form a brush. Wrap the thread forward to the eye platform then follow with the dubbing brush. Tie it off and clip the waste end from the hook.

Step 3: Wrap the oval tinsel forward forming a five-turn rib, tie it off, and trim the unused portion. Use a bodkin to fluff out the dubbing or Jeff's favorite picking tool, a cleaning brush for a rifle.

Step 4: Advance the hackle placing each turn tight against the rib. Stroke the fibers back after each wrap to produce a swept-back, Spey-body hackle. Tie off the feather and clip the waste end.

Step 5: Tie a black saddle hackle feather on the front of the hook by its tip. Fold the fibers then wrap a three-turn collar. Tie off the feather and trim the waste end from the hook.

Step 6: Match four white saddle hackle feather. Even the tips and tie them on the shank as wings that are long enough to reach the end of the hook. Trim off the waste ends, wrap a thread head, whip finish, and remove the thread from the hook. Apply a coating of Aqua Flex to the head to finish the fly. Place the fly on a rotating wheel so the Aqua Flex will dry to a smooth, even finish.

BRUCE STAPLES

It took a few years for Stan Yamamura, Bruce's colleague in analytical chemistry at the Idaho National Engineering Laboratory, to convince him that fly-tying would make him a better fly-fisher. Bruce was sure it was a waste of time for him to tie flies when he could buy them from Stan at the same price per dozen that a single Rapalla minnow cost. Stan finally wore Bruce down and he took up fly-tying during the winter of 1973. By the end of the following summer he definitely understood what Stan had been trying to tell him.

The Upper Snake River Chapter of TU, now the Snake River Cutthroats (a combination FFF/TU Club), was formed in the early 70's. One of its functions each winter was a fly-tying class that Stan taught. Bruce, now totally hooked on fly tying, became his helper. By 1976 Stan moved to Arizona to take up private employment and Bruce assumed the responsibility of teaching the class, starting a 26-year tenure as a fly tying instructor. Later, as club president, Bruce became familiar with the Federation of Fly Fishers goals and joined the organization. About that time Charlie Brooks was one of the club's banquet speakers where he extended an invitation for all present to attend the FFF Conclave, then held in West Yellowstone, Montana. Bruce tells us, "I attended my first Conclave in 1983 and there met Darwin Atkin heading up the fly tying demonstrations. I asked him how one got to take part. His reply was, 'All you have to do is ask.' That was my start at a twenty-plus-year tour as a demonstration fly tier." *Author's note: Bruce is such a good demonstrator that he received the 2001 Buz Buszek Memorial Award for fly tying excellence (the highest award a fly-tier can receive).*

Bruce Staples

By the mid 80's, fly-tying and fly-fishing had expanded into more than just the pursuit of large trout for Bruce. The urge to put something back into this great sport emerged. Bruce further advises, "What easier way could there be than writing to pass on experiences and skills to others? Thus began my contributions to fly-tying and fly-fishing magazines. Within a few years this did not seem as fulfilling as I first thought. I had begun to visit tying shows around the West and saw misrepresentation with respect to fly-tying creativity. Some involved east Idaho patterns, and I resolved to see due credit given to tiers from that region." This goal in conjunction with his conviction that east Idaho hosted some of the finest, yet unheralded trout waters inspired his first book, *Snake River Country Flies and Waters,* published by Frank Amato Publications. It was a great success and is still selling today. A few years later Frank Amato agreed to publish his second book, the *Yellowstone Park River Journal.* Its purpose was to show the fly-fishing world that the Park's best fishing was not just along its roads. Bruce closes, "From that time to the present, while working with Frank Amato's staff to produce my third book, *Trout-Country Flies,* I have realized that real joy in fly-fishing includes preserving its heritage and educating with respect to its many facets." *Author's note: Bruce and his lovely wife Carol make their home in Idaho Falls, Idaho. We are certainly proud to call them friends!*

Tri-Color Marabou Muddler

Dan Bailey gets credit for creating the Marabou Muddler. Since its inception in the 1940's this pattern has become one of the world's most popular streamers. Bailey tied it with various colored wings. It has been used for trout, warmwater species, and saltwater sport fish. Many trout fishers credit it with being perhaps the most effective brown-trout pattern available. Not long after Bailey's original appeared, modifications began, including multi-colored wings. Bruce has tied the Marabou Muddler with three wing colors for at least two decades. In his versions, Bruce places the lightest shade of marabou on the bottom, an intermediate color in the middle, and the darkest on top. The color scheme we

present here today is one he finds particularly effective.

His favorite place to fish this fly is Shoshone Lake in Yellowstone Park. Bruce uses a float tube or boat to present it on a full-sink line to get the fly deep into the water around the weed beds. In streams he presents the pattern on a sink-tip line using both weighted and non-weighted flies on short leaders based on the water's depth. Bruce tells us, "The Tri-Color Marabou Muddler is one of my most effective patterns on the Lewis, Salt, Madison, Snake, Little Wood, and the lower Henry's Fork rivers." We certainly agree with Bruce's assessment, it's a pattern that has served us well for a number of years.

Tri-Color Marabou Muddler

Hook:	Size 2-12, Mustad 9672
Thread:	Gray
Tail:	Red bucktail
Body:	Gold or silver Sparkle Braid
Wing:	Three colors of marabou
Topping:	Peacock herl
Collar & Head:	Deer hair

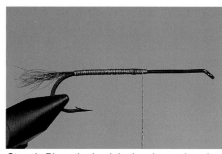

Step 1: Place the hook in the vise and apply a thread base that covers the back half of the hook shank. Select a sparse clump of red bucktail and clean out the under fur. Stack the hair and tie it on the hook as a tail that is as long as 1/4 the length of the shank. Trim off any waste ends and leave the thread near the center of the hook.

Step 2: Form the body by wrapping Sparkle Braid around the rear 3/4 of the shank. Durability is improved if the Sparkle Braid is spiraled around the tying thread in the same manner performed on dubbing and then wrapping the body. Tie it off at the 1/4 point and trim away the waste end.

Step 3: Select a clump of white marabou and tie it on the hook near the 1/4 point. Apply a clump of orange marabou then follow it with a bundle of purple to finish the wing assembly. Trim any waste ends.

Step 4: Select several peacock herls and even the tips. Tie them on the hook as a wing topping and trim off the waste ends.

Step 5: Select a clump of deer hair, remove the under fur, even the tips in a stacker, and spin it to form a deer-hair collar. Spin a couple more clumps of deer that will eventually form the head. Whip finish and remove the thread.

Step 6: Use a pair of scissors to shape the head. Apply a coating of Aqua Head to finish the fly allowing the liquid to soak into the spun/trimmed hair.

MARK STEVENS

Mark Stevens

Mark Stevens was introduced to fly-fishing and fly-tying by his family on the streams and reservoirs of central Colorado, most notably on the various sections of the South Platte River.

When his family relocated to northern Virginia in 1980, Mark learned to chase bluegills and largemouth bass with flies he'd learned to tie from his brothers and from books he'd read on the subject. After graduating George Mason University with a bachelor's in History, Mark began to take fly-fishing more seriously and started chasing smallmouth bass on Virginia's Shenandoah River and its tributaries, where he also introduced his longtime friend, Tom Hawley (featured elsewhere in this book), to fly-fishing. Soon, trout were calling his name again, and he began fishing the spring creeks of the Shenandoah Valley, as well as the native brook trout streams of Shenandoah National Park.

In 1995, Mark's professional life took him to State College, Pennsylvania where he had the opportunity to learn more about eastern spring creeks and freestone streams. In his free time, he fished for trout on such notable streams as Spring Creek and the Letort. He also spent many hours learning more advanced fly-tying techniques for both trout and bass flies and began studying entomology.

From Pennsylvania, he moved to Boise, Idaho in 1996. Idaho proved to be important to his career, both in business and in fly-fishing. Mark soon began working part-time at Anglers, a local Orvis fly shop

and tying flies on the side. There he began teaching casting, entomology, and fly-tying classes. When he wasn't working, Mark plied the many rivers of Idaho, including Silver Creek, the Big Wood, the South Fork of the Boise, and the Henry's Fork. Mark also developed a strong fondness for Yellowstone National Park and its famous streams, including the Firehole, Gibbon, and Slough Creek.

Diversity is important to Mark with regard to fishing opportunities and he soon drifted into the warm-water options of Idaho, including carp. He became something of a local cult-figure on carp fishing on the Snake River, and gave a number of seminars to local clubs and fly-fishing shows on carp and carp tactics. He also delved into high-mountain lake fishing and steelheading on the Salmon River.

Mark continued to teach fly-tying and branched into specialty classes, teaching applied entomology and advanced tying techniques, including deer-hair spinning, flaring, and stacking. Teaching classes naturally led him to guiding and he began working for a local outfitter, guiding on Oregon's Owyhee and Grande Ronde rivers.

In addition to teaching, Mark had the opportunity to write a weekly fly-fishing column for a local newspaper.

Ed Sullivan

A mayfly emerger Mark had seen tied on a swimming nymph hook served as the inspiration for the Ed Sullivan. The original design was focused on this style of hook and he tied it to represent an emerging adult brown drake (*Ephemera simulans*).

While fishing this prototype pattern on Idaho's Silver Creek, Mark realized he was sitting on top of a gold mine. Fish took this fly more readily than any other brown drake pattern he had ever used. He told his fishing partner that the fly was like Ed Sullivan, "It put on a really good show".

However, the fly had a fatal flaw; it wouldn't hook fish. While the

swimming nymph hook presented a great profile to the fish, when tied upside down to support a dry fly, the hook point sat above the fly. Mark realized during the hook-set that the point actually rolled out of the fish's mouth.

To correct the problem, he opted to use a hopper hook, bent at midshank. With the hook point now under the fly, not only did fish greedily take the pattern, it hooked them as well. Mark suggests a slightly exaggerated wing to improve visibility since brown drakes hatch at dusk and into the night. He also explains that this style of emerger, tied on smaller hooks, can be used to represent many species of mayflies.

Ed Sullivan

Hook:	Size 10, 3XL streamer
Thread:	Golden olive
Tail:	Mixed brown Z-lon and marabou fibers
Abdomen:	Brown marabou
Rib:	Copper wire
Thorax:	Golden olive dubbing
Wing:	Brown polypropylene
Hackle:	Grizzly dyed brown, parachute style

Step 1: Use a pair of pliers to place a bend in the hook shank then place it in the vise. Wrap thread from the eye to the top of the bend. Tie on a sparse clump of brown Z-lon for an under tail then top it with the tips of a marabou feather. Do not cut off the excess marabou. Tie on a section of copper wire to later use as the rib.

Step 2: Wrap the waste ends of marabou forward to the center of the hook, tie them off, and trim the excess. Counter wind the copper rib forward to meet the thread, tie it off, and also trim the remainder.

Step 3: Advance the thread forward to the middle of the front half of the hook. Select a clump of brown poly yarn and tie it to the under side of the hook with several cross wraps, like tying on a spinner wing. Pull up on the yarn bringing it on both sides of the hook then construct a parachute platform and the wing post as well.

Step 4: Select a dyed grizzly hackle and strip the fuzzy material from the base end of the stem. Tie the prepared feather to the hook making certain to bind it to the parachute post.

Step 5: Apply dubbing to the thread and construct a thorax behind and in front of the wings. Leave the thread hanging at the hook eye.

Step 6: Wrap the hackle around the post parachute style and tie it off at the hook eye. Trim the waste end of the feather, whip finish, and remove the thread. Trim the poly yarn at a slight angle to better represent a mayfly wing. Apply a coating of Aqua Head to finish the fly.

Big Wood Green Drake Nymph

One of Mark's favorite rivers in Idaho is the Big Wood River in Sun Valley. Although it is a great year-round fishery, he particularly likes to fish it in the winter.

While fishing the "Wood" one winter, Mark came across quite a few green drake nymphs in the water. The river is known for its great summer hatch, it has nymphs in the water all year. He began experimenting to create the ultimate pattern. What Mark ultimately settled on was a cross between the LePage Bead Head Mayfly Nymph and A.K. Best's Tri-color Nymph.

Nymph-fishing winter streams usually requires the use of small nymphs, but he finds that by fishing a larger fly, in combination with smaller droppers, one's catch rate goes up dramatically. The Big Wood Green Drake Nymph's "sandwiched bead head" offers several advantages. It weights the fly sufficiently enough to reach fish quickly and it adds just enough flash to help attract fish, without being so flashy as to startle them. In addition, Mark believes the more realistic look provided by the shellback encourages fish to strike that have "seen everything."

Big Wood Green Drake Nymph

Hook:	Size 10, nymph hook
Thread:	Olive
Weight:	Gold bead head
Tail:	Pheasant-tail fibers
Body:	Olive dun rabbit dubbing
Rib:	Gold wire
Shellback:	Turkey-tail fibers
Legs:	Dyed olive hen back

Step 1: Slip a bead on the hook, mount it in the vise, and slide the bead all the way to the eye. Apply a thread base that starts behind the bead and goes to the end of the shank. Tie on the gold wire for the rib while advancing the thread back to the hook center. Store the rib in a material keeper for now. Select several pheasant-tail fibers and tie them to the hook as a tail that is as long and 3/4 of the shank. Trim off any excess and leave the thread at the back of the hook.

Step 2: Select a slip of turkey tail that is about as wide as the distance of the hook gape. Tie it to the back of the hook with the shiny side facing down; it will be up when folded over in a future step. Dub the back half of the hook with rabbit dubbing. Leave the thread hanging at the front of the dubbed abdomen.

Step 3: Pull the turkey slip over and bind it to the hook in front of the abdomen. Do not cut off the excess. Remove the rib wire from the material keeper and wrap it over the abdomen. Tie if off and trim away the waste. Pull the turkey slip back and wrap a couple of turns to anchor it in that position.

Step 4: Select a hen back feather, tie it on top of the turkey by its tip, and trim off the waste. Dub a small segment to cover the thread wraps. Whip finish and remove the thread.

Step 5: Attach the thread in front of the bead. Force the bead head back into the dubbing and dub in front of body (sandwiching the bead head into the thorax). Pull the hen back feather over the bead head, tie it off, and trim away the waste end. The legs should fall along both sides of the fly.

Step 6: Pull the turkey slip over to form the wing case, tie it off at the hook eye, and trim off the excess material. Whip finish and remove the thread. Complete the fly with an application of Aqua Head over whip finish.

Shenandoah Crayfish

Fly-fishing for smallmouth bass on Virginia's Shenandoah River was an early passion for Mark. While honing his skills as a fly-caster, he also spent many hours practicing fly-tying.

Smallmouth bass are particularly fond of crayfish and Mark soon began experimenting with those patterns. A number of features stood out and became important in the development of the fly. Soft rabbit claws not only imitated molting crayfish, they also gave the fly a more realistic look and didn't "plane" in the water like stiffer materials would. Deer hair proved to be a great shellback because individ-ual fibers could be left long to imitate the antennae. As fish chewed the deer hair, it splayed out, making the fly even more effective. Chenille had the advantage of being very durable and very easy to work with.

The result was the Shenandoah Crayfish. This fly has effectively taken smallmouth bass in Virginia, Pennsylvania, and Idaho. It is also a deadly carp fly. One option is to tie the fly "upside down" on the hook and add lead eyes below the tail. This version works particularly well when fishing very stony waters, as the fly is less likely to snag.

Shenandoah Crayfish

Hook:	Size 4-8, 3XL streamer
Thread:	Rusty brown
Weight:	Non-lead wire or dumbbell eyes
Body:	Rusty-brown chenille
Claws:	Rusty-brown rabbit fur
Shellback:	Brown-dyed deer hair
Legs:	Brown hackle
Rib:	Tying thread
Crayfish Tail:	Brown deer hair

Step 1: Place the hook in the vise and apply a thread base that covers the complete shank. Leave the thread at the back of the hook. Select, clean, and stack a clump of dyed-brown deer hair. Tie it to the end of the shank by the butts then add a section of chenille. Trim any waste ends then coat the thread base with head cement. Wrap several turns of non-lead wire covering most of the hook. Wrap back and forth over the wire with the tying thread to further secure it. Leave the thread at the back of the hook.

Step 2: Wrap a couple of turns of chenille stopping at the hook point. Tie it off and place the loose end in a material keeper for future reference. Tie a clump of rusty brown rabbit fur/guard hairs to the off side of the hook tight against the wrapped chenille. Repeat the process on the near side of the hook.

Step 3: Prepare a brown hackle feather by removing the fuzzy material at the base of the stem and tie it to the hook above the point. Wrap the thread forward to the 1/3 position, then wrap the chenille forward to meet it. Tie the chenille off, but do not trim the excess.

Step 4: Palmer the hackle forward to meet the thread. Tie it off and trim away the waste end. Wrap the thread forward to the hook eye.

Step 5: Wrap the chenille forward to the hook eye, tie it off, and trim away the waste end. Wind the tying thread back over the chenille until it meets the palmered hackle. Trim the top of the hackle.

Step 6: Pull the deer hair across the back of the fly and secure it at the end of the palmered hackle. Advance the tying thread forward to the hook eye binding the deer hair into a carapace. Allow the remaining hair to hang over the eye to form the crayfish tail. Whip finish under the hair then trim the thread from the hook. Apply a coating of Aqua Head to finish the fly.

PAUL STIMPSON

Paul tells us, "My father was a fly tier and I should have learned from him, but I delayed too long and he passed away before I got around to it. I felt so bad that I took a fly-tying class within months of his passing. I took the fly-tying kit he willed me and learned from Mims and Bruce Barker at the Fly Line in Ogden, Utah." He claimed to be a slow learner with his wife Char fairing much better in the class than Paul did. Even though he didn't have the natural aptitude, he became obsessed with tying and practiced every day. Paul ended up cutting more flies off their hook than ended up on the stream with him. He stuck with it though and years later Paul was selling flies to the very same shop where he learned to tie.

Because of his interest in fishing and tying Paul found himself giving up on his other hobbies and dedicating himself to spending virtually all of his time at the vise or on the stream. Paul met Steve Shiba from Clearfield, Utah who started a business selling foam flies for bass and saltwater fishing. Paul tied thousands of flies for the new business, Edgewater Fishing Products constructing most of their prototype flies as well as some of their production patterns.

Paul started working in some of the area shops teaching fly-tying classes. Those shops are Eagle Outfitters in Layton, Wild Country Outfitters in Ogden, and Anglers Inn in Salt Lake City. While on a fishing trip to Yellowstone Park, he met Arrick Swanson owner of Arrick's Fly Shop in West Yellowstone. Paul has been tying flies for Arrick's shop for the past eight years.

Paul Stimpson

While attending a seminar in Salt Lake City put on by the Traveling Fly Fishermen, Jack Dennis, Mike Lawson, and Gary LaFontaine, he became interested in Gary's flies. He started tying and fishing them throughout the West with great success. Soon Paul was teaching fly-tying classes of LaFontaine patterns. The next time he met Gary at a show in Provo they discussed flies for hours and a friendship followed. When Gary was diagnosed with ALS he asked Paul to become his "hands" at the shows. From then on Paul tied the steps while Gary manned the microphone.

Paul is a regular demonstrator for the FFF International Conclave so when Gary was presented FFF Man of the Year Award naturally Paul and his wife Char demonstrated fly-tying for him while Gary talked about how to fish them. At that show Paul tells us, "I had a discussion with Al Beatty about how many flies Gary had developed over the years and we decided to approach Gary with the idea of videotaping all of his patterns. Gary was very enthusiastic about the idea." Two years later there are seven videos of Gary LaFontaine's flies featuring instruction by Gary's daughter Heather, Paul and Char Stimpson, and your authors, Al and Gretchen Beatty. It was our pleasure to work with Heather, Gary, Char, and Paul bringing Gary LaFontaine's legacy (his flies) to video.

Bead Thorax Cased Caddis

Paul replaced a dubbed thorax with the chartreuse bead to change a fly originally developed by René Harrop. The turkey slip abdomen very closely resembles the cases built out of bottom debris by many caddis species. Paul has enjoyed super success with this fly for his own fishing and sells many dozens to Arrick's Fly Shop in West Yellowstone, Montana for use on the Madison River.

Paul fishes it as a searching pattern for those days when nothing seems to be happening on the river. Maybe it's because of Gary LaFontaine's theory that caddis are the only aquatic insect to perform a behavior drift during the day; that stoneflies, midges, and mayflies do so at night. Whatever the reason, this is one of our favorite searching patterns because it just seems to work in a variety of situations.

Bead Thorax Cased Caddis

Hook:	Size 8-18, 2XL nymph
Thread:	Black
Thorax:	Chartreuse bead
Rib:	Copper wire
Weight:	Non-lead wire, optional
Case/abdomen:	Turkey tail over dubbing
Legs:	CDC
Head:	Black dubbing

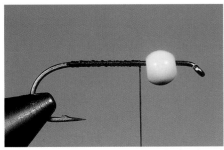

Step 1: Slip a chartreuse bead on the hook and slide it to the front part of the shank. Apply a thread base that starts and returns to the 2/3 position on the hook.

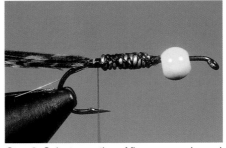

Step 2: Select a section of fine copper wire and tie it to the hook to later use as a rib. Tie a 1/4-inch slip of turkey tail to the end of the shank and trim the waste end. Wrap several turns of non-lead wire if you want to increase the fly's sink rate or leave it off if the bead provides enough weight. If you add the additional weight, then crisscross wrap over the wire to further anchor it in place.

Step 3: Apply any type of dubbing to the thread (we used gray muskrat because it was handy) and wrap an underbody, covering the wire turns. Wrap the turkey quill forward, tie it off, and trim the waste end. Counter wrap the rib, tie it off, and trim away the excess. Whip finish and remove the thread. Place a drop of glue on the whip finish then slide the chartreuse bead back tight against the abdomen/case. Re-attach the tying thread in front of the bead.

Step 4: Select a clump of natural CDC and tie it to the hook in front of the bead. Trim the waste end.

Step 5: Separate the CDC in half, pull it to the off side of the hook, and bind it back to form legs. Repeat the process on the near side of the hook.

Step 6: Apply black or dark brown dubbing to the thread and construct the head. Whip finish and remove the thread. Apply a coat of Aqua Head to the thread wraps to finish the fly.

Enchanted Prince

We first learned about this fly while scripting one of the LaFontaine videos with Gary. Paul was sharing his fishing experience on the Provo River the prior weekend. He had "terrorized" the trout there with a fly he called the Enchanted Prince. Ever curious, Gary immediately wanted to know which fly Paul was using and he sheepishly admitted it wasn't a LaFontaine pattern, but instead it was a Bead Head Prince with a double-magic body (a mix of Antron and pea-cock herl). He wanted to see one so Paul sat down at the vise and tied it for him. Gary wanted it in the next video and that's just what we did.

Since then we have all tested it in various western waters and then compared notes regarding its results. In all instances it outfished a standard Prince better than two to one. We've added double-magic bodies to many of our flies. The technique has not let us down and it seems to be equally effective on either dry or wet flies.

Enchanted Prince

Hook:	Size 6-18, 2XL nymph
Thread:	Black
Bead:	Gold
Tail:	Brown biot
Body:	Peacock, Antron Touch Dubbing
Rib:	Copper wire or silver tinsel, optional
Hackle:	Brown
Wing:	White biots

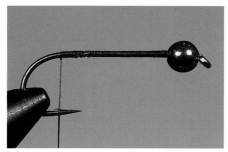

Step 1: Slip a bead on a hook and place it in the vise. Start a thread base behind the bead and wrap it to the end of the shank.

Step 2: Select two brown biots and tie them to the hook as a tail that is about as long as the width of the gape. Trim any waste ends then advance the thread to the bead. Here we will illustrate a method of tying on the white wings that makes them much more durable. Select two white biots and tie them to the hook so they are pointing forward as illustrated. We will reposition them in the last step.

Step 3: Select several peacock herls and tie them to the end of the shank by their tips. Wax the thread then touch the Antron Touch Dubbing to it. The wax will grab the fibers. Do not twist the dubbing into a noodle like you normally would. Fold the thread over to make a dubbing loop then anchor the peacock herl and touch-dubbed thread together in an electronics test clip or hackle pliers. Wrap the bobbin/thread forward to the bead. Here we used green Touch Dubbing because it is very effective in our Idaho waters. Paul usually uses orange because it goes well with the surroundings along the Provo River in Utah.

Step 4: Twist the peacock/dubbing loop to form a chenille rope. Wrap it forward to form a body. Tie it off and trim away the waste ends. Notice the Antron provides additional highlights to the peacock body. Gary LaFontaine calls this technique, double magic. A rib is optional and we elected to leave it off.

Step 5: Prepare a brown hackle feather by stripping the fuzzy material from the base of the stem. Tie it on the hook and wrap a two- or three-turn collar. Tie it off and trim the waste end.

Step 6: Fold the wings over and wrap a thread collar to hold them down. Apply a coating of Aqua Head to the whip finish to complete the fly.

Klod Hopper

Paul advises, "I hate tying hoppers but I love fishing them. I took this problem to the vise to develop a quick, easy tie that would imitate a mature grasshopper, float well, and fool some of the selective fish I've had to deal with lately."

He started with a basic foam design, but when his first attempts were not as successful as Paul felt they should have been he went to the field and caught several hoppers to more closely study them. He got a real surprise when he inspected them up close. First the hoppers from his area did not have yellow bodies instead they had a tan variegated body. Also the kicker legs were large and red. Back at the vise the Klod Hopper was born and became an instant success with the fish and Paul. We must admit it's become our favorite hopper pattern as well and recommend it to all of you.

Klod Hopper

Hook:	Size 6-10, Mustad 9671
Thread:	Dark brown
Body:	Tan craft foam
Hackle:	Brown
Over Body:	Tan dubbing
Wing:	Elk hair
Legs:	Red/black rubber legs

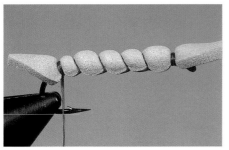

Step 1: Place the hook in the vise and attach the tying thread behind the hook eye. Cut 2mm craft foam into a strip as wide as the hook gape and trim one end so it comes to a blunt point. Position the foam strip so the pointed end sticks out beyond the end of the hook a short distance. Tie it on starting at the front and ending at the end of the shank. Leave the thread there for the next step and do not trim off the extra foam sticking out front.

Step 2: Prepare and tie on a brown hackle. Dub a body that covers the back 3/4 of the shank. Palmer the hackle forward, tie it off, and trim away the waste end. Notice the hackle is sized smaller than normal.

Step 3: Select, clean, and stack a clump of elk hair. Bind it to the hook to form a wing that is as long as the body. Trim away the excess fibers.

Step 4: Select two sections of red/black rubber leg material and tie them both on the near side of the hook with a couple of snug wraps. Reposition one of the leg segments to the off side of the hook then bind them both in place with several tight wraps. Use your scissors to trim them to length.

Step 5: Grab the foam strip remaining from Step 1, pull it over, and bind it to the hook to form the head. Trim away the excess foam. Notice the trimmed end of foam helps hold the wing fibers in place. Whip finish and remove the thread. Apply a coat of Aqua Head to seal the whip finish.

Step 6: A top view of the same fly.

ROGER SWENGEL

Roger Swengel

Since his retirement as a Dispensing Optician, Roger has enjoyed dividing his time between traveling, fly-fishing, fly-tying, and helping his son in his dispensing business. He lives with his wife Nancy in Poulsbo, Washington, a small Norwegian town on the Olympic Peninsula west of Seattle. They have taken several trips to Europe, Canada, and destinations within the States. Roger tells us, "Where ever I travel at home or abroad, I seek out fly shops to visit. I have found some interesting ones in London, Bergen, and Oslo. His travels have included demonstration fly-tying at the Northwest Fly Tyers Exposition in Eugene, Oregon every year since 1994 and the Federation of Fly Fishers 2001 Conclave in Livingston, Montana.

His introduction to fly-fishing came in the early 60's when Roger was living in Grants Pass, Oregon on the Rogue River. A friend took him on a steelhead float trip down the Rogue with a fly-fishing-only guide. Roger remembers, "I hooked my first steelhead, which threatened to drag us all the way down to the Pacific Ocean. He got away, but I was the one that was really hooked!"

Soon after that trip he purchased his first fly rod and reel. In a short time he decided to go the next step when he bought a Herter's fly-tying kit and a copy of Roy Patrick's book, *Pacific Northwest Fly Patterns*. Now Roger was really set!

A career move changed his priorities and pushed fly-fishing to the back burner for the next fifteen years. In the late 70' Roger's son, then newly married, became interested in fly-fishing and tying. He dusted off his equipment and was off again! This time Roger was lucky enough to take a basic and intermediate fly-tying class from renowned instructor Darrell Martin from Tacoma, Washington.

As often happens with people in fly tying, they are first the student and then become the instructor; this happened to Roger. Today he stays busy tying flies, fishing, and teaching fly-tying classes at area fly shops. He comments with a grin, "Now I am really "hooked" on fly tying!"

Liljo

This pattern was a collaborative effort between Roger and his brother-in-law who is sometimes called "Little Joe," thus the name of the fly. They were searching for a candlefish pattern and decided glass beads for the head would be a good idea. The final version grew out of several prototypes as they worked toward their goal.

It is particularly effective when used on the incoming tide, fishing from the beach employing a fast sinking line and retrieving the fly very fast. Sometimes Roger will even place the rod under his arm to facilitate the two-hand retrieve.

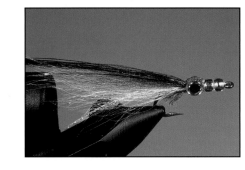

Liljo

Hook:	Size 2-4, salt water
Thread:	White
Head:	Clear glass beads
Eyes:	Spirit River 3-D Molded Eyes, silver
Belly:	White artic fox
Throat:	Red Neon UNI-Yarn
Wing:	Olive over white artic fox
Wing accent:	Pearl Krystal Flash
Topping:	Marine green Sparkle Flash
Eye finish:	Green and red sparkle material
Coating:	Epoxy or Aqua Flex

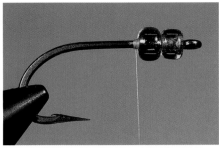

Step 1: Slip two glass beads on a hook and place it in the vise. For the moment, leave the beads at the back of the hook. Attach the thread directly behind the hook eye and build up a thread base large enough to anchor the beads. Whip finish and remove the thread. Coat the thread base with Krazy Glue then slip the two beads into position. Attach the tying thread to the hook again this time behind the beads.

Step 2: Select a small clump of white arctic fox and tie it to the underside of the hook. Tie on two strands of red Neon UNI-Yarn, trim it even with the hook barb, and use a bodkin to pick out the fibers. Trim away any waste ends.

Step 3: Select another small clump of white arctic fox and tie it on top of the hook so it blends in with the belly placed in the last step. Add two strands of pearl Krystal Flash as a wing accent then top that with a small clump of olive arctic fox. Top the arctic fox with several strands of green Sparkle Flash. Trim any waste ends, whip finish, and remove the thread.

Step 4: Flatten the thread base behind the beads using needle-nose pliers. The flattened area is the base on which to install the eyes in the next step.

Step 5: Secure two 3-D Molded Eyes on the flattened thread base with Krazy Glue or epoxy. Allow the glue to dry before continuing.

Step 6: Place a drop of head cement between the eyes (top) and apply a few green sparkle flakes. Turn the fly over and repeat the process with red sparkle flakes. Coat the area between the eyes (top and bottom) with epoxy or Aqua Flex and place fly in a rotating dryer to allow the coating to set up evenly. We like to apply a second coat of epoxy or Aqua Flex that covers the eyes and the glass bead, but this is an optional step.

MIKE TELFORD

Mike has always felt that he was extremely lucky to have grown up in rural areas along the Columbia River near Baker City and Pendleton, Oregon. Outdoor activities were abundant and easily accessed on foot or by riding his bicycle beyond the city limits in pursuit of fish and game. He fondly recalls spending cool summer mornings shooting larger hoppers with his Daisy BB gun and using them as bait in the afternoon honing both his shooting and fishing skills in the same day.

Mike was fortunate also to have adult mentors willing to spend the time and effort to teach him about the outdoors. Among them were Ernie Morrison, Duane Haman, "Doc" Holderness, Bill Herrmann, "Mac" MacDonald, Jerry Allen, Tommy Leggler, Larry Naney and of course his father, Lee Telford. His earliest conscious memory is fishing for perch with his father off the jetties of the Oregon coast, and angling has been a preoccupation in his life since then. Most of all, Mike thanks his father for giving him a love of fishing.

Mike was always curious about fly-fishing and flies, but in remote eastern Oregon there were no opportunities for exposure. The magazine *Outdoor Life* and the television show "American Sportsman" filled his mind with fantasies of exotic trips and fish. He seized the chance to fulfill these fantasies when he was recruited to fill a spot on a trip to Belize in the late 80's where Phil Davis and "Mac" McDonald introduced him to fly-fishing. He was immediately hooked.

Seeking to save some money on flies, Mike purchased some of his

Mike Telford

first patterns from Bob Scheidt a local tier of some renown whom he first met as an equipment repair technician in his business. Seeking to save even more money, he decided to take tying lessons and tie his own flies. Mike bought his first tying kit from one of California's finest tiers, Tommy Leggler. He laughs as he recalls disappearing from his wife and business spending the time driving Tommy crazy with questions about tying techniques. Tommy became his tying "guru" and Bob became an important tying mentor and a treasured fishing companion.

He enjoys tying flies for trout, bass, and salt water and is a self-confessed dubbing junkie. His work may be seen in *Trout Flies of the West* and the *Fly Pattern Encyclopedia*. Mike, his wife Susan, and son Richard currently live in Fresno, California. After a career in the oil industry and as a small businessman, he currently teaches math and science to "at risk" students. His home waters are the lakes and streams of the Sierra Nevada Mountains, Yosemite Park, and the San Joaquin Valley, which offer a diversity of fish species and waters. Mike's passion is creek fishing, but given one last chance to fish, it would be for bluegills, a species that always takes him back to his childhood and that he admires for its tenacity and enthusiasm.

F-86 Damsel

This fly is an updated version of an adult damselfly that the late Ned Long once told Mike was the best he had ever seen. Perhaps Ned was just encouraging a neophyte by asking him for a sample, but Mike received two of Ned's Para-Loops in exchange, along with detailed tying instructions. Mike named this fly after the swept-wing Korean War era fighter because of the swept back wings of the pattern and his awe of the adult insect's flying prowess reminded him of the airplane.

Mike fishes this fly primarily when searching for actively feeding or surface-oriented trout in still water. Spent or trapped adult damsels are a food item routinely seen and eaten by trout. He also fishes the fly as an indicator with a nymph dropper. Mike feels the real advantage of it is the flexible tail, which he feels enhances the hooking capability. Patterns with tails made of stiffer materials can sometimes impede hooking. Mike says he has had bluegills suck the whole fly in so deep that it took forceps to remove it.

F-86 Damsel

Hook:	Size 14, scud
Thread:	Black
Body:	Blue foam strips
Post:	Orange poly yarn
Wings:	Zing Wing material

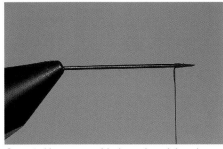

Step 1: Use a razor blade and straight edge to cut a very thin piece of foam at least two inches long. Insert a thin needle in the vise, mount the thread to the end, and trim the waste end. We probably don't need to caution about the needlepoint but we will anyway: be careful!

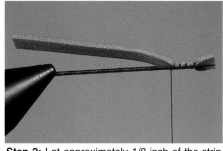

Step 2: Let approximately 1/8 inch of the strip stick out over the needlepoint and make two wraps of thread around the foam and the needle forming the first segment. Lift the foam and place a couple of thread turns around the needle. Pull the strip back down and bind it with a couple of thread turns to form the second segment. Repeat this process constructing a third segment.

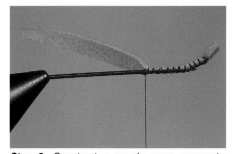

Step 3: Construct a couple more segments then slip the first three off the needle. Continue making segments and slipping them off the needle every three or four applications until an extended body unit is formed that is one inch long. Trim the tail end so it is round and remove the foam from the needle.

Step 4: Remove the needle from the vise and replace it with the hook. Attach the thread to the hook and wrap back on the shank until it is positioned above the point. Bind the extended body to the hook, trim the excess foam, whip finish, and cut the thread from the hook.

Step 5: Use a razor blade and straight edge to cut another piece of foam about one inch long. It should be wider than the strip used in the body. We suggest a strip a little bit narrower than the hook gape. Fold it in half and use a bodkin to punch a hole through it. Slide the eye of the hook through this hole and push the foam back along the shank until it meets the extended body. Reattach the thread to the hook tight against the foam. Cut a strip of Zing Wing two inches long and 1/4 inch wide. Center the wing material and bind it to the hook. Pull the top piece of foam over the wing material and anchor it to the hook. Repeat the process with the foam located on the underside of the shank.

Step 6: Bring the thread forward of the foam and tie on a clump of poly yarn as a parachute post application. Split the top section of foam in half, bring it around the post, bind it to the hook at the eye, and trim the waste ends. Bring the bottom piece of foam forward, tie it to the hook, and trim off the excess material. Apply a whip finish and trim the thread from the hook. Pull the wings back and trim them even with the end of the extended body. Round the wing ends with a pair of scissors leaving them swept back F-86 style. Trim the poly post to length then complete the fly with a coat of Aqua Head on the thread wraps. Mike tells us he also ties another version of this fly in which he adds a parachute hackle to the post.

PD Special

Mike says this pattern has been evolving among his fishing buddies for several years. It is a direct descendant of Denny Rickard's callibaetis nymph. One of Mike fishing buddies, Fred Rameriz added the marabou tail. The fly got its name because another friend spotted it in Fred's box and promptly pointed out that it wouldn't hook fish because the tail was too long. After watching Fred catch more than his fair share of trout they finally agreed that maybe the tail wasn't too long after all and the Pretty Darned Special was born.

Mike likes to fish this fly on an intermediate sinking line using two or three six-inch strips followed by a pause. Repeat the process until a fish takes it. Vary the speed of the retrieve until the fish identify the one they prefer for that day. He often fishes it on an eighteen-inch dropper behind a woolly bugger.

PD Special

Hook:	Size 8-18, 2XL streamer
Thread:	Black
Tail:	Olive marabou
Rib:	Copper wire
Body:	Peacock and ostrich herl, twisted
Back:	Dyed brown mallard
Hackle:	Grizzly dyed burnt orange

Step 1: Place the hook in the vise and lay down a thread base that covers the complete hook shank. Tie on a length of copper wire to later use as a rib and secure it temporarily in a material keeper. Pull a sparse clump of marabou from a feather and tie it on as a tail that is at least as long as the complete hook. Trim any waste ends. We suggest using the waste ends of the materials in this and the next steps as an under body to avoid a lump at the back of the hook. The thread should be located at the end of the shank.

Step 2: Select a slip of dyed-brown mallard flank and trim it from the stem. It should be about as wide as the hook gape. Tie the fibers on the hook by their tips starting at the end of the shank and wrapping forward to the eye. Trim any waste ends then leave the thread there for the next step.

Step 3: Select two peacock herls and one dark ostrich. Starting at the hook eye bind them to the shank ending at the back of the hook.

Step 4: Form a dubbing loop with the thread at the back of the hook, store it for a moment in the material keeper, and advance the tying thread forward to the hook eye. Select a hackle feather (grizzly dyed burnt orange), prepare it by stripping the fuzzy material from the base of the stem, and tie it on the hook just behind the eye. Retrieve the dubbing loop from the material keeper, bring it and the peacock/ostrich herl together, and twist them into a chenille strand. Wrap the unit forward to the hook eye forming the body. Tie it off and trim away the waste ends. Be sure to leave plenty of working room at the hook eye for future steps.

Step 5: Grab the hackle in a pair of pliers and wrap it to the back of the hook palmer style. Retrieve copper wire from the material keeper and use it to anchor the hackle feather. Wrap it forward as a rib that also binds the hackle to the hook. Tie it off and trim away the waste end. Clip the hackle fibers from the top of the body.

Step 6: Trim off the excess feather at the back of the hook, pull the dyed mallard fibers over, and anchor them at the hook eye. Trim off the waste ends, apply a whip finish, and remove the thread from the hook. Apply a coat of Aqua Head to the whip finish to complete the fly.

Rich's Slow Water Caddis

Mike named this fly after his favorite fishing partner, his son Richard. He designed it for fishing slow, flat waters during caddis hatches where a low profile is critical to success. The body sits in the surface film where the fish can get a good look at the segmented abdomen and the soft-hackle fiber legs.

Even though Mike tied it for slow-water conditions, he finds it produces well in any water because of its floatability. He often fishes it as an indicator fly with a Bead Head Soft Hackle, Caddis Pupa, or Pheasant Tail on a dropper system.

Rich's Slow Water Caddis

Hook:	Size 12-20, scud
Thread:	Olive
Abdomen:	Two colors of elk hair
Thorax:	Dubbing to match body
Hackle:	Brown or color of choice
Wings:	Elk hair
Head:	Trimmed hair

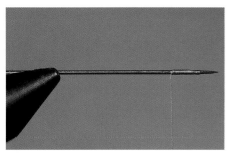

Step 1: Place a needle in the vise with the point to the right. Apply a short thread base slightly back from the needlepoint. Caution! The needle is sharp.

Step 2: Select a clump of green elk hair, remove the under fur, and tie it to the top of the needle by its tips. Repeat the process on the under side of the needle with a clump of tan elk hair. Trim any waste ends.

Step 3: Wrap the thread toward the needle-point. Pull the green bundle of hair over and tie it to the needle. Repeat this process with the tan hair on the under side of the needle. Notice Mike has captured each bundle of hair with a couple of loose turns of thread to keep them under control.

Step 4: Lift the hair bundles, slip the thread back on the needle, and tie a second segment. Repeat this process to construct a third segment completing the extended body.

Step 5: Slip the body off over the point, remove the needle from the vise, and place a hook in the jaws. Apply a thread base from the hook eye to a position directly above the point. Tie the newly formed extended body (tan color down) to the hook there and trim off the waste ends. Prepare a wet-fly saddle feather by removing the fuzzy material at the base of the stem and tie it to the hook at the front of the abdomen. Trim the waste end of the stem from the hook and apply dubbing to the thread. Wrap a thorax then palmer the hackle over it. Trim off the waste feather end then clip the hackle fibers both top and bottom. Be sure to leave enough room to tie on the wing in the next step.

Step 6: Select, clean, and stack a clump of elk hair. Tie it to the hook Troth's Elk Hair Caddis style with the waste ends trimmed as a head. Whip finish and remove the thread from the hook. Apply a coating of Aqua Head to the whip finish to complete the fly.

Spent Wing Para-Ant

Mike developed this fly to imitate the large carpenter ants found in the riparian habitat of the small Sierra Nevada streams and lakes. He designed it to be durable, highly visible, and to float forever.

The Para-Ant is fished primarily as a searching pattern because it is a food source trout often see on a regular basis. We really like the design and how well it floats. It has gained a permanent spot in our terrestrial fly box.

Spent Wing Para-Ant

Hook:	Size 14-20, dry fly
Thread:	Black
Body:	Black foam and dubbing
Post:	Orange poly yarn
Hackle:	Grizzly

Step 1: Place the hook in the vise and apply a thread base that covers the back half of the shank. Use a straight edge and razor blade to cut a strip of foam about as wide as the hook gape. Tie it to the end of the hook shank and trim off the waste end. Cover this tie-down point with black dubbing leaving the thread at the center of the hook.

Step 2: Pull the foam strip over and bind it to the center of the shank slightly forward of the hook point. Pulling slightly on the foam while tying it down produces a more rounded segment.

Step 3: Pull the foam strip up, advance the thread a couple of turns, and cover them with a bit of dubbing. Bring the foam back to the hook shank and bind it to the hook. Again a more rounded profile will result if the strip is tied to the shank while under tension.

Step 4: Cut the tag end of foam in half. Tie the poly yarn to the hook at the 1/3 point on the shank, stand it up, and wrap a parachute platform. Prepare a grizzly hackle feather by removing the fuzzy material at the base of the stem, tie it to the hook in front of the post, and bind it to the parachute platform. Trim the waste end and leave the thread just behind the hook eye.

Step 5: Pull the split foam sections around each side of the post/feather and bind them to the hook at the eye. Tie them down under tension to make this last segment smaller than the first. Do not cut the waste ends. Wrap the hackle parachute style and tie it off on top of the foam. Whip finish and trim the thread from the hook.

Step 6: Stretch each foam tag and cut it from the hook as close to the tie-down point as possible. Use the tips of a pair of sharp scissors to cut off the hackle fibers to the front and rear of the post, leaving a spent wing. Apply a coat of Aqua Head to finish the fly.

Terminator Ladybug

Mike is an avid small-stream fly-fisher and favors terrestrial patterns, especially on his home waters in the Sierra Nevada Mountains. He developed this pattern as a response to blizzard hatches of ladybugs that trout key on in the lakes and streams in his area. Ladybugs are also available year around as a food item in a trout's diet. Mike named this fly the Terminator Ladybug because it just keeps on catching fish and when they finally beat all the hair off it, a foam ant is exposed.

Because trout sip this fly so naturally the take is hard to detect. Mike usually fishes it as a dropper behind a more visible parachute pattern. He is convinced part of the pattern's attraction is the acoustic "plop" it produces when landing on the water. It's like a ringing dinner bell to the hungry trout.

Terminator Ladybug

Hook:	Size 14-16, scud
Thread:	Black
Body:	Orange elk rump
Under Body:	3mm black foam strip
Legs:	Elk hair
Head:	Black foam
Finish:	Black marker, Aqua Flex

Step 1: Insert the hook into the vise then apply a thread base that starts at the eye and travels to a position in the hook bend straight above the barb. Select a clump of orange elk hair, clean out the under fur, and trim off the tips. Tie the trimmed clump (tip end) to the end of the shank. Leave the thread at the back of the hook.

Step 2: Use a razor blade and a straight edge to cut a strip of 3mm foam that is about as wide as the distance of the hook gape. Tie this strip of foam on top of the elk hair at the end of the shank. Advance the thread forward to a position even with the hook point.

Step 3: Pull the foam strip over and secure it with three snug thread wraps. Be careful not to cut it with the thread wraps by tightening too hard on them. Adjust the size of the foam bubble by stretching the strip while tightening the thread. Pull the foam up and wrap to the center of the hook. This completes the first body segment.

Step 4: Construct two more body segments with the last one even with the hook eye. Leave the tag end of the foam extending over the eye for the moment.

Step 5: Pull the hair over the foam making sure the fibers evenly cover the top of the body. Secure the hair at the same point as the foam just behind the hook eye. Pull three hair fibers back on the off side of the hook and anchor them to form legs. Repeat the process on the near side of the hook. Trim the waste ends of the hair, whip finish and clip the thread from the hook.

Step 6: Pull slightly forward on the waste end of the foam strip while cutting it from the hook. The cutting-under-tension technique helps shape the foam head. Trim the legs to length, coat the shell back with Aqua Flex or nail polish, and set the assembly aside to dry. Once it is dry place several black dots on the shell back with a black felt-tip marker. Apply a second coat of Aqua Flex or nail polish to complete the fly.

TOM TRIPI

Approximately forty-five years ago Tom purchased a tarpon fly from a local sporting goods store. At that time he didn't know what it was or how to fish it, but the clerk had assured him it was a good lure to catch fish. Back then his family lived on a small "farmstead" on the Mississippi River with hundreds of chickens and ducks. So it was inevitable he would wrap a stray white hackle around a hook to see if he could catch a fish. He fished that fly using a fresh-cut bamboo pole and caught a white perch on it. Tom was hooked on fishing in general, but became addicted to fly-fishing when he caught his first brown trout on an Orvis rod he had built from a kit.

Since then Tom has become involved in all aspects of fly-fishing. He is a life member of the Federation of Fly Fishers, has been a FFF Certified Master Casting Instructor since 1995, and is considered a master-level fly-dresser and designer.

Tom's fly-fishing background has taken him from eastern Canada and Maine to the Gulf of Mexico, with guiding stints on coldwater streams in the mountains of upstate New York and Vermont. While in New England he became involved in stream-management programs and was a watercolor landscape artist and wildlife illustrator. Tom is also an avid collector, builder, and restorer of bamboo fly rods. At one time he had over forty bamboo rods, as well as sixty more modern rods. Tom jokingly comments, "Compulsive Obsessive Behavior Syndrome has been a definite problem in my life."

After returning to his native New Orleans in 1982 he found a bamboo rod didn't fit the fishing conditions of the Gulf of Mexico and backwater sloughs. The situation required more distance casting and none of the mending he used on moving water. Tom set out to become

Tom Tripi

proficient with the distance cast and the fact he is a Master Casting Instructor is evidence of the skill he developed.

Fly tying is a fundamental part of the sport and through out Tom's growth as a fly-fisher he strove to master the tying of all major fly categories—dries, wets, nymphs, full-dress salmon, and salt water. The learning process in mastering the different categories opened the door to the designing side of fly tying. Tom really excels in this area; we consider him to be one of the most innovative fly tiers we know. We think the flies presented here in this section prove our point.

Over the years Tom has worked with many fly-fishing related companies, including Orvis and Thomas & Thomas. He is actively involved in teaching in all areas of fly-fishing, doing seminar presentations, outdoor photography, writing, and wildlife illustration. The Crabnet, a sporting art gallery in New Orleans, has exclusively represented his fly-fishing art since 1985.

Today Tom makes his home in La Place, Louisiana with his wife Cheryl. There he pursues his fly-fishing avocation and his hobby, astronomy. He has more than a dozen telescopes, some computer driven, and a workshop where he teaches beginning astronomy. His current fly-tying projects include designing and tying "monumental flies" on 10/0 hooks, some of which are over twelve inches long and six inches high. We can hardly wait to see them.

Copper Cyclops

The Cyclops has had a detrimental affect on the population of redfish in south Louisiana for about ten years. Tom designed it to meet three criteria: ease of casting, doesn't tangle, and lots of flash for use in dirty brackish water. He tells us, "There are many patterns that fit the requirements I've listed, but I also wanted to be able to tie it quickly, and not copy the patterns of other tiers." Tom also felt a predator will chase a prey

with an eye more often than one without so he included stick-on eyes.

It is a redfish pattern used for specific fishing circumstances, dark skies and dirty water conditions. Tom often uses a sink-tip line because the fly is plastic and tends to be buoyant. The line pulls the fly under the water and the plastic keeps it off the bottom. He prefers a slow strip retrieve giving the fish plenty of time to see the fly.

Copper Cyclops

Hook:	Size 1/0-2, saltwater
Thread:	Red
Tail:	Copper Krystal Flash
Body:	Copper Krystal Flash
Eyes:	Stick-on with black pupils
Head:	Thread, gold Mylar tinsel
Over coat:	Epoxy

Step 1: Place a hook in the vise and apply a thread base that covers the complete hook shank. Select a three-eighths inch clump of copper Krystal Flash and bind it to the hook at the end of the shank. Leave enough of the clump forward of the tie-in point to later use as the body. Trim the tail using an uneven cut. Tie on a section of gold Mylar tinsel and place several turns to cover the thread wraps. Trim off the excess and set it aside for use in the next step. Advance the thread almost all of the way back to the hook eye.

Step 2: Form a humped body from the Krystal Flash and bind it to the hook near the eye. Tie on the gold Mylar tinsel, wind it over the thread wraps, and trim the excess. Set it aside to use in the next step. Whip finish and remove thread temporarily.

Step 3: Trim off the waste ends of Krystal Flash. Reattach the thread and tinsel at the hook eye. Wrap the tinsel back over the trimmed Krystal Flash then forward to meet the thread. Tie off the tinsel and remove the unused portion. Whip finish and remove the thread. Fan the fibers in the hump so they form a bubble over the top half of the hook.

Step 4: Prepare a puddle of mixed epoxy and apply it to the body. We suggest using a true rotary vise while applying and setting the epoxy. Also use a bodkin to help shape the body while rotating the fly.

Step 5: Place the stick-on eyes one per side. Coat the body and eyes with one more coat of epoxy. Again rotate the fly in the vise until the epoxy sets up.

Step 6: Apply a coat of high-gloss lacquer over the body. Place it on a rotating wheel to dry.

Deceiving Popping Spoon

Tom tell us about his thought process when developing this combination fly, "The four base flies I selected for designing this pattern were the Muddler Minnow, a Lefty's Deceiver, a classic spoon fly, and a standard bass popper—tied both ways—popper and cone shaped (reversing the popper body). The deceiver had to go in the rear so there would be no fouling of materials on the hook; the spoon was a natural for the body, and of course the popper had go in the front." Many flies later the Deceiving Popping Spoon crawled off

Tom's vise ready to fool even the most selective fish.

One of his preferred fishing tactics is to find a clean cut-bank on a deep bayou, cast the fly onto the shore, plop it into the water, and strip-pop-strip like crazy. Tom talks about the results, "If any bass are lurking, they nail the fly. The same can be said for small alligators...now that's fly fishing!" Check Tom's photo with his bio to see what he's talking about. It gives us nightmares just to think about it!

Deceiving Popping Spoon

Hook:	Size 1/0-2, keel
Thread:	Red
Tail:	Black over chartreuse over white buck tail
Tail accent:	Red and green Krystal Flash
Tail flank:	Grizzly dyed chartreuse
Body:	Gold braided Mylar tubing
Head:	Cork popper head
Coating:	Black, green, yellow, and red acrylic paint

Step 1: Place the hook in the vise and apply a thread base that covers the complete shank. Tie on a clump of black bucktail at the end of the hook. Follow with bundles of chartreuse then white. Add a few strands of red and green Krystal Flash between the chartreuse and white clumps of bucktail. Trim any waste ends. Remember this fly is fished hook-point up so the black bucktail is on the top of the fly.

Step 2: Pick two grizzly dyed chartreuse saddle feathers and remove the fuzzy material from the base of the stem. Tie them to the sides of the bucktail to serve as tail flanks (actually they are part of the wing of the Deceiver portion of the fly). Trim off the waste stems. Use an iron to flatten a section of gold Mylar tubing. Slip it on the hook and tie it to the end of the shank. Trim the waste ends then cover them with several thread wraps.

Step 3: Whip finish and remove the thread from the back of the hook. Tie the thread back on the front of the hook at the first bend while binding the Mylar tubing to the shank. Cover the whole front part of the hook with a thread base.

Step 4: Prepare the cork popper head by opening a slit using a razor blade. Slip the popper head on the front of the hook.

Step 5: Whip finish and remove the thread. Anchor the popper head by placing epoxy in the slit. The glue holds the head in place and also fills the gap in the cork.

Step 6: Coat the Mylar body with Super Glue and allow the application to dry. Paint the popper head with black paint and allow it to dry. Use yellow, green, red, and black paint to apply random dots over the head and belly of the body. Allow each application of paint to dry before placing another color.

Step 7: Here we photographed the fly with the vise rotated to illustrate the posture it takes in the water.

Step 8: Rotating the vise a bit more provides an even better view of the random dot distribution on the belly of the spoon.

Doc Chris' Crab

This pattern is the result of a request from one of Tom's friends to downsize a crab pattern originally designed for use on a twelve-weight rod. The friend who fishes for redfish wanted a fly he could easily cast on an eight-weight rod. After several test patterns, this fly emerged from Tom's vise. It is a fairly large fly for the hook size, but is constructed of light, easy-to-cast materials.

The fly is time-consuming to tie, approximately twenty minutes each, and there are no shortcuts to the final product. However, preparing some of the parts in quantity can save time. Tom advises, "Don't forget to experiment with various dyed feathers to match natural patterns on the carapace and bottoms of crabs in your area."

Tom fishes the crab as often as he can for reds and sheep head and even uses it for largemouth bass in some of Louisiana's brackish-water marshes. Black drum, large croakers, and a few specs have also fallen for the pattern. Tom recommends using a very slow, steady retrieve after letting the fly sink until it is on or near the bottom.

Doc Chris' Crab

Hook:	Size 3/0-1/0, circle
Thread:	Red
Appendages:	Tan, olive, and white calf tail
Accent:	Red, blue, and green Krystal Flash
Pincers:	Brown hackle feather, trimmed tip
Pincer edge:	Red, blue, bronze, and green nail polish
Swimming (rear) legs:	Two pheasant body feathers
Body:	Oval section of fox fur
Eyes:	Eighty-pound monofilament, melted, bent ninety degrees
Carapace:	Four pheasant body feathers
Bottom:	Two church window pheasant feathers
Glues:	SOFTEX, epoxy, and super glue

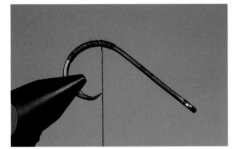

Step 1: Place a hook in the vise with the eye tilted down to make accessing the hook bend easier. It is the place where all the materials are tied or laminated. Place a thread base in the bend of the hook.

Step 2: Select a small clump each of tan, olive, and white calf tail. Mix the colors and tie them in the bend of the hook pointing to the right. Trim off the waste ends. Select two short strands each of red, blue, and green Krystal Flash. Tie them on top of the calf tail also pointing to the right. Trim any waste ends. Repeat the process with mixed calf tail and Krystal Flash pointing to the left.

Step 3: Select two brown hackle feathers and trim the tip off each. Cut off a short section of the base of each stem and bind the feathers to the hook, one to the left and the other to the right. The feathers need not be the same length because seldom are the claws of a crab equal in size. Select two pheasant body feathers and strip off the fuzzy material at the base of the stem. Tie them to the right and left, angled down to form the swimming legs. Whip finish and remove the thread from the hook as all future steps are glued or laminated. Coat the area between the claws with super glue. While the super glue dries, highlight the edges of the claws with coats of red, blue, bronze, and green fingernail polish. Let the fingernail polish dry between the different color applications.

Step 4: Prepare a "tab" of fox fur on the hide that is one inch long and 3/4-inch wide (rabbit on the hide is a good alternative). Place a coating of SOFTEX over the thread area between the claws. Divide the fox "tab" in half, separate the hair midline, and coax it to divide longwise towards the ends of the section. Fold it around the SOFTEX-coated thread wraps, hair side in, as if you were placing the glue-covered area inside a taco shell. Coax the fur from under the hide so it sticks out fan-like from the edges.

Step 5: Prepare four pheasant body feathers by stripping off the fuzzy material at the base of the stems. Place a coat of SOFTEX on the exposed fox hide on the top of the fly. Press a prepared feather on top (and centered) of this area we will refer to as the carapace. Apply another coat of SOFTEX over this feather and position two more feathers to the sides of the first application. The final step in laminating the carapace is to glue the last feather in the center of the assembly over the other three.

Step 6: Prepare two church window pheasant feathers by stripping the fuzzy material from the base of the stem. Turn the pattern over and construct the apron (or bottom) of the fly using the same method as outlined for the carapace in Step 5. Set this assembly aside to dry for at least fifteen minutes. Note that we photographed the fly with the vise rotated one-half turn.

Step 7: Prepare a set of eyes by first melting a single end of two one-inch sections of eighty-pound monofilament. Next place a ninety-degree bend in each about 1/4 inch back from the melted eye. Coat the longer ends of the eye assemblies with five-minute epoxy then slip them between the carapace and apron. Hold them there until the epoxy sets up. If the fly in this step looks different than the one in the last it's because we wanted to illustrate how this pattern's color can be easily adapted to match your local crab population. All you need to do is change feather colors. We'll go back to our original illustration in the next step.

Step 8: Trim off the waste ends of the carapace and apron located on the inside bend of the hook. Apply a coating of SOFTEX to the trimmed ends to form a bond and contour between the carapace and apron. When this coating is dry, place several layers of the different colors of nail polish used in the fly earlier. Allow each layer to dry before going to the next. Tom advises us, "When dried, place the crab in a strong plastic box—preferably opaque; the opaque box hides the crab from overzealous redfish."

The Mohawk or Pic's Special

Many saltwater fly-fishers are familiar with the gold spoon fly made popular by Jon Cave from Geneva, Florida. It has become a mainstay in almost everyone's fly-fishing arsenal for reds and specks; some even use it for largemouth and striped bass. Like many creative fly tiers, Tom wanted to make a few changes to an already successful pattern. His main goal was to stabilize the fly for a very slow, even wobble along with a little organic movement and more flash. Flashabou and a Zonker strip provided the needed alteration.

After making the changes he asked Tom Piccolo to act as his field tester because "Pic" fished and guided the marshes of south Louisiana almost daily. After four months of testing the pattern on a daily basis they concluded it was one of the best flies for redfish either had ever used. It is particularly effective when retrieved using a very slow three-inch strip followed by a pause. The strip-pause-strip retrieve allows the fly to work its magic.

The Mohawk or Pic's Special

Hook:	Size 2/0-2, salt water
Thread:	Red
Tail:	Olive Flashabou over olive marabou
Tail flank:	Two pheasant flank feathers
Eyes:	Yellow barbell
Body:	Wide Mylar tubing, olive Zonker strip
Legs:	Red rubber strips
Coating:	Clear nail polish with gold and green flecks

Step 1: Mount the hook in the vise and apply a thread base that extends over the whole shank and into the bend. Tie on a clump of olive marabou that is twice as long as the hook. Select several strands of olive or pearl Flashabou and tie them to the shank to accent the tail. Leave the thread at the back of the hook.

Step 2: Select two well-marked pheasant feathers and strip the fuzzy material from the base of the stem. Tie one on the off side of the hook parallel with the tail. Repeat the process on the near side of the hook to complete the tail flank.

Step 3: Pick a section of olive Zonker strip and tie it on the hook in the bend. It must be upside down and the natural direction of the fur should be pointing forward so the fur will sweep back when it is folded over in a future step. Use an iron to flatten a section of gold Mylar tubing. Slip it over the hook and anchor it in the bend on top of the Zonker strip. Press the tubing flat with the thumb and forefinger.

Step 4: Anchor the barbell eyes in the bend of the hook with several crisscross wraps, whip finish, and remove the thread. Move forward to the front of the hook and tie the thread back on while binding the tubing to the shank just behind the eye. Trim off any waste tubing then wrap a thread head covering the clipped ends.

Step 5: Pull the Zonker strip over the body, anchor it behind the hook eye, and trim the excess material. Tie on the red rubber strips to form four legs. They should be long enough to reach to the center of the tail flank feathers.

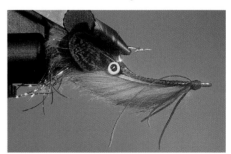

Step 6: Whip finish and remove the thread from the hook. Turn it over in the vise or rotate the jaws like we did. Apply a line of super glue to the Mylar tubing on either side of the shank so it will soak through and anchor the Zonker strip to the top of the body (which is really the bottom of the fly because it travels through the water hook-point up). When the super glue has dried, apply a coat of clear fingernail polish to the bottom of the Mylar (top of the fly) and accent it with sparkle flecks; Tom likes gold and light green.

DAVID TUCKER

David grew up in Boise and the Pacific Northwest with a mother and father in the education field. His father taught him about the outdoors on family vacations spent in the Sawtooth Mountains and the Salmon River Wilderness area. Those vacations were primarily backpacking adventures where David learned the basics of backcountry survival, hunting, fishing, astronomy, native plant life, and entomology. His grandfather introduced him to fishing for salmon and steelhead in the Puget Sound and western Washington rivers.

At twelve years of age Bob Freidly taught David the basics of fly-tying with an emphasis on high-mountain lake type patterns. He spent many hours striving to tie the perfect Humpy, Royal Wulff or Muddler Minnow. It amazed him to watch the speed and precision of other tiers. He studied their techniques, used what he could, and practiced every day, perfecting his own style.

By age seventeen David had a good handle on trout flies and became interested in Atlantic salmon flies after finding the great book by Poul Jorgenson, *Salmon Flies*. No longer was he satisfied with the mundane smaller flies, David began tying the bigger more complex full-dress salmon patterns. He soon discovered the materials for these beauties were more expensive, so he started tying commercially to offset their cost. He bought his materials from Ken Magee owner of Streamside Adventures. Ken really liked David's tying style and took

him under his wing. He mentored David over the next years and purchased his flies for sale in the store. David is totally self-taught and one of the best salmon-fly dressers we know. As a result, many of his techniques are quite unique, developed from many long hours at the vise.

David Tucker

Not long after David started selling flies to Streamside Adventures, Ken hired him to stock shelves and package materials. By the time he was twenty-two he was managing the store and at age twenty-six he became a partner. During his time at Streamside Adventures guiding was an important part of the business, including llama pack trips into the wilderness, several fly-tying contests, and appearances on fly-fishing televisions shows. Unfortunately in 1996 a major road construction project affected traffic and business dwindled forcing the shop to close.

Since then, David ties flies commercially while performing the duties of a stay-at-home dad with his children Ryan, Joshua, and Holli. He also had experience with accessory manufacturing at Loon Outdoors, managed the Idaho Angler fly shop, and is currently pursuing his passion; guiding/teaching others (especially children) how to fly-fish.

Crane Fly Skater

Skating crane flies on the South Fork of the Boise River has always been a fun way to fish in the fall. David has used everything from a large Elk Hair Caddis to a Blonde Wulff. About five years ago the guys at the Idaho Angler Fly Shop in Boise suggested he tie a Bomber-style fly for the hatch. It worked well, creating a wake but it did not skate like he wanted so it was back to the drawing board. His next attempt hit the mark when he added an extra body hackle and a

stiff front collar constructed from spun elk mane. He told us in his quiet unassuming way, "It worked wonders!"

David advises, "The only wrong way to fish this fly is to dead-drift it. The pattern has to move to be effective. I fish it by holding my rod tip high, allowing the line to belly below me, and dragging the fly across the water. The fish can't resist it. The way they attack a skated crane fly is awesome!"

Crane Fly Skater

Hook:	Size 6-14, curved nymph
Thread:	Tan
Body:	Light tan to rusty brown dubbing
Tail:	Bleached elk mane
Body Hackle:	Two ginger hackles, palmered together
Rib:	Fine silver wire
Collar:	Elk mane hackle

Step 1: Mount the hook in the vise and wrap a thread base that covers the back 2/3 of the shank. Select a clump of bleached elk mane and clean out the under fur. Even the tips in a hair stacker then tie the fibers to the hook to form a tail that is as long as the shank. Trim the waste ends.

Step 2: Select two ginger hackle feathers and strip the fuzzy material from the base of the stems. Tie them both to the hook at a position directly above the barb. Tie on a section of fine silver wire while advancing the thread forward almost all the way to the hook eye.

Step 3: Select another clump of bleached elk mane, clean out the under fur, and even the tips in a stacker. Tie the fibers to the hook tips pointing forward with three loose thread wraps. Bring the thread under tension and spin the bundle of hair around the hook. Trim the hair butts at a severe angle to blend them with the tail. Stand the spun hair up and wrap several thread turns tight against the front to force them into position. Wrap the thread to the back of the hook.

Step 4: Apply dubbing to the thread using a good tacky wax and twist it to form a noodle. Wrap it forward shaping the body. Leave the thread hanging behind the spun elk hackle.

Step 5: Palmer the two feathers forward over the body, tie them off, and trim the unused portion from the hook. Leave the thread hanging in front of the spun elk hair.

Step 6: Counter wrap the wire forward to form a rib over the hackle, tie it off, and trim away the waste end. Wrap a thread head, whip finish, and cut it from the hook. Apply a coat of Aqua Head, let it dry, and go "skating."

Green Hornet

The Green Ant has always been one of David's favorite flies for steelhead. It does have one problem: it is constructed of hard, textured material. David really prefers to fish flies tied from soft materials so they have the illusion of life. He changed the pattern to include a blue-eared pheasant hackle and a bronze mallard wing. The modification really made a difference and today David considers the Green Hornet to be one of his top five flies.

It produces in both fast and slower water. Fished using the standard grease-line technique, it has accounted for numerous steelhead on the Deschutes, Grande Ronde, Clearwater, and Salmon rivers. We've noticed something about the patterns in David's fly box—they all seem to have fluorescent green somewhere in their construction. He is of the opinion that any color is fine for a steelhead pattern as long as it's fluorescent green. We certainly can't argue because he is one of the most successful steelhead guides we know.

Green Hornet

Hook:	Size 3/0-1.5, Alec Jackson Spey
Thread:	Black
Tag:	Silver oval tinsel
Rib:	Silver oval tinsel remaining from the tag
Rear Body:	Peacock herl
Under Body:	Silver flat tinsel
Front Body:	Fluorescent green floss
Collar:	Blue ear pheasant
Wing:	Bronze mallard, tent style

Step 1: Place a hook in the vise and apply a thread base that starts at the looped-eye platform. Wrap back on the shank to a location directly above the hook point. Tie a length of silver oval tinsel to the bottom of the hook while advancing the thread to the center of the shank. Trim the waste end of tinsel. Tie several peacock herls to the hook by their tips starting the tie-in process at hook center, wrapping back to a position above the point, and then winding the thread back to its starting location. Wrap the peacock herl to form the back half of the body, tie it off at the hook center, and trim the waste ends.

Step 2: Wind the thread forward to the eye platform and tie on a length of silver flat tinsel. Wrap it back to the peacock and then forward to its starting point. Tie it off and trim the excess tinsel. Tie on a section of fluorescent green floss. Wrap it back over the tinsel underbody to the peacock and then forward to hook eye. Tie it off and trim the waste end. Wrap the silver oval tinsel five turns behind the peacock part of the body to make the tag and then forward forming a seven-turn rib. Tie it off and cut the waste end from the hook.

Step 3: Tie a blue-eared pheasant feather to the hook by its tip and wrap a couple of turns to form a collar. Tie off the feather and trim the unused portion.

Step 4: Select two slips from matching bronze mallard feathers and tie them on the hook as tent-style wings. Cut off the waste ends, wrap a thread head, whip finish, and trim it from the hook. Coat the thread wraps with Aqua Head to complete the fly.

Steelhead Akroyd

During the fall of 2001 the Salmon River ran the color of chocolate milk after every rainstorm. David tried all of his usual flies but they just disappeared in the brown water. The only color that was visible for more than one foot was fluorescent green, so he tied an Akroyd using this material and started catching fish. It quickly became one of his "go to" patterns.

David has learned larger size flies (3/0-2) fish better when the water is cold or off color and the smaller sizes (4-6) seem more productive when the water is clear and warmer. He uses the usual grease-line presentation fishing the fly as slow as possible through holding water.

Steelhead Akroyd

Hook:	Size 3/0-1.5, Alec Jackson Spey
Thread:	Black
Tag:	Silver flat tinsel
Tail:	Golden pheasant crest
Back ribs:	Fine silver oval tinsel, fine silver wire
Under Body:	Flat silver tinsel
Back Body:	Fluorescent green floss
Back body Hackle:	Lime green
Front ribs:	Medium silver oval tinsel, fine silver wire
Front Body:	Black floss
Front body Hackle:	Blue-eared pheasant dyed black
Collar:	Widgeon
Wings:	Argus pheasant strips, Dee style

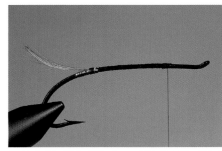

Step 1: David tied his fly on odd-sized hooks. If yours are even size, no problem use one of them. Whichever you have, place it in the vise, apply a thread base that starts at the looped eye platform and ends at a position slightly forward of the hook point. Tie on a strip of flat silver tinsel and wrap a tag over the bare hook that goes down into the bend (ends even with the throat of the barb) and back to the starting point. Tie on a golden pheasant crest feather to form a tail that is about as long as the hook gap. Wrap the thread forward to the eye platform.

Step 2: Select a section of fine silver oval tinsel and bind it to the underside of the shank starting at the eye platform and ending at the tail. Tie on a piece of fine silver wire while advancing the thread back to the front part of the hook. Bind a section of flat silver tinsel to the hook starting at the eye platform and stopping in the center of the shank. Wrap it from its center position to the tail and back to the starting point, forming the tinsel underbody. Tie it off and trim the waste end. Note: All waste materials in this step are bound to the bottom of the shank and trimmed off at the eye platform. Pick a fairly long piece of fluorescent green floss and tie it to the top of the shank starting at the eye platform and stopping in the center of the hook. Wrap it from the center to the tail and back over the tinsel forming the back half of the body. Tie off and trim the waste end. Retrieve the oval tinsel and wind it forward over the body using five evenly spaced turns. Tie it off and trim the waste end. Prepare a lime green saddle hackle feather by stripping the fuzzy material from the base of the stem. Tie it to the underside of the hook and wrap it around the body following the rib to the back of the hook. Use the silver wire to tie it off at the back then counter rib over the hackle to the hook center. Tie off the wire and trim the waste end.

Step 3: Cut off the unused portion of the body feather at the back of the hook. Tie on a dyed blue-eared pheasant feather by its tip binding it to the underside of the hook and trim the excess feather at the eye platform. Tie on a section of fine silver wire and another of medium oval tinsel to later form ribs over the front half of the body. Tie on a length of black floss at the eye platform, wrap it to the hook center, and back to the starting point. Tie it off and trim away the waste end. Wrap the medium oval tinsel forward over the black floss using five evenly spaced turns. Tie it off and trim away the excess tinsel.

Step 4: Wrap the pheasant feather forward placing each turn tight against the rib. Tie it off at the eye. Counter wrap the silver wire over the feather, tie it off, and trim away the waste ends of the feather and the wire.

Step 5: Tie a widgeon feather on the hook by its tip. Wrap a two-turn collar, tie it off, and trim away the excess feather.

Step 6: Select two Argus pheasant strips from matching feathers and tie them to the hook as Dee-style wings. Trim off the waste ends, wrap a thread head, whip finish, and remove it from the hook. Apply a coating of Aqua Head to the thread wraps to finish the fly.

ROBERT WILLIAMSON

Robert Williamson

Robert's first memories of fly-fishing come from family trips to a beautiful, small creek in southeast Idaho. His father was a fly-fisher and many weekend camping trips were spent on this beautiful stream. Robert remembers following his dad up and down the creek with his older brother Jerry. It was a magical time. His dad's fly line would travel through the air and it seemed that every time it landed on the water a nice cutthroat trout would attack it. Robert was fascinated with the sights and sounds of the creek, and especially with the colorful trout.

As he got older Robert decided he wanted to catch trout like his dad and would spend time with his own equipment tying to catch a fish. Robert remembers becoming very frustrated at first because all he seemed to catch was the branches of willows and pines. By the age of thirteen he gained the casting skills he needed to be a successful angler. Most of his fishing consisted of casting Potts hair flies down and across stream, catching eager cutthroats from the creek.

Robert, his brother Jerry, and their dad have pursued trout on this same little creek for over thirty-five years now. It is a place of memories and a place where memories are still made.

Early on Robert learned from his dad he only needed one or two flies. They were the Potts Fizzle and the Rock Worm. He spent all of his teenage years fishing these two patterns catching his fair share of trout. These flies were purchased and the thought of tying them never crossed Robert's mind until he was into his twenties and the flies became increasingly difficult to find. He would just have to learn to tie them himself and Robert did so by taking apart the originals to study their construction secrets. Robert's version caught fish as well as the original, and certainly added a new excitement and dimension to his fly-fishing. He became fascinated with the "old time" western tiers like George Grant. Again he went to work studying and replicating Grant's flies. Soon Robert was experimenting on his own using new materials with old techniques and vice versa; designing patterns he could call his own.

Robert works as a commercial and residential lighting consultant to pay the bills. He has also dabbled in professional fly-tying and writing about the outdoors. His pieces have appeared in *Utah Fishing, Fly Tying, Fly Fishing,* and *Fly Fishing & Tying Journal.* Robert wrote a book on his favorite subject entitled *Creative Flies: Innovative Tying Techniques,* published by Frank Amato Publications. He lives in Roy, Utah with his wife Phyllis and three children, Kassie, Mikel, and Ryan. The Williamson family enjoys spending time at their cabin in Bear Lake, Idaho where they relax, swim, camp, and, most importantly, fish.

O₂ Stonefly Adult

Robert tells us about this great new pattern, "I work in the electrical/lighting industry. One day I was talking to a sales representative who was filling our shelves with heat shrink tubing. As the rep was putting the different diameters of tubing on the shelf, I noticed that the orange-colored tube was about the same diameter as an adult stonefly body (funny how that thought popped into my head while I was at work). The tubing was made of polyolefin and had a glue coating inside allowing it to be sealed. I also learned a design could be printed on it with a special machine. I drew up a simple design, took it to the factory, and they printed me samples for experimentation." With this great, newly-adapted material Robert was able to develop this innovative pattern. It's another example of the many flies we've seen tied from materials developed for industries other than fly-fishing.

The pattern should be used to imitate *Pteronarcys californica* (salmonflies) which hatch on many western rivers from late May through early July. Robert fishes it using standard dry-fly techniques. Its air-filled design makes it virtually unsinkable and it is certainly easy to tie.

O₂ Stonefly Adult

Hook:	Size 6, 3XL dry fly
Thread:	Orange
Body:	Pre-marked O₂ Body Material
Wing:	Light elk hair
Head:	Natural deer or black closed-cell foam
Legs:	Black rubber leg material

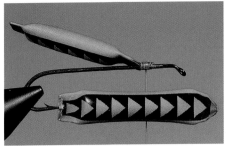

Step 1: Cut a section of O2 Body Material that is equal in length to the hook shank and taper one end with a pair of scissors. Heat a set of wing burners then use them to seal that end of the material. Seal the other end of the body using the same process. Place a hook in the vise and apply a short thread base about 1/4 of the way back on the shank from the eye. Tie the body to the hook by the tapered end. Here we've illustrated a body temporarily stuck to the hook point and another identical body already mounted on the shank. Note the un-tapered end of the body is stuck to the hook point.

Step 2: Select, clean, and stack a clump of elk hair. Tie it to the hook as a Trude-style wing slightly longer than the body. Trim off the waste ends and advance the thread to the hook eye.

Step 3: Cut a clump of elk hair from the hide, remove the under fur, and even the tips in a stacker. Tie them to the hook with the tips pointing forward from the eye. Trim off the waste ends then cover wrap them with the tying thread. Leaving the thread back at the 1/4 position on the shank. Sweep the fibers back, form a bullet head, and bind them in place with several thread turns.

Step 4: Select two sections of black rubber leg material each about 1 1/2 inches long. Tie one of them on the off side of the hook in the center of the piece and then repeat the process with the other on the near side of the shank. Whip finish and remove the thread. Apply a coating of Aqua Head to the thread wraps to finish the fly.

TERRY WILSON

Terry Wilson from Bolivar, Missouri tell us, "During my twelfth summer, I watched a family friend casting cork poppers to bedding bluegills at a local lake. Attempts to duplicate the beautiful casting loops with my 5 1/2-foot steel casting rod forced me to learn to "chuck and duck"—and to begin begging for a real fly rod. A glass rod and a rusted reel spooled with level line, a monumental find at a rummage sale, enabled my lifelong obsession."

Hardware-store poppers and wet flies, supplemented by streamers and deer-hair bugs from rare visits to a fly shop in a neighboring town, fueled the fly-fishing of Terry's formative years. Eventually he bought a tying kit that included an inexpensive vise and assorted scraggly feathers and hair. Unfortunately the kit did not lead to satisfactory flies as he had hoped. Without a fly tier in his acquaintance, Terry purchased a book by the legendary Helen Shaw and in no time he began to tie some flies acceptable to him and the fish.

Using skills honed by thirty-eight years of public school teaching, Terry and his wife Roxanne began writing for outdoor magazines in the early 1980's. They've published nearly 100 articles in *The FlyFisher, Flyfishing & Tying Journal, Bassmaster, Warmwater Fly Fishing, Fly Fishing Quarterly, Ontario Out of Doors, The Hunting and Fishing Journal, Thickets Outdoor Journal, Outdoor Guide,* and many others. Their books, *Blueguill Fly Fishing & Flies* (c1999) and *Largemouth Bass Fly Fishing: Beyond the Basics* (c2001), were published by Frank Amato Publications, Inc.

Terry Wilson

Terry closes with his thoughts regarding the Federation of Fly Fishers, "Belonging to the Federation has given us the opportunity to share our enthusiasm for warmwater fly-fishing with others. We're convinced that the organization, through club meetings, conclaves, and publications, provides an unparalleled forum for sharing information about flies and warmwater fly-fishing. At this writing, we are members of the Federation's Warmwater Conservation Committee, which oversees the preservation and restoration of warmwater fisheries habitat."

Wilson's Craw Bully

Terry shares with us how the Bully Series of flies evolved, "Thirty-five years ago, I watched a cane-pole fisherman catch huge bluegills on live crickets. I wanted to duplicate his success with a fly that incorporated the same enticing leg action as his live bait. Eventually Bully's Bluegill Spider emerged after my wife and fishing partner, Roxanne, and I spent hours in our backyard swimming pool taking turns dropping weighted versions into the water while the other observed its descent from below. After years of passing them out to our fishing friends, we were asked to tie them commercially in the late 1980's. That initiated the Bully Series. Wilson's Bass Bully was designed to fish like the bait-casters' jig and eel for largemouth bass. Wilson's Craw Bully was created in the mid 1990's for smallmouth bass, but it is equally effective at catching largemouth bass."

It is best when fished among rock outcroppings, boulders, or riprap areas that harbor crayfish. In rivers, Terry and Roxanne fish it on floating lines casting upstream to pocket water. When the fly reaches the bottom, lift the rod tip and impart a short strip, then drop the rod tip and repeat the process. Crayfish are poor swimmers and thrust themselves backward in an effort to utilize the current in making their escapes. In lakes, fish the Craw Bully along steep rocky bluffs, around rocky points, or along the face of riprap dams. Here they frequently use a sink-tip or full-sinking line, again, allowing the fly to settle to the bottom before lifting and stripping to simulate escape.

Wilson's Craw Bully

Hook:	Size 4-8, curved nymph
Thread:	Brown
Tail/mouth parts:	Orange over ginger marabou, copper Krystal Flash
UnderBody:	Copper Krystal Flash
Body:	Clear Jelly Rope, sand-colored E-Z Shape Sparkle Body
Legs:	Brown rubber leg material
Eyes:	Small (1/36) red barbell with black pupils
Head:	Sand colored E-Z Shape Sparkle Body

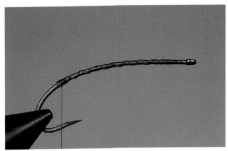

Step 1: Place the hook in the vise and apply a thread base that starts at the end of the shank, travels almost to the eye, and back to its starting point. On this style of hook we identify the "end of the shank" as a position directly above the barb (or where the barb would be if the hook had one).

Step 2: Tie on a ginger marabou feather at the end of the shank that is as long as the complete hook. Top it with several strands of copper Krystal Flash and an orange marabou feather both the same length as the first application. Trim off the waste ends and leave the thread here at the end of the shank for the moment.

Step 3: Select two segments of brown rubber leg material and tie them to the end of the shank so they extend away from the hook at a ninety-degree angle. Trim all four legs so they are about 2 1/2 inches long.

Step 4: Tie on the barbell eyes slightly forward of the rubber legs using several tight crisscross wraps. We like to further anchor them with a drop of super glue.

Step 5: Tie on a clump of copper Krystal Flash and section of clear Jelly Rope. Use a pair of scissors to taper the end of the Jelly Rope to maintain a smooth body over the tie-in position. Wrap the thread to the hook eye then follow with the Krystal Flash forming an under body. Tie off the Krystal Flash and trim the waste ends. Wrap the Jelly Rope forward to the eye, tie it off, and trim the excess material. Whip finish and remove the thread from the hook.

Step 6: Apply sand-colored E-Z Shape Sparkle Body around the eyes to form the head, making certain to leave them exposed. Finally, add a bit of E-Z Shape Sparkle Body around the thread wrappings at the hook eye. Allow 24 hours to completely dry. We've photographed this step with the vise rotated a half turn to illustrate the position the fly takes in the water column.

TIM WITSMAN

Growing up in Illinois, Tim spent a lot of time fishing with his father. They enjoyed many days together on the lakes of Illinois, Wisconsin, and Minnesota where bass, panfish, and northern pike were plentiful. This is also the time when theories on fishing with relation to structure, depth, and water temperatures were expanding in the print media.

Years later, after graduation from pharmacy school, Tim moved his family to Colorado where fly-fishing soon became his passion. He read books on entomology and tying by Rick Hafele, A. K. Best, and Swisher & Richards that soon had him looking at fishing from a different perspective. He used a net to study the aquatic life and observed how structure/water effected his fly line. Tim's fishing success boomed!

Using his improved fishing skills he started guiding in the Black Canyon of the Gunnison River when he was not working at his regular job in the pharmacy. It was a great opportunity to share the beauty and explain the fragile environment of the canyon with other people. He joined the Federation of Fly Fishers because of its focus on education about, and conservation of, places like the Black Canyon.

Tim Witsman

As Tim learned more about rivers and their environment, he realized many of the flies sold in shops just didn't match with nature, so he formed Bogus Bugs, a tying company whose name was suggested by his daughter Samantha. He began tying for shops and giving classes on entomology, nymph fishing, casting, and tying. Tim is an instructor who successfully shares with his students what he sees in the water and what intrigues him about rivers.

Today he continues to tie flies, fish with his dog Gunnison, and share his love affair of rivers with anyone who will listen. He makes his home with wife Debbie in Grand Junction on Colorado's Western Slope. We have known Tim for several years and his skill at the vise is awesome; he is a true fly-tying master.

Bogus Damsel Dry

Fishing the Grand Mesa Lakes in Colorado in July has always been a pleasant passion for Tim and searching for lakes with damsel hatches with big fish was also great fun. Even during a midge hatch, a properly placed damsel dry will take fish.

In developing this fly, Tim settled on Z-lon for the body and wing material because it was light enough for the imitation to land on the water like a natural insect. It will also collapse allowing the fly to be retrieved sub-surface as an egg-laying adult.

Tim likes to locate feeding fish close the weed beds and just vibrate the fly to simulate a struggling insect. He cautions, "The fish usually take the fly very hard so watch the hook set." Tim uses a nine-foot leader tapered to 4X then adds three to six feet of fluorocarbon tippet before tying on the fly.

Bogus Damsel Dry

Hook:	Size 8-12, scud
Thread:	Blue
Eyes:	Melted monofilament
Extended Body:	Blue Z-lon
Wing:	Light dun and black Z-lon, mixed
Body:	Blue dubbing
Hackle:	Medium dun, optional

Step 1: Place the hook in the vise and apply a short thread base just behind the hook eye. Use a cigarette lighter to melt monofilament eyes or select a commercially made pair. Tie them to the hook with several crisscross thread wraps. Wind the thread back on the shank so it is hanging near the hook point.

Step 2: Select a sparse length of blue Z-lon and tie it to the shank. Use a test clip or hackle pliers to twist the strand very tight.

Step 3: Fold over the twisted Z-lon, tie it to the shank, and release it allowing it to "furl" into an extended body. Trim off the excess material and set it aside for use on the next fly.

Step 4: Separate a half strand of light dun and a quarter of black Z-lon. Hand mix the two colors then tie them to the hook to form wings using crisscross wraps. Position the wings slightly behind the eyes. Trim each so they are about as long as 3/4 the length of the extended body.

Step 5: Apply a small amount of blue dubbing to the thread, then prepare a dun hackle feather by stripping off the fuzzy material at the base of the stem. Wrap the dubbed thread a couple of turns then tie on the prepared feather while continuing to dub the area behind the eyes. Dub around the eyes, ending up behind them. Wrap two turns of hackle, tie it off behind the eyes, and trim away the waste end. Whip finish behind the eyes and remove the thread from the hook. Apply a drop of Aqua Head to the whip finish.

Step 6: Use a black felt-tip marker to color stripes on the extended body. Apply a drop of Aqua Flex to the extended body where it joins the hook. Pull up slightly on the body to set its angle and allow the Aqua Flex to dry.

LEARN MORE ABOUT FISHING WITH THESE BOOKS

TYING EMERGERS
Jim Schollmeyer and Ted Leeson

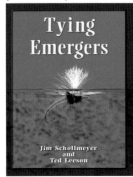

Two of fly-fishing's most well-respected writers collaborate once again, this time discussing emergers. Emergence is itself a behavior, and it puts the tier in a challenging and rather unusual position—not that of imitating a fixed and recognizable form of the insect, but rather of representing a process. This book shows you how, including: emerger design and materials, basic tying techniques, many specialized tying techniques, fly patterns, and more. When you buy a book by these two authors you know what you will get—up-to-the-minute information, well-written text, and superb photography, Tying Emergers will not let you down. 8 1/2 x 11 inches, 344 pages.

SB: $45.00   ISBN: 1-57188-306-1
UPC: 0-81127-00140-8

Spiral HB: $60.00   ISBN: 1-57188-307-X
UPC: 0-81127-00141-5

FEDERATION OF FLY FISHERS FLY PATTERN ENCYCLOPEDIA
Over 1600 of the Best Fly Patterns
Edited by Al & Gretchen Beatty

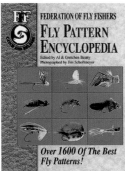

Simply stated, this book is a Federation of Fly Fishers' conclave taken to the next level, a level that allows the reader to enjoy the learning and sharing in the comfort of their own home. The flies, ideas, and techniques shared herein are from the "best of the best" demonstration fly tiers North America has to offer. The tiers are the famous as well as the unknown with one simple characteristic in common; they freely share their knowledge.

As you leaf through these pages, you will get from them just what you would if you spent time in the fly tying area at any FFF function. At such a show, if you dedicate time to observing the individual tiers, you can learn the information, tips, or tricks they are demonstrating. Full color, 8 1/2 x 11 inches, 232 pages.

SB: $39.95   ISBN: 1-57188-208-1
UPC: 0-66066-00422-2

ROD CRAFTING
Jeffrey L. Hatton

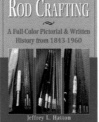

This unique, one-of-a-kind book is a must for anyone interested in the history of our great sport and collectors of antique fishing tackle. It takes a look at the history of fishing rods from the early 1800s to the 1970s, through text and hundreds of color photographs. With access to five private and extensive collections, Hatton covers the first three ages of rod-making: The smith age, up to 1870; the expansion era, 1870-1900; and the classic era, 1900-1970s. Forty-nine beautiful rods are featured, each with a description, history, notable features, and much more. Be warned: once you get into this book, you may look up to discover that several hours have gone by.

SB: $45.00   ISBN: 1-57188-356-8
UPC: 0-81127-00190-3

HB: $65.00   ISBN: 1-57188-357-6
UPC: 0-81127-00191-0

Limited HB: $150.00   ISBN: 1-57188-358-4
UPC: 0-81127-00192-7

MAYFLIES: TOP TO BOTTOM
Shane Stalcup

Shane Stalcup approaches fly-tying with the heart and mind of both a scientist and an artist. His realistic approach to imitating the mayfly is very popular and effective across the West, and can be applied to waters across North America. Mayflies are the most important insects to trout fishermen, and in this book, Shane shares his secrets for tying effective, life-like mayfly imitations that will bring fly-anglers more trout. Many tying techniques and materials are discussed, Mayflies: Top to Bottom is useful to beginner and expert tiers alike. 8 1/2 x 11 inches, 157 pages.

SB: $29.95   ISBN: 1-57188-242-1
UPC: 0-66066-00496-3

Spiral HB: $39.95   ISBN: 1-57188-243-X
UPC: 0-81127-00116-3

CURTIS CREEK MANIFESTO
Sheridan Anderson

Finest beginner fly-fishing guide due to its simple, straightforward approach. It is laced with outstanding humor provided in its hundreds of illustrations. All the practical information you need to know is presented in an extremely delightful way such as rod, reel, fly line and fly selection, casting, reading water, insect knowledge to determine which fly pattern to use, striking and playing fish, leaders and knot tying, fly tying, rod repairs, and many helpful tips. A great, easy-to-understand book. 8 1/2 x 11 inches, 48 pages.

SB: $7.95   ISBN: 0-936608-06-4
UPC: 0-81127-00113-2

WESTERN MAYFLY HATCHES
Rick Hafele & Dave Hughes

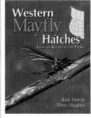

Western Mayfly Hatches introduces the mayflies important in the western states and provinces, shows how to recognize them, helps in the selection of fly patterns to match them, and provides the best presentation methods. Also included is: matching hatches, collecting and observing mayflies, recognizing species and stages, fly-tying techniques, and more. For each species there's a detailed illustration labeled with the characteristics of each life stage, and individual charts of emergence times and hatch importance provide even more information. Western Mayfly Hatches leaves no stone unturned. 8 1/2 x 11 inches, 268 pages.

SB: $39.95   ISBN: 1-57188-304-5
UPC: 0-81127-00138-5

HB: $60.00   ISBN: 1-57188-305-3
UPC: 0-81127-00139-2

Limited HB: $125.00   ISBN: 1-57188-337-1
UPC: 0-81127-00171-2

FLY TYING MADE CLEAR AND SIMPLE
Skip Morris

With over 220 color photographs, expert tier show all the techniques you need to know. 73 different materials and 27 tools. Clear, precise advice tells you how to do it step-by-step. Dries, wets, streamers, nymphs, etc., included so that you can tie virtually any pattern. 8 1/2 x 11 inches, 80 pages.

SPIRAL SB: $19.95   ISBN: 1-878175-130
UPC: 0-66066-00103-0

SOFTBOUND: $19.95   ISBN: 1-57188-231-6
UPC: 0-81127-00131-6

SMALL-STREAM FLY FISHING
Jeff Morgan

There are many myths surrounding small streams—they only hold small fish, they're for beginners and kids, they aren't a challenge, don't allow for versatility in techniques, and so on—in this book, Morgan addresses these myths and shares the realities of small-stream fishing. Topics covered include: the myths; best small-stream equipment; ecology; entomology and fly patterns; small-stream types; fly-fishing techniques; casting; reading the water; and more. If you're up for the challenge, maybe it's time to explore this fun and unique facet of fly-fishing. 8 1/2 x 11 inches, 142 pages.

SB: $24.95   ISBN: 1-57188-346-0
UPC: 0-81127-00180-4

**ASK FOR THESE BOOKS AT YOUR LOCAL TACKLE OR FLY SHOP.
IF UNAVAILABLE CALL, FAX, OR ORDER ON THE WEB AT WWW.AMATOBOOKS.COM**

Frank Amato Publications, Inc. • PO Box 82112 • Portland, Oregon 97282   0094

TOLL FREE 1-800-541-9498 (8-5 Pacific Time) • FAX (503) 653-2766